# CONGENITAL ADRENAL HYPERPLASIA

## A Parents' Guide

By

C. Y. Hsu and Scott A. Rivkees, M.D.

*1663 Liberty Drive, Suite 200*
*Bloomington, Indiana 47403*
*(800) 839-8640*
*www.AuthorHouse.com*

*First published by AuthorHouse 09/07/05*

*ISBN: 1-4208-0649-1 (sc)*

*Library of Congress Control Number: 2004099212*

*Printed in the United States of America*
*Bloomington, Indiana*

*This book is printed on acid-free paper.*

*CHSR Enterprises, LLC*

*NOTICE*

*This book is written for educational and informative purposes only. It is not meant to replace the advice and counsel of your personal physician. Readers should be aware that the expression of Congenital Adrenal Hyperplasia (CAH) can be very different from person to person; that professionals in the field may have experiences and opinions different than those stated in this book; and that standards for the treatment and monitoring of CAH are constantly changing.*

*It is the responsibility of the treating physician, relying on his or her experience and knowledge of the patient, to determine the best treatment for each patient, including the adjusting of all medication dosages. Neither the authors nor publisher assume any liability for any injury and/or damage to persons or property arising from this publication. Nor can they be held responsible for any errors or omissions.*

*For Jack*

~

*For Nick*

# Table of Contents

# *Foreword*

***By John D. Crawford, M.D.***

***Dr. Crawford is the Emeritus Chief of the Section of Pediatric Endocrinology at Massachusetts General Hospital in Boston, Massachusetts, and a Professor Emeritus at Harvard Medical School.***

**THESE** days, you can walk into a bookstore or the public library and find books on almost any medical condition—cancer, diabetes, eating disorders, or osteoporosis. But there is nothing for the layperson on Congenital Adrenal Hyperplasia—CAH. Admittedly, there are a few booklets and pamphlets on the subject, but nothing comprehensive or authoritative. This new book for parents fills that large void. It is written by a mother who has "been there," and a pediatric endocrinologist who has cared for many children with this potentially life-threatening—yet little known—chronic disorder. Both authors are special people.

You will instantly come to know C. Y. Hsu as a real live anguished mother and keen observer, as she describes how she stumbled upon the diagnosis in her six-and-a-half-year-old son Nicholas. The Prologue that Ms. Hsu has written is intimate and engaging. After decades witnessing situations similar to hers, it was still difficult for me not to be moved.

Dr. Rivkees is a special person, too. As I reflect on my sixty years at Massachusetts General Hospital, where none but the top medical school graduates are recruited for residency training, I can recall perhaps half a dozen stars of the first magnitude that have come through our training program. Scott Rivkees is one of them. He is a scientist "at the cutting edge" in the laboratory; an able teacher and administrator; as well as a pediatrician who can charm a two-year-old and is never too busy to soothe a distraught parent.

These two special people have teamed together to fill the void of information for parents of children with this rare and demanding condition. Ms. Hsu contributes her firsthand understanding of parents' questions and concerns. Dr. Rivkees contributes his twenty-plus years of knowledge and experience, caring for children as one of medicine's brightest young lights. Both possess the analytical skills and critical eye needed to shape this book into a reference that parents can easily understand and use.

Nowadays it is not always the bookstore or public library that parents turn to for information, but the Internet. Recognizing this, the authors make it easy for readers to find support groups and other sources of online information. But medical information gotten on the Internet can often be misunderstood or misinterpreted. It can also be difficult to find the answers to practical, everyday concerns such as how to adjust medication schedules when crossing time zones; how to find a knowledgeable doctor in a new community; and what information to give to schools and other child care providers, so that they can properly care for the child with CAH. These and many more coping strategies are covered in this truly comprehensive and medically accurate volume.

Medicine often has a language of its own; this book is written in plain English. The use of some technical terms is unavoidable, but the authors include ample diagrams, charts, and line drawings, as well as an extensive glossary, to help readers negotiate this treasure trove of information.

As parents, you will find this book understandable, complete, and comforting in its upbeat approach. It is a resource to which you will turn repeatedly as your child grows and you become more confident in your ability to care for him or her. Any pediatrician caring for a CAH child will also be well advised to obtain a copy. I wish I had had one sooner.

♦♦♦

*Authors' Note:*

***While this book was in press, on April 19th, 2005, Dr. John D. "Jack" Crawford passed away after a celebrated life devoted to Pediatric Endocrinology; the training and education of medical students, residents, and fellows; and the care of young men and women, and boys and girls.***

***This book is dedicated to Jack for all that he has done for the children in his watchful and gentle care, and for all that he has done for the physicians—young and old—that he touched with his brilliance, wisdom, grace, kindness, and friendship.***

***Thank you Joanna, Becky, Tom, and Jud for sharing Jack with us.***

# Introduction

***By Scott A. Rivkees, M.D.***

IN my experience as a practicing pediatric endocrinologist, I have come across few conditions as complicated as CAH. CAH can be a life-threatening disorder that leaves newborn infants extremely ill, connected to IVs in intensive care units, with parents white-knuckled, praying for their baby's life. It can also touch on the extremely delicate issue of gender. Eager to welcome the arrival of a new son or daughter, some parents are instead told by doctors that they are uncertain if their child is a boy or a girl.

CAH can remain unrecognized for many years, as happened with my co-author's son, who was not diagnosed until he was six and a half years of age. While the condition can be milder in late-recognized children, it can be just as shocking for parents to learn that their child—once thought to be perfectly healthy—has a condition that will influence physical development, makes the child more vulnerable to common infections, and requires the child to take medication for the rest of his or her life. Thus, CAH is not a simple medical problem, but one that leaves parents vulnerable and hungry for more information.

Not only is CAH difficult for parents and children, it is also a difficult condition for treating physicians. Because CAH is uncommon, the average pediatrician or general practitioner will never see a child with this condition. Thus, when faced with a child with CAH, many MDs will be as thirsty for information as parents.

CAH can test the mettle and skill of even the most experienced pediatric endocrinologist. Some children are easy to treat and control, while others are not. Some children gain weight easily on glucocorticoids, others do not. Some children go into puberty early, others do not.

Medical treatment of CAH has been around for more than fifty years. Yet, we, as a discipline, are still asking, "How can we best and better treat CAH?" Thus, the medical treatment of CAH varies from center to center, and from physician to physician.

Reflecting this variability and our need to learn more about CAH, "consensus committees" have yet to generate a standard approach for CAH treatment and monitoring. Parents asking questions of different experts will often get different answers to the same questions. For example, some physicians prescribe long-acting medications, others short-acting medications. Some monitor hormone levels in blood, others in urine. Some doctors recommend testing before a child's morning dose, others insist on getting tests two hours after medication. Some consider the prenatal treatment of mothers at risk of carrying a child with CAH as routine medical care; others view it as still experimental. Understandably, this wide variability in approach can result in confusion, frustration, and the empty feeling that important concerns are going unanswered.

However, despite there being areas of uncertainty in the field, it is important to emphasize that children with CAH can do very well now. With adrenal hormone replacement therapy, parents are empowered to prevent adrenal crisis during illness. With newborn screening in many—though, sadly, not all—states, the unfortunate deaths of infants born with clinically unrecognized CAH can be prevented. Early detection and treatment have also made it possible for other children, who might otherwise have gone undiagnosed for many years, to develop normally and avoid the penalty of late diagnosis. Even if complicating factors—such as central precocious puberty—should develop, interventions can be started to address those problems.

We in the medical profession cannot answer all your questions because we do not yet have all the answers ourselves. Although there is still much work to be done, our knowledge of CAH has increased significantly in the last half century and a lot is now known about this condition. Thus, children with CAH can, should, and do lead normal lives.

***

This book came about after my co-author helped me realize that families need much more information about CAH than can easily be obtained without having to go to the complicated medical literature. Internet message boards are filled with queries from parents and patients, asking each other basic and important questions about CAH, often because they feel they have nowhere else to turn. Thus, when Carol would present me with lists of wonderful and probing questions, and I saw that others were as eager for detailed information, we decided that it was time to draft a comprehensive book about this condition.

Our book is comprised of eleven chapters. Starting with a general overview of CAH, we go on to discuss genetics; symptoms; diagnosis; glucocorticoid treatment and monitoring; mineralocorticoid treatment and monitoring; other medications used in CAH treatment; stress coverage during illness; surgery in girls with CAH; and prenatal treatment of mothers with dexamethasone. At the end of each chapter, we address many commonly asked questions.

We are indebted to Dr. Dix P. Poppas and Dr. Rosalia Misseri for contributing the chapter on surgical restoration in girls with CAH. Parents faced with this difficult decision will undoubtedly find this information invaluable.

After the chapters is an appendix, where you can find listings of patient support groups; sources to help you find a qualified physician in your area; names of gene-testing laboratories; and organizations from which you can order medical alert jewelry. You will also find copies of standard growth charts, and templates of letters that can be given to schools, emergency room doctors, and airline security personnel, to explain the protocols that need to be followed if your CAH child should become ill. A glossary of terms follows the appendix, as well as a comprehensive list of references.

In preparing this book, we have tried to give you the in-depth, nuts-and-bolts information that parents and patients deserve. However, as the title of our book suggests, our emphasis is on CAH in the pediatric patient. Thus, we do not delve into some of the topics that may be of special interest to CAH adults.

I must also emphasize that this book is ***not*** to be used as a treatment manual to change or manage your child's treatment on your own. Our aim is to help you to have a better and more meaningful dialogue with your physician, not to promote a specific approach to treatment. ***As such, specific questions about treatment, monitoring, and medication adjustments—as it relates to your child—should always be addressed to your pediatric endocrinologist.***

***

I wish to thank the parents and physicians who have reviewed earlier versions of this manuscript for their helpful comments. I especially wish to thank my co-author, C. Y. Hsu, for her tremendous and tireless efforts in working to put this book together. In the process, she has learned so much about CAH that she has made me consider issues I never thought of and has taught me a great deal about the impact of CAH on parent and child. We hope that you may have a better understanding of CAH from our words.

♦♦♦

# Prologue: A Mother's Story

***By C. Y. Hsu***

**MY** son was six and a half years old when he was diagnosed with Congenital Adrenal Hyperplasia. I will never forget being told that he had a serious medical condition that I had never heard of. We were in a small conference room in the Pediatric Specialty Clinic at the Yale Children's Hospital. It was a Friday afternoon, one week before Christmas and two weeks before the New Millennium.

***

A week before, I was in the bathroom toweling off after a shower, when Nick walked in on me. Looking at me intently for a moment, he said, "I have some of that." He meant pubic hair. I asked him to show me, and—sure enough—there were a few long, dark strands at the base of his penis.

I looked in the home medical book after I took him to school. It said only that boys started developing signs of puberty—at the earliest—around the age of nine. It didn't mention the possibility of other problems. I figured that that was a good sign, but decided to call the pediatrician anyway.

As it turned out, she was away for the week, so it was not until the following Tuesday that I could ask what she thought. I half expected her to say what doctors always seemed to say: "Yes, it's a little unusual, but nothing to be overly concerned about. Let's keep an eye on it, and if things change, we can look into it further."

To my surprise, she didn't say that. In fact, she came right out and said we needed to worry. When signs of precocious puberty happened in girls, she said, it was usually nothing. But when you saw them in a boy, there was often an underlying problem.

I asked what she meant by "underlying problem" and was relieved when she mentioned a hormone imbalance. I had been afraid she would say something really dreadful like cancer. She said Nick needed to see a specialist called a pediatric endocrinologist.

The problem was that it was two weeks before Y2K, one of the biggest holidays of all time, and she wasn't sure who would be around. Someone she knew was practicing up in Westchester. There was also a doctor at Yale. She didn't know him personally, but had heard him lecture. She wavered for a moment then decided to call the guy at Yale.

I waited while she tried to reach his office. In a short while, she came out, waving a piece of paper in her hand. He could see us that Friday, she said. His name was Scott Rivkees.

***

The next three days were spent scouring the home medical books for clues. I looked for anything related to early puberty or a hormone imbalance. Nothing really fit.

There was something called "acromegaly," or gigantism. People with acromegaly produced too much growth hormone and could grow to be over eight feet tall.

Nick had always been unusually tall. His dad, Patrick, was just shy of six foot one, but I was barely five feet tall. Was it really possible that we had spawned a giant?

But people with acromegaly were also supposed to have exaggerated features and oversized hands and feet. I imagined Lurch from *The Addams Family*. That was not Nick at all. He was tall, but well proportioned. If anything, his features were fine and delicate.

Patrick called his internist, who—as it turned out—had specialized in endocrinology in medical school. He thought that the worst-case scenario was a tumor or cyst of the pituitary gland. The tumors were not cancerous and didn't spread. In some cases, they could even be removed from the nose.

A benign tumor was not a happy prospect, but I supposed we would deal with it if we really had to. At least it was curable.

***

Our afternoon at Yale that Friday was a long one. The doctor took Nick's medical history then said he wanted to run some blood tests and get some x-rays. After he had had the chance to review the preliminary results, he would see us again to answer our questions.

We were sent to get something called an ACTH stimulation test, where they took Nick's blood twice, an hour apart. They also x-rayed his hand, abdomen, and testicles.

In the lab, we asked if the doctor had ordered an MRI or CT scan. The technician said no. We also asked if anything unusual had shown up on the ultrasound. Again the answer was no.

By the time the doctor summoned us at the end of the day, I was feeling pretty confident. Nothing we had told him about Nick's prior history had seemed to make a special impression, and the abdominal and testicular scans had been clean. Since the doctor had not even found it necessary to check for a pituitary tumor, it must mean we were home free.

It was now almost four hours after we had first arrived. The waiting room was empty except for the occasional intern, and the cleaning crew had already started its nightly rounds.

The doctor sat across a small table from us. He started by saying he was pretty certain he knew what was causing Nick's signs of early puberty. He wrote the words on the blackboard behind him. "Congenital Adrenal Hyperplasia." I wasn't sure where the adrenal glands were, but knew that, whatever this was, "congenital" meant that Nick had been born with it.

I waited for the doctor to tell us that it was nothing, an inconsequential familial tendency towards being an early bloomer. Instead he said that Nick couldn't produce a hormone called "cortisol." Cortisol was known as the "stress" hormone. Without cortisol, he could have trouble handling stress and illness.

The condition was very rare. Some children who had it died in infancy. Nick appeared to have a milder variant. He would be okay in the long run, but would need to take medication to replace the cortisol that he couldn't make. There was no cure, and treatment was for the rest of his life.

When you couldn't make cortisol, you ended up overproducing androgens, he continued. Androgens were male sex hormones. Excess androgens caused some girls with Congenital Adrenal Hyperplasia to be misidentified as boys, at birth. They also caused other children, like Nick, to develop signs of early puberty.

The hand x-ray showed that Nick had a bone age of about thirteen. This meant that he had been growing at a pace close to that of a thirteen-year-old. It was why he was so tall. The problem was that when you matured too quickly, the growth plates in your skeleton closed prematurely. Once the growth plates closed, you couldn't get any taller.

Boys normally stopped growing around age seventeen, when their bone age was also about seventeen. Since Nick's bone age had been advancing at twice the rate of his actual age, his growth plates could have closed by the time he was eight or nine years old. Had we not caught this, he would probably have ended up less than five feet tall.

With treatment, we could hope to slow things down, but a six-year advancement in bone age was significant. With treatment, he could possibly reach five-two or five-four, but we would not be able to buy back all the time that we had lost. A lot also depended on genetics.

The doctor pulled out a copy of Nick's growth chart. I saw how, each year, the black circles jumped higher and higher above the lines on the chart. At the age of three, Nick was already a little above the 95$^{th}$ percentile line in height. Now, at the age of six and a half, he was as far above the $95^{th}$ percentile line as the $95^{th}$ was above the $25^{th}$ percentile line in height.

As the doctor spoke, my confidence gave way to rising panic. As desperately as I wanted to believe that there was some sort of mistake, everything he said struck a familiar chord. I couldn't believe we had been playing Russian roulette all these years without knowing it.

I tried to hold myself together. I focused my questions to the doctor on the practical issues. Could we expect any side effects from the medication? Were there any foods that Nick couldn't eat? Any medications that might cause an adverse effect? Aspirin? *Tylenol*? What about his allergy shots?

But then I faltered. I was grateful that the doctor didn't look away in embarrassment or stop to ask if I was okay. He held my gaze and, without missing a beat, pushed a box of *Kleenex* towards me and kept on talking.

We stopped at a friend's house to pick up our daughter. I was glad when she skipped past me and on into the car. My friend came out after her, all smiles. The words "Is everything all right?" died on her lips as I started sobbing and couldn't stop. A few times, I tried to explain, but couldn't catch my breath. When she said we could talk in the morning, all I could do was nod.

***

People often ask what you tell your child about CAH and when. For me, there was never any question that I would tell Nick everything. As bereft as I felt, I knew that anything we omitted would be made that much worse in a little boy's imagination.

I couldn't say much that first night because I couldn't find my voice. I was sure Nick thought he was dying. I told him he was okay. Yes, we were upset, but everything would be okay.

The next day I pulled out the home medical book. I showed him a picture of the human body. I showed him a picture of the adrenal glands. I told him he would need to take medicine to make up for the cortisol that he couldn't make.

I told him about bone age. I told him he was six and a half, but his body thought he was more like a thirteen-year-old. I told him why he was so tall. I explained it in terms of timing and he seemed to understand.

The following week, I went to the school. I met with the principal. I met with Nick's teacher and the school nurse. I ordered a *MedicAlert* bracelet. We called our family. We called all our friends. Everyone was sympathetic.

***

It was the irony of the situation that got to me. Since he was a toddler, everyone had commented about how tall Nick was. In the school pictures, he was always the one in the center, in the back row. Not only that, he was almost a full head taller than the next tallest child. Sometimes I'd stand with the other mothers at school, watching him walk down the hallway with his class. *He looks like the kid that's been left back*, I joked.

At his last well child checkup, even the pediatrician had done a double take. "Wow," she said. "He is really tall … *really* tall!"

Why had no one ever said that being too tall could be a warning sign of something wrong? How had he sprung up under all our noses without anyone saying, *wait*! We were all smart, educated, responsible.

And why hadn't I charted Nick's heights and weights, the way I had done with Hayley's? As soon as the doctor had pointed out the abnormal growth pattern, I had understood what he meant. I was an architect. I was used to evaluating things visually. Maybe if I had seen that pattern sooner, I would have thought to ask if it was unusual.

But Nick was the second child, so I had not obsessively chronicled the details of his birth and early childhood the way I had done with Hayley. Now we were left fighting for every inch. Now there was no room to make a mistake.

I had never had trouble sleeping, and now I was restless every night. If I dozed off, I would wake again at 2 or 3 a.m., my mind racing. There was anger, regret, guilt, and wanting to go back to the time before we knew anything about CAH. But there was also the pang of wondering what would have happened had things not played themselves out the way they had, albeit so late in the game.

What if Nick had never walked in on me that morning? What if I had decided to lock the bathroom door? What if he had decided that a few stray hairs were not worth mentioning, or had been too embarrassed to say anything? Would we have trapped him inside his eight-year-old self for the rest of his life? Would he have gone to bed one night with the flu or a fever, and never woken up?

***

I was desperate for information. I went to the public library. I went to Barnes and Noble. I looked in all the medical encyclopedias. There was nothing written on this condition anywhere. I complained to Dr. Rivkees and he graciously agreed to copy some medical articles for me.

We met with him again before the New Year, this time without Nick. He gave me three papers, two that he had co-authored and one by a colleague.

But, though I had clamored for more information, I couldn't bear to look at these articles, at first. For three days, they sat untouched in the yellow manila envelope. And when I was finally able to face them, I read with a combination of fascination and horror.

***

After the diagnosis, it was hard not to wonder how much of Nick's early history had been due to unrecognized CAH. He had always been a funny study in contradictions. I could never quite decide if he was a really healthy kid or a really sick kid. He was often at both extremes of the spectrum.

From the time he was born, he had been plagued with medical problems that often had an odd or unexpected twist. They started at the age of three days old, when he was readmitted to the hospital for neonatal jaundice.

I remember looking at him in the sunlight as I was getting ready to go to an OB appointment, and asking Patrick if he looked just a little bit yellow. We had been discharged with the usual instructions to keep an eye out for jaundice, but had no idea if this would be obvious. The pediatrician's office was on the way home, so we decided to take him in, just to be sure.

The doctor chuckled, saying Nick would have to look like the yellow on a box of *Kodak* film before there was anything to worry about. But he did a heel stick anyway, just in case.

By the time we got home, less than fifteen minutes later, there was already an urgent message on the answering machine. The bilirubin number was through the roof. We needed to get Nick to the hospital ASAP. We got right back into the car. I didn't even stop to pack a bag.

I cried when the nurses brought Nick back into the room, after his bath. He was in a rolling bassinet equipped with an incubator light, an IV taped to the back of his small hand. His skin was noticeably dry and chapped. At the same time, with his hair sticking straight up after being shampooed, and completely naked except for a diaper and a pair of sunglasses, he looked like Joe Cool on the beach. I couldn't help laughing, in spite of myself.

Bilirubin levels in a newborn were supposed to be between 0 and 12 percent. Nick's was 21.6. In spite of this, the doctor was not concerned. Newborn jaundice was very common, he said. The numbers should come down quickly after phototherapy.

But, maddeningly, things didn't happen the way they were supposed to. After a day under the fluorescent lights, Nick's bilirubin level went down. But, by the next morning, it had shot back up again. The same thing happened the following day. The number was always high in the morning and low in the late afternoon or evening.

The doctor said he had never seen this happen. He suggested that Nick might be allergic to my breast milk, so I stopped breast-feeding. It didn't make a difference. The strange up-down pattern continued.

Finally, the doctor said he thought the high-low numbers were a result of the laboratory using two different machines to run the tests. Because the numbers, overall, seemed to be following a downward trend, he discharged us after three days. We were sent home with a special light pad to strap around Nick's torso. A visiting nurse came twice a day to draw blood.

So that was how Nick spent the first two weeks of his life: plugged into an electrical outlet; wearing his fluorescent green biliblanket; a B-X cable trailing out of the Moses basket he slept in. And getting stuck with a needle every morning and night.

In time, the jaundice went away, but then the ear infections and sleep problems started. Newborns were supposed to sleep more than they were awake, but with Nick, the pattern seemed to be reversed. He never slept—or so it seemed—and when he did, it was always fitfully. During the day, he would sleep for no more than ten or fifteen minutes at a stretch. At night, I would put him down by 8:00 or 8:30, but within a few hours, he would be up again, making little groaning noises.

When he was seven months old, the doctors finally recommended ear tube surgery. The ear infections got better, but the sleeping didn't.

We tried letting him cry it out. Gradually increasing the amount of time before we would rescue him from his crib. Switching him to a soy formula, then to a hypoallergenic formula called *Alimentum*. Nothing helped. Once, he stayed awake for an entire twenty-four-hour period after taking a prescription decongestant.

We were in the pediatrician's office constantly, but nothing was obviously wrong. Nick had reached all his developmental milestones. He was growing and putting on weight. He was irritable, but didn't quite appear sick. The doctor was sure he would outgrow this phase.

That March, we took him to a pediatric gastroenterologist. The doctor listened to our complaints, but still wasn't moved. He thought Nick's problems were behavioral, but—as a parting concession—suggested a teaspoonful of *Maalox* each night.

To our astonishment, the *Maalox* worked like a charm! For the first time in eight months, Nick slept through the night. The following morning, he took a two-hour nap. I didn't care that the magic bullet had come in the form of something as ordinary as an over-the-counter antacid. I was just so grateful that something had worked.

But, to my dismay, the relief was temporary. After six weeks, the fitful sleep and nightly waking resumed. Next, the doctor scheduled a barium x-ray.

I knew something was wrong as soon as the radiologist looked up from his screen. He told me Nick had multiple ulcers. I was almost relieved ... at least, we finally had a diagnosis. But, then the nagging doubts took over. *Why would an eight-month-old infant have ulcers? And not just one, but—apparently—several?*

An endoscopy followed. It was the second time in three months Nick had been put under general anesthesia.

When the doctor marched into his office immediately after the procedure to phone our pediatrician, I was sure it was going to be devastating news. So when he came back out and told us that there were no ulcers, I could not believe that we had dodged a certain bullet.

The doctor did see evidence of inflammation, however. He termed it "mild, esophageal reflux" and put Nick on a six-month course of *Pepcid*. Shortly thereafter, the sleep problems resolved.

As Nick approached his toddler years, things finally started to settle down. There was a swollen lymph node on the back of his neck that never went away. A cold that turned into pneumonia two winters in a row. Allergies to grass, trees, cats, dogs, and mites. But compared to the first year of his life, these events seemed routine.

The odd thing was that, in spite of all these different ailments, Nick was not a frail, sickly looking child. On the contrary, he often gave the impression of being healthier and more robust than everyone else.

For one thing, he was bigger than all the other kids his age. When he was three, he was often mistaken for a five- or six-year-old. By the time he was in kindergarten, he was taller than most of the eight-year-olds in Hayley's third-grade class.

He was also a natural athlete, with remarkable hand-eye coordination. From a very young age, he could hit, catch, and throw with incredible accuracy. He could dribble a basketball down the length of the driveway before the age of two; volley a tennis ball at the age of four.

He never sat still. While other kids were content with Legos or Lincoln Logs, he was happy only when he was moving. He spent hours and hours shooting hoops, hitting pucks, diving for imaginary touchdowns. He slowed down only when he was sick, but—even then—as soon as the *Tylenol* kicked in, he was ready to go bowling.

He never had a child's soft body. He was tall, slender, and perfectly proportioned. As an infant, I joked that he was the only baby I knew who had muscle instead of baby fat. At the age of six, he was shaped like a miniature Statue of David.

At school, his physical stature and athletic ability gave him an exalted status among his peers. Even the older boys eyed him with grudging respect. But, though he was bigger, faster, and stronger than everyone else, he never used his size to bully or intimidate. He had a maternal streak, and was especially kind to babies and small animals.

At home, it was sometimes a different matter. In spite of a soft heart and gentle spirit, Nick could have a hair-trigger temper. He was easily frustrated, sometimes by the smallest things. He was prone to tantrums. He did not always cope well with new or unexpected situations. In a word, he was not very good at handling stress.

So, while I could never have foreseen a diagnosis of Congenital Adrenal Hyperplasia on that December afternoon, I also knew there was no mistake. The contradictions of this enigmatic illness seemed to fit my little boy to a T.

Not treating him was never a consideration. At the same time, I worried about the effects of the medication. Would Nick's personality change after treatment? Would he find himself suddenly unable to do the things he loved? Would we be caught in that frustrating catch-22 where the treatment was as bad as the disease?

***

Dr. Rivkees was wonderful. He was very well versed in CAH and always sounded genuinely interested when he asked how things were going for Nick. And when he told me that he was a parent, too, and understood how difficult this was, I almost cried.

But, soon after the New Year, we heard of a doctor who was considered to be the world expert on CAH. She was just down the road in New York City. We saw her for a second opinion on Valentine's Day. She was trying an experimental drug to improve height in CAH children. With so few options and nothing to lose, we decided to give her program a try. We discussed this with Dr. Rivkees and he gave us his blessing. Sadly, we said goodbye.

I discovered the Internet. While there was little to no information available in print, I found pages and pages online. Much of the more in-depth information was written for a medical audience, but I could generally understand enough to grasp the concepts. I read whatever I could find.

I found an Internet message board, frequented by many parents with CAH children. In the beginning, I avoided it. I didn't want to hear any more about sick children and frightened parents, girls who had been diagnosed as boys in infancy. There were too many sad stories.

But, eventually, I was drawn back. I found that most parents had questions similar to mine. When was the best time to give medication? Was it better to test before or after a dose? What hormone levels were considered acceptable? I was anxious to compare notes and share experiences.

In time, I learned who was who. I even started putting up my own responses and comments on the message board. Writing helped me sort out the issues that were still confusing. It became my therapy.

It didn't work out in New York City. After three months, we went back to Yale and Dr. Rivkees. In time, I even got him to start reading the message board. When he asked me, some time later, if I would collaborate with him on a CAH handbook for parents, I did not have to think twice.

***

Writing this book has not been easy. CAH is a complex disorder that is widely thought to be poorly understood and poorly managed. Trying to simplify an inherently complex subject has been a challenge. In addition, standards for treatment and monitoring are still evolving.

As a parent, I know all too well what it is like to be told that your child has a serious medical condition, yet feel completely powerless to help him or even yourself. It is difficult to know what questions to ask when you have no idea what it is you're dealing with. So—while no book can ever be definitive enough or comprehensive enough—this book is for all those whose lives are affected by CAH, with the hope that we have bridged this information gap in a meaningful and useful way.

And, of course, this book is also for Nick. From his mother with great pride, hope, and love. And it is for his children, and his children's children. We have come a long way in these last few years, but there are still lifetimes yet to go.

♦♦♦

# 1

# What is Congenital Adrenal Hyperplasia?

*For most parents, the news that their child has Congenital Adrenal Hyperplasia comes as a shock. Whether they are the parents who have just been told that their baby boy is, in fact, a baby girl; or the parents whose newborn becomes critically ill and is in danger of failing to thrive; or the parents of an older child who starts showing signs of early puberty. For most, the shock comes not only from the realization that the child has a potentially life-threatening condition, but also from the notion that the condition is one that no one seems to have ever heard of or knows much about.*

*In this introductory chapter, we give you a general overview of CAH—what this condition is, the systems in the body that are affected, the different types of CAH, and the different ways that CAH can present itself. We also tell you about the problems that can arise when you have CAH, and give you an idea of what you might expect, if your child is diagnosed with CAH.*

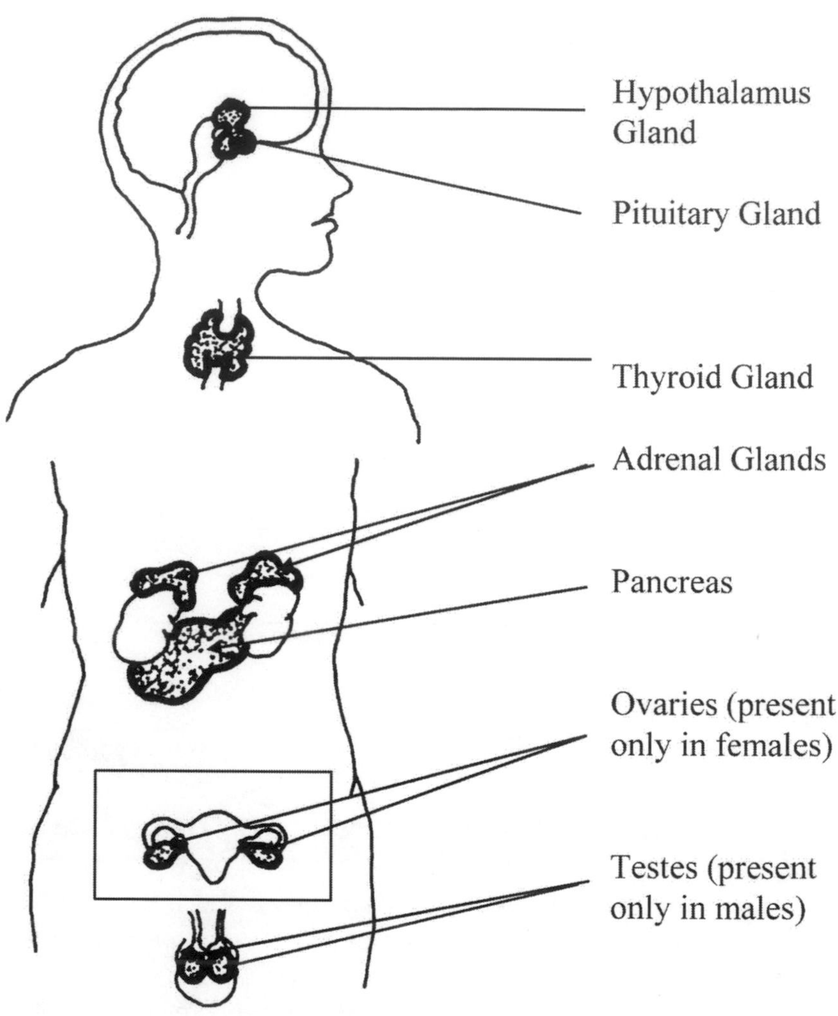


THE ENDOCRINE SYSTEM

**CON**genital Adrenal Hyperplasia (CAH) is an inherited disorder of the adrenal glands. When CAH occurs, the adrenal glands cannot properly make the hormones "cortisol" and "aldosterone" and, instead, overproduce "androgens" (male hormones). This can result in serious illness and growth problems, though, with proper treatment and care, those with CAH can lead normal and healthy lives.

The adrenal glands are part of the body's endocrine system. The pituitary gland, thyroid gland, pancreas, ovaries, and testicles are also part of the endocrine system.

## THE ENDOCRINE SYSTEM

The endocrine system is made up of small organs called "glands." Glands produce important chemicals called "hormones." Hormones are directly responsible for delivering instructions from the brain to your cells. Thus, hormones are called "chemical messengers."

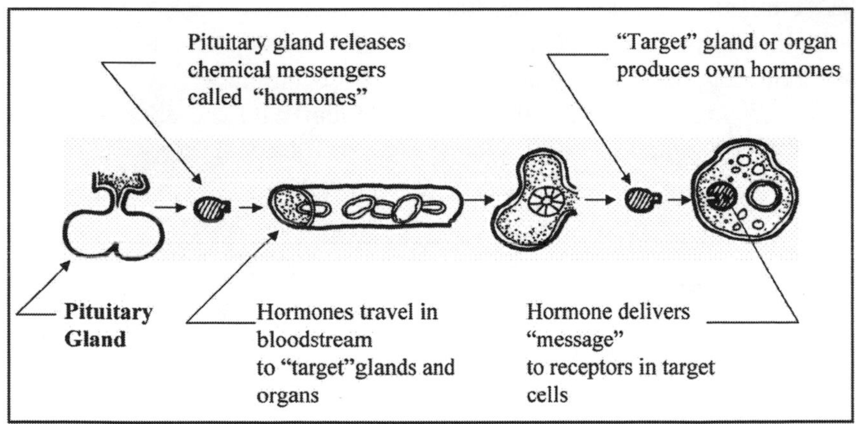


### Hormones and Enzymes

Hormones regulate many bodily functions including growth, metabolism, and reproduction. They are made in one part of the body, and then travel through the bloodstream to affect the activity of "target" cells and organs in other parts of the body. In some cases, release of a hormone from one gland will trigger the release of a different hormone from a different gland.

Some hormones are made from protein and some are made from cholesterol. The hormones affected by CAH are all made from cholesterol. Hormones produced from cholesterol are known as "steroid" hormones.

There are more than twenty different steroid hormones produced in the adrenal glands. Each involves different changes to the chemical makeup of cholesterol. These changes are made by cell proteins called "enzymes."

In people with CAH, an enzyme necessary to convert cholesterol to the hormones cortisol and aldosterone is impaired or defective. As a result, when you have CAH, you cannot properly produce one, or both, of these important adrenal hormones.

## The Adrenal Glands

The adrenal glands are small, triangular-shaped structures that sit on top of the kidneys. Each gland consists of two parts.

The outer layer, called the "adrenal cortex," makes a number of different hormones including cortisol, aldosterone, and androgens. The inner layer, the "adrenal medulla," makes hormones including "epinephrine" and "norepinephrine." Epinephrine is commonly known as "adrenaline," the hormone responsible for the instinct to "fight or flight."

When you have CAH, there is a problem with the adrenal cortex. However, in some people with CAH, the adrenal medulla is also abnormal.

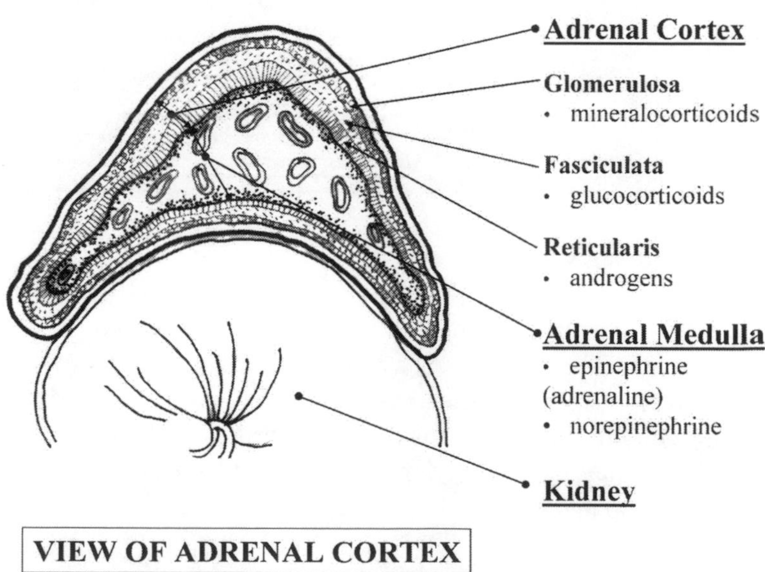


VIEW OF ADRENAL CORTEX

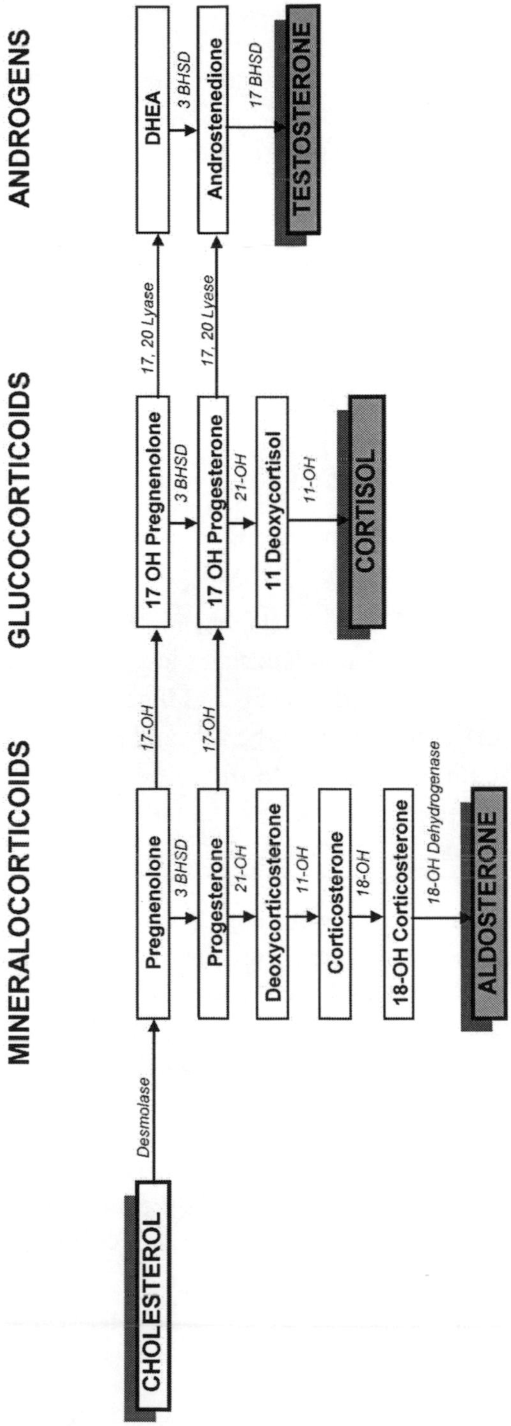

MINERALOCORTICOIDS | GLUCOCORTICOIDS | ANDROGENS

CHOLESTEROL → *Desmolase* → Pregnenolone

Pregnenolone → *17-OH* → 17 OH Pregnenolone → *17, 20 Lyase* → DHEA

Pregnenolone ↓ *3 BHSD* Progesterone

17 OH Pregnenolone ↓ *3 BHSD* 17 OH Progesterone

DHEA ↓ *3 BHSD* Androstenedione

Progesterone → *17-OH* → 17 OH Progesterone → *17, 20 Lyase* → Androstenedione

Progesterone ↓ *21-OH* Deoxycorticosterone ↓ *11-OH* Corticosterone ↓ *18-OH* 18-OH Corticosterone ↓ *18-OH Dehydrogenase* ALDOSTERONE

17 OH Progesterone ↓ *21-OH* 11 Deoxycortisol ↓ *11-OH* CORTISOL

Androstenedione ↓ *17 BHSD* TESTOSTERONE

**KEY:**

XYZ (in a box) = Hormone

*Italics* = Enzyme

**ABBREVIATIONS:**

*3BHSD = 3-Beta Hydroxysteroid Dehydrogenase*
*21-OH = 21 Hydroxylase*
*11-OH = 11 Beta Hydroxylase*
*18-OH = 18 Hydroxylase*
*17-OH = 17 Hydroxylase*

**ENZYME PATHWAYS IN ADRENAL CORTEX**

## THE ADRENAL CORTEX

The hormones produced in the adrenal cortex are grouped into three major categories, known as "mineralocorticoids," "glucocorticoids," and "androgens." Each of these groups of hormones is made by a different layer of the adrenal cortex.

### Zona Glomerulosa

The outer layer of the adrenal cortex, called the "zona glomerulosa," makes mineralocorticoids. Mineralocorticoids help the body regulate salt and fluid levels, and maintain normal blood circulation. Aldosterone is the most important mineralocorticoid made by the adrenal glands. To produce aldosterone, six modifications of cholesterol are needed.

### Zona Fasciculata

The middle layer of the adrenal cortex, the "zona fasciculata," produces glucocorticoids. Glucocorticoids regulate sugar levels, maintain normal blood pressure, and help you respond to stress and illness. Cortisol is the most important glucocorticoid made by the adrenal glands. To produce cortisol, five modifications of cholesterol are needed.

### Zona Reticularis

The innermost layer of the adrenal cortex, the "zona reticularis," produces androgens (male hormones). Androgens play an important role in the development of the genitals and the development of sexual characteristics such as armpit hair, genital hair, and adult-type body odor. They also help to speed up growth. Both males and females normally produce androgens.

The androgens produced in greatest quantity by the adrenal cortex are "dehydroepiandosterone" (DHEA) and "androstenedione." A portion of these hormones is then made into "testosterone," which is the most potent androgen. To produce testosterone, five modifications of cholesterol are needed.

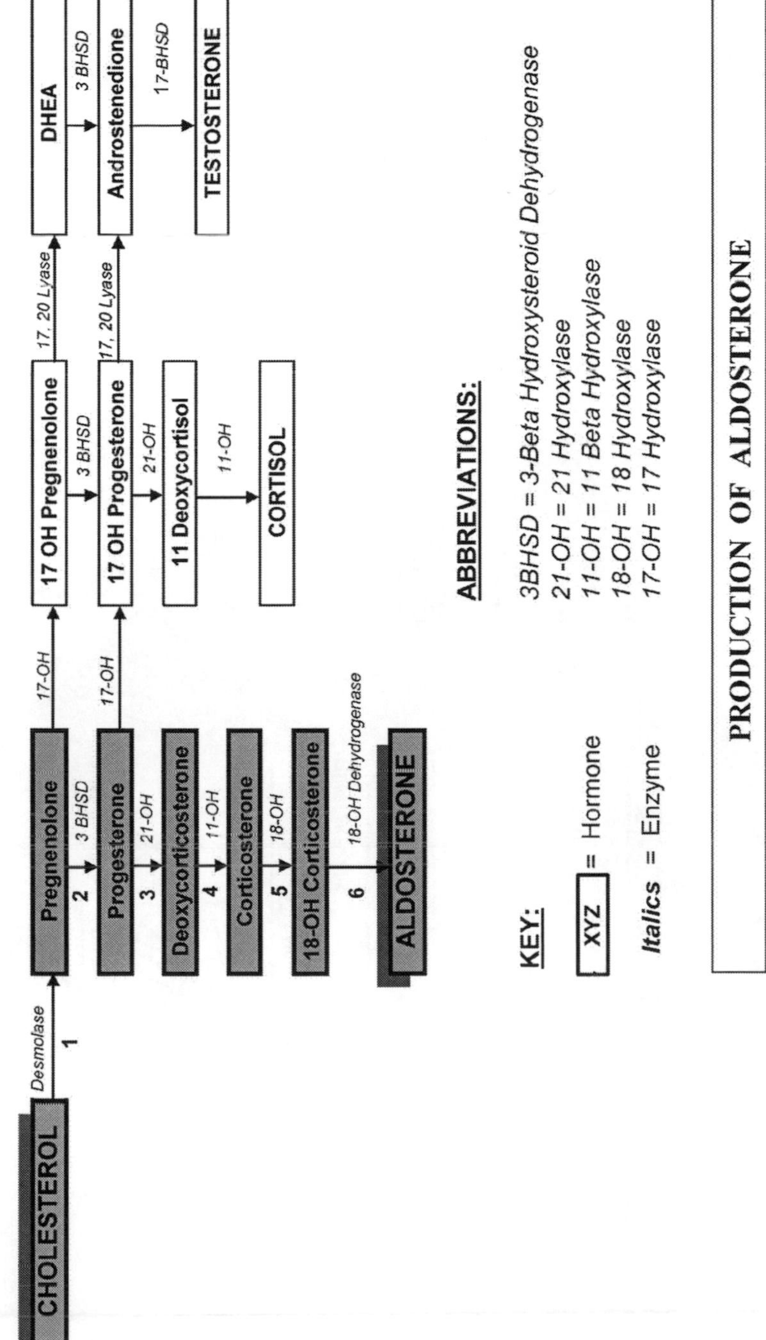


PRODUCTION OF ALDOSTERONE

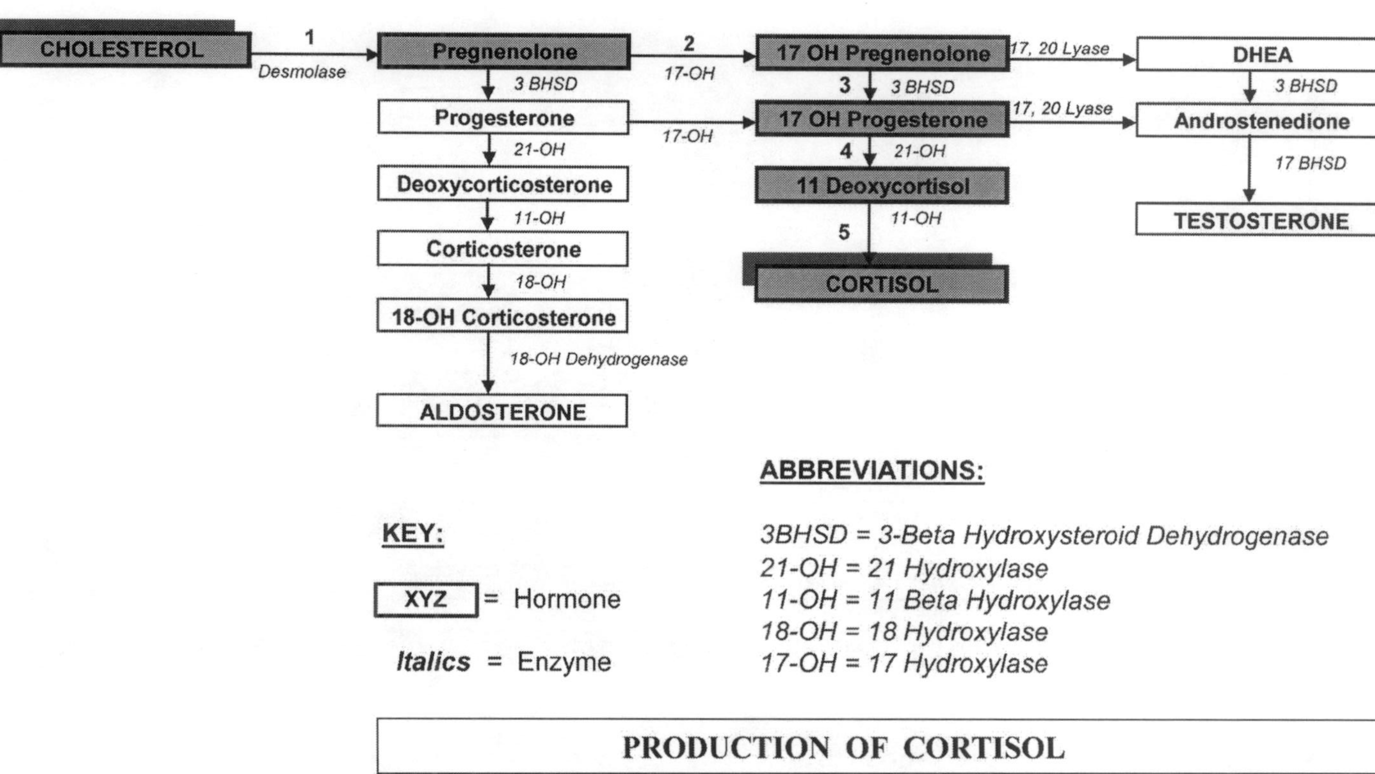
MINERALOCORTICOIDS
GLUCOCORTICOIDS
ANDROGENS
CHOLESTEROL
1
Desmolase
Pregnenolone
3 BHSD
Progesterone
21-OH
Deoxycorticosterone
11-OH
Corticosterone
18-OH
18-OH Corticosterone
18-OH Dehydrogenase
ALDOSTERONE
2
17-OH
17-OH
17 OH Pregnenolone
3
3 BHSD
17 OH Progesterone
4
21-OH
11 Deoxycortisol
5
11-OH
CORTISOL
17, 20 Lyase
17, 20 Lyase
DHEA
3 BHSD
Androstenedione
17 BHSD
TESTOSTERONE
KEY:
XYZ = Hormone
Italics = Enzyme
ABBREVIATIONS:
3BHSD = 3-Beta Hydroxysteroid Dehydrogenase
21-OH = 21 Hydroxylase
11-OH = 11 Beta Hydroxylase
18-OH = 18 Hydroxylase
17-OH = 17 Hydroxylase
PRODUCTION OF CORTISOL

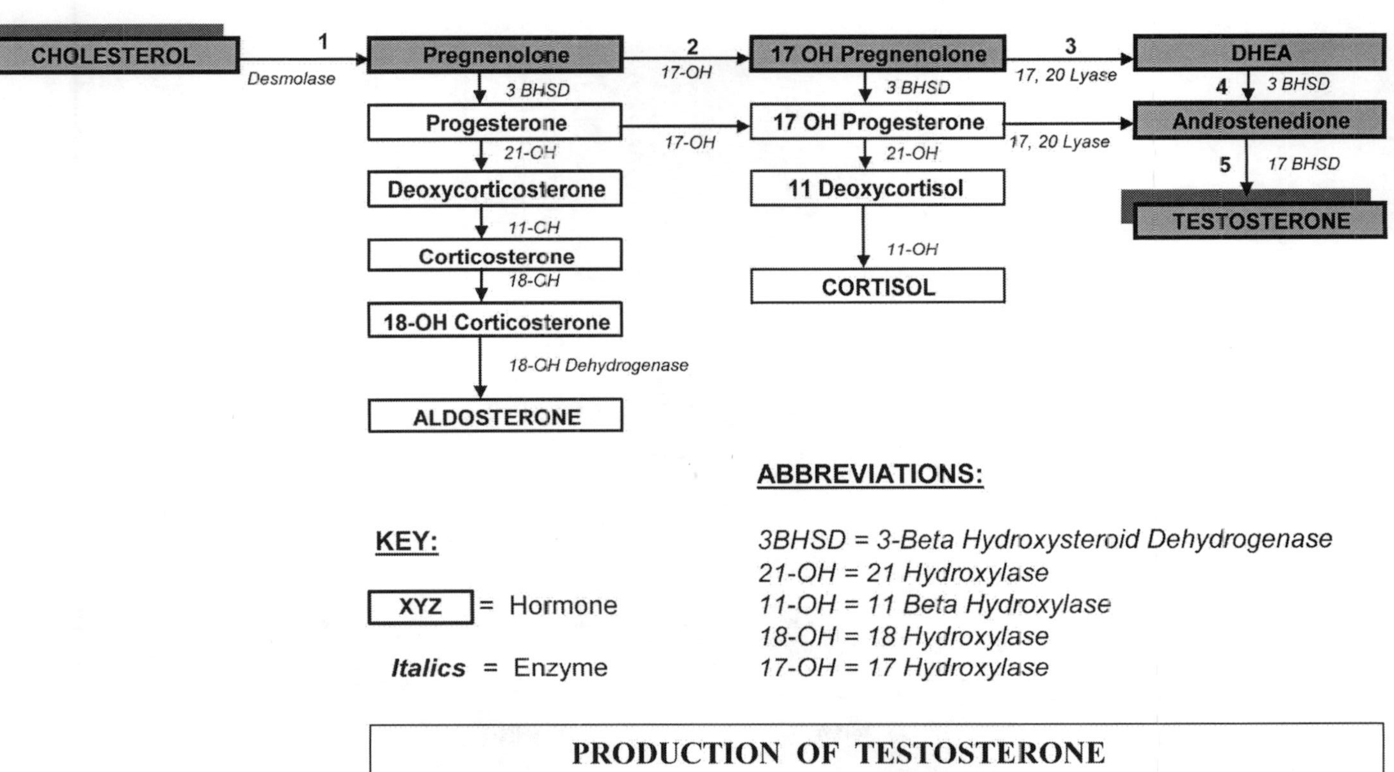
MINERALOCORTICOIDS
GLUCOCORTICOIDS
ANDROGENS
CHOLESTEROL
1
Desmolase
Pregnenolone
3 BHSD
Progesterone
21-OH
Deoxycorticosterone
11-CH
Corticosterone
18-CH
18-OH Corticosterone
18-CH Dehydrogenase
ALDOSTERONE
2
17-OH
17 OH Pregnenolone
3 BHSD
17-OH
17 OH Progesterone
21-OH
11 Deoxycortisol
11-OH
CORTISOL
3
17, 20 Lyase
DHEA
4
3 BHSD
17, 20 Lyase
Androstenedione
5
17 BHSD
TESTOSTERONE
KEY:
XYZ = Hormone
Italics = Enzyme
ABBREVIATIONS:
3BHSD = 3-Beta Hydroxysteroid Dehydrogenase
21-OH = 21 Hydroxylase
11-OH = 11 Beta Hydroxylase
18-OH = 18 Hydroxylase
17-OH = 17 Hydroxylase
PRODUCTION OF TESTOSTERONE

## THE HYPOTHALAMIC-PITUITARY AXIS (HPA)

The adrenal glands are regulated by parts of the brain called the hypothalamus gland and the pituitary gland. Release of the hormone CRF ("Corticotropin-Releasing Factor") from the hypothalamus gland triggers the pituitary gland to release its own hormone, ACTH ("Adrenocorticotropin Hormone"). ACTH, then, triggers the adrenal glands to produce cortisol.

### Normal Cortisol Production

Normally, cortisol is secreted when ACTH levels rise. When cortisol levels increase, ACTH levels then diminish. This is known as "negative feedback." If cortisol levels do not rise, ACTH continues to elevate, leading to increased adrenal gland activity. This is known as "positive feedback."

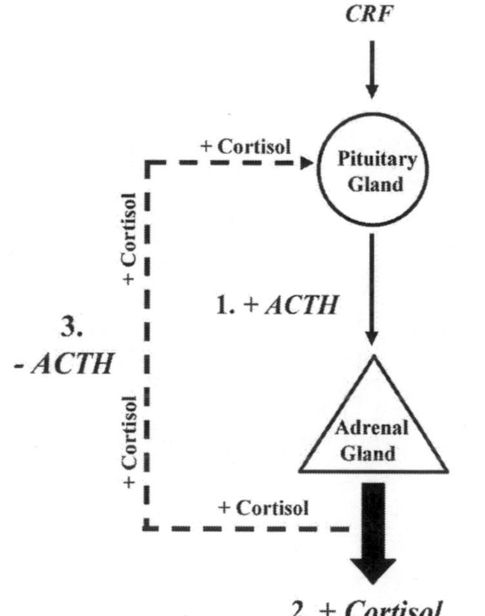


**NORMAL
ADRENAL GLAND FUNCTION:**

1. Pituitary Gland produces ACTH when Hypothalamus releases CRF.
2. Adrenal Gland produces cortisol in response to release of ACTH.
3. Production of cortisol stops continued release of ACTH.

ACTH and cortisol production is not the same at all times of the day. Normally, they are highest in the morning and low in the late afternoon and evening, following a day-night, or "circadian," rhythm. Production of many of the other adrenal hormones, including the adrenal androgens, also follows this same circadian pattern.

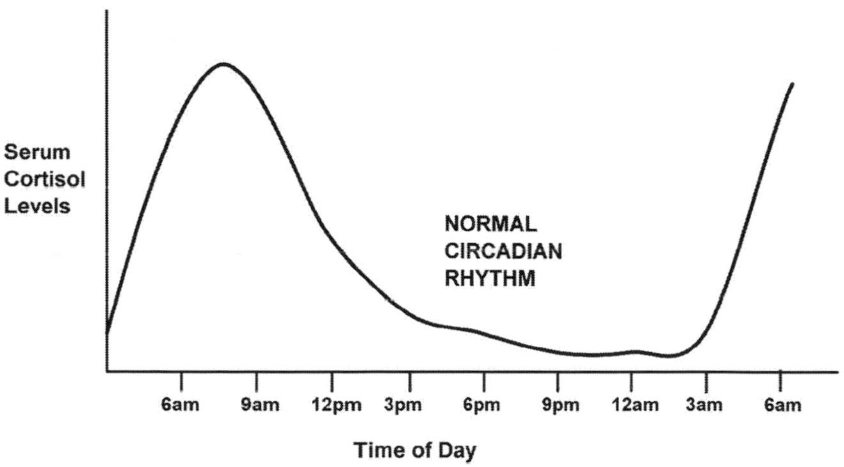


## Normal Aldosterone Production

Unlike with cortisol, ACTH does not regulate the production of aldosterone. Rather, aldosterone production is controlled by changes in blood pressure and blood volume, and the release of hormones from the kidneys.

Aldosterone production is normally triggered when the kidneys release a hormone called "angiotensin." In turn, angiotensin is released when there are high levels of another kidney hormone called "renin." Renin is produced when blood pressure and blood volume are low.

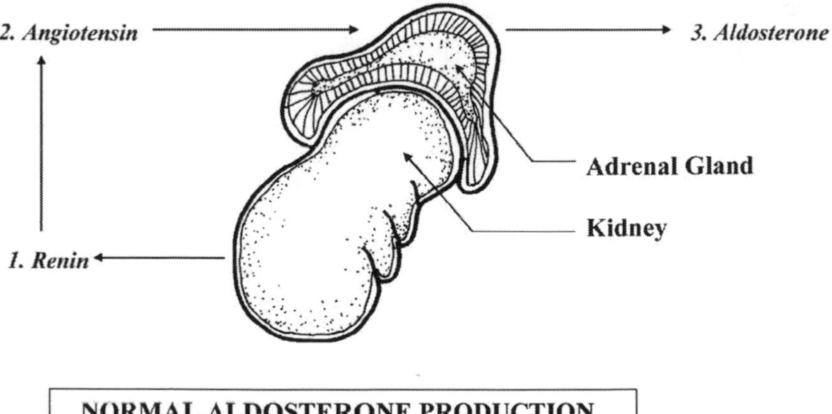


NORMAL ALDOSTERONE PRODUCTION

### What Happens in CAH?

When you have CAH, you cannot properly produce cortisol. Your brain then senses that the adrenal glands are not functioning properly. To compensate for this problem, the pituitary gland will release more ACTH.

High levels of ACTH will cause the adrenal glands to continue to try to make cortisol. This overactivity will cause the adrenal glands to increase excessively in size (what is known as "hyperplasia"). Thus, Congenital Adrenal Hyperplasia refers to an inborn (or "congenital") condition, involving adrenal gland enlargement (or "hyperplasia").

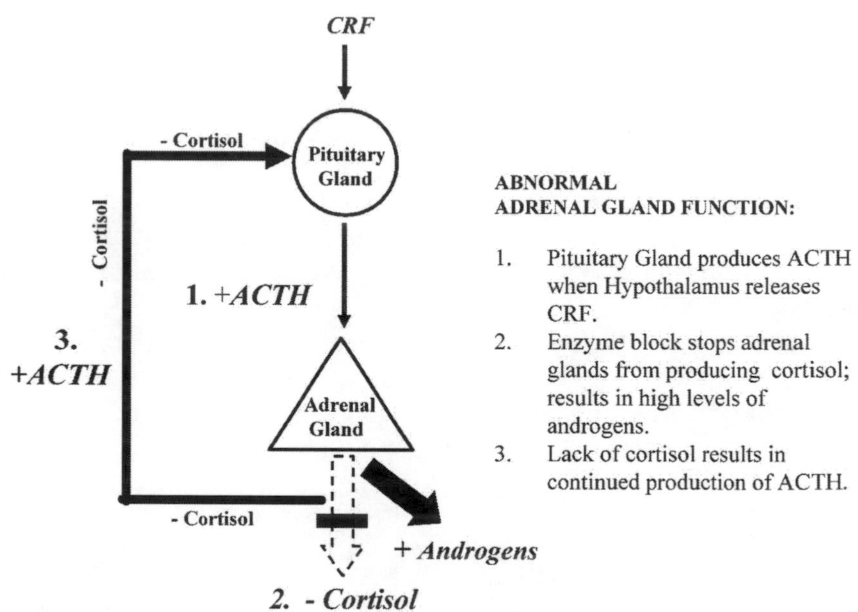


## THE PROBLEMS RESULTING FROM CAH

When the adrenal glands cannot produce enough cortisol and aldosterone, they instead overproduce androgens. Thus, CAH is usually characterized by deficiencies in cortisol and aldosterone production, *and* excesses in androgen production. Each of these problems can damage health.

In some uncommon forms of CAH, androgen production is also compromised or impaired. However, these account for a small percentage of all CAH cases.

## Lack of Aldosterone

Aldosterone helps the body maintain a proper balance of salts (also known as "minerals" or "electrolytes") and fluids. It does this by causing cells to retain "sodium" and lose "potassium." Without aldosterone, your body will end up doing the opposite, i.e., you will lose too much sodium and retain too much potassium. Thus, the severest form of CAH—in which you make little to no aldosterone—is termed "salt-wasting" (or "salt-losing") CAH.

Sodium is a mineral that helps to keep fluid in your blood vessels. A deficiency in sodium leads to low blood pressure and poor circulation. In some situations, blood circulation can stop altogether, a state known as "shock." If you are in shock, you are in danger of suddenly dying.

Low sodium levels can also cause a condition called "hyponatremia." Hyponatremia can lead to seizures. Seizures occur when your brain cells fire in an erratic pattern, causing uncontrollable movements and loss of alertness.

Potassium plays an important role in regulating the electrical charges of cells. The inability to get rid of potassium results in a condition known as "hyperkalemia." When you suffer from hyperkalemia, your heart can beat irregularly. This is called a heart "arrhythmia." Heart arrhythmias can also lead to shock and death by stopping your blood from circulating.

## Lack of Cortisol

Cortisol is essential for maintaining your general health and well-being. Commonly referred to as the "stress" hormone, it helps your body cope with physical stress, including the stress of illness. Without cortisol, you can have difficulty coping with infections, surgery, or trauma. These routine situations can lead to shock or sudden death, if you have CAH, unless proper precautions are taken.

Cortisol also helps to maintain normal blood sugar levels. A lack of cortisol can cause blood sugar levels to become too low, a condition known as "hypoglycemia." Because sugar (glucose) is needed for your brain to work properly, mental confusion or seizures can result, if you are hypoglycemic.

In addition, cortisol is essential for maintaining normal blood vessel tone, by allowing the walls of blood vessels to contract normally. Like low aldosterone, low cortisol levels can lead to low blood pressure, poor circulation, and shock.

## The Overproduction of Androgens

The inability to produce cortisol and aldosterone results in the overproduction of androgens. Because androgens are male hormones and influence fetal genital development, baby girls with CAH may develop masculine looking genitalia and be mistaken for boys, at birth.

After birth, high androgen levels can result in more rapid than normal physical development and growth. High androgen levels can also cause children to have signs of early puberty, including the development of body odor, axillary (armpit) hair, pubic hair, and acne at a young age. Excessive androgen production can also make the growth centers of the skeleton calcify prematurely, causing some CAH children to lose several inches of adult height.

There may also be problems with infertility. In women, high androgen levels can cause irregular periods, or a complete absence of periods. In men, small pieces of adrenal tissue (known as "adrenal rests") may develop within the testes. These rests produce hormones that can cause low sperm counts and reduced fertility. However, problems with infertility appear to affect CAH women more than men.

Lastly, high androgen levels can produce cosmetic problems such as severe acne, hirsutism (excessive hairiness), and male pattern baldness. While not life threatening, these problems can still adversely affect quality of life.

## The Basic Principles of CAH Treatment

Treatment of CAH is based on providing the hormones that your body cannot naturally produce. This is accomplished by replacing deficient cortisol and aldosterone with synthetic glucocorticoids and mineralocorticoids, usually in the form of oral medications. This treatment also helps to reduce androgen overproduction.

| FUNCTION OF MAJOR ADRENAL HORMONES | | | | | |
|---|---|---|---|---|---|
| **Cortisol** | | **Aldosterone** | | **Androgens** | |
| **Needed to:** | **Lack Causes:** | **Needed To:** | **Lack Causes:** | **Needed to:** | **Overproduction Causes:** |
| • Maintain normal blood vessel tone<br>• Maintain normal blood sugar levels<br>• Combat stress and illness | • Low blood sugar (hypoglycemia), leading to mental confusion and seizures<br>• Inability to fight stress and illness, leading to collapse of circulation (shock) and possibility of sudden death | • Maintain proper balance of fluids and minerals | • Low blood volume (hypovolemia), leading to low blood pressure (hypotension) and collapse of circulation (shock)<br>• High potassium levels in blood (hyperkalemia), leading to heart arrhythmias<br>• Low sodium levels in blood (hyponatremia), leading to seizures, coma, and mental confusion | • Promote proper growth<br>• Promote normal pubertal development | • Masculinization of external female genitalia<br>• Premature sexual development, incl. adult-type body odor; premature pubic hair growth; premature axillary hair growth; acne<br>• Premature bone maturation, leading to excessively rapid statural growth and loss of adult height |

## THE MOST COMMON TYPES OF CAH

There are more than six different types of CAH, each resulting from the lack of a specific enzyme. With each different type of CAH, cortisol production is somewhat impaired or abnormal, while the other adrenal hormones may be either under-produced or over-produced.

The three most common types of CAH are caused by problems with the "21-hydroxylase," "11-beta hydroxylase," and "3-beta hydroxysteroid dehydrogenase" enzymes. Each of these types of CAH may be either mild or severe, and may be detected in early infancy, in adolescence, or in adulthood.

| TYPES OF CONGENITAL ADRENAL HYPERPLASIA | | |
|---|---|---|
| **Missing Enzyme** | **% All Cases** | **Incidence per number of individuals** |
| ***21-Hydroxylase*** | 90% | 1: 10,000-20,000 |
| ***11-Beta Hydroxylase*** | 5% | 1:100,000 |
| ***3-Beta Hydroxysteroid Dehydrogenase*** | 3% | <1:500,000 |
| ***17-Alpha Hydroxylase*** | <1% | Rare |
| ***Corticosterone 18-Methloxydase Type II*** | <1% | Rare |
| ***Cholesterol Desmolase*** | <1% | Rare |

### 21-Hydroxylase Deficiency

The most common type of CAH, accounting for more than 90 percent of all cases, is 21-hydroxylase (21-OH) deficiency. Deficiency in 21-hydroxylase activity causes impaired production of aldosterone and cortisol. The inability to make cortisol and aldosterone results in the overproduction of androgens.

The most severe impairment of 21-hydroxylase activity results in salt-wasting. Salt-wasting occurs when you produce little to no cortisol and aldosterone. Salt-wasting is the most life-threatening form of CAH.

A milder form of 21-hydroxylase deficiency, resulting from a less severe enzyme problem, is "simple-virilizing" CAH. Simple-virilizers can make some aldosterone and cortisol, and are not at as great a risk for developing early life-threatening illnesses. However, like salt-wasters, simple-virilizers make high levels of androgens.

The mildest form of 21-hydroxylase deficiency is known as "late-onset" CAH (LOCAH). This form of CAH is often not detected until adolescence or even into adulthood.

Not normally life threatening, because aldosterone and cortisol production is near normal, late-onset CAH is also characterized by problems resulting from high androgen levels. In contrast with simple-virilizing CAH, the lesser degree of enzyme impairment—and, consequently, lower androgen levels—generally leads to different symptoms of androgen excess, at diagnosis.

## 11-Beta Hydroxylase Deficiency

The second most common type of CAH, accounting for about 5 percent of all cases, is 11-beta hydroxylase (11-OH) deficiency. Like with 21-hydroxylase deficiency, lack of 11-beta hydroxylase results in impaired aldosterone and cortisol production. However, unlike 21-OH deficiency, 11-OH deficiency does not normally result in salt-wasting. This is because those with 11-OH CAH normally produce high amounts of other salt-retaining hormones called "deoxycorticosterone" (DOC) and "11-Deoxycortisol" (commonly known as Compound S). High levels of these hormones will compensate for the lack of aldosterone and prevent you from wasting salt.

The inability to produce cortisol and aldosterone also results in the overproduction of androgens. In this way, 11-OH deficiency is not unlike simple-virilizing 21-OH CAH, with the difference that there may be problems with high—rather than low—blood pressure, due to the high levels of DOC and Compound S.

## 3-Beta Hydroxysteroid Dehydrogenase Deficiency

The third most common type of CAH is 3-beta hydroxysteroid dehydrogenase deficiency. Similar to 21-OH and 11-OH CAH, aldosterone and cortisol production is impaired. As a result, 3-beta deficiency can also result in salt-wasting. However, unlike with 21- and 11-hydroxylase deficiencies, androgen production is also impaired.

| COMPARISON OF 3 MOST COMMON TYPES OF CONGENITAL ADRENAL HYPERPLASIA | | | | | | | | |
|---|---|---|---|---|---|---|---|---|
| **Missing Enzyme** | **Major Deficient Hormones** | | | **Major Excess Hormones** | | | **Physical Characteristics** | |
| | **Mineralo-corticoids** | **Gluco-corticoids** | **Androgens** | **Mineralo-corticoids** | **Gluco-corticoids** | **Androgens** | **Salt-Wasting** | **Genital Ambiguity** |
| ***21-Hydroxylase*** | Aldosterone | Cortisol | - | Proges-terone | 17-OH Proges-terone (17-OHP) | DHEA; Androstene-dione; Testos-terone | Yes | Female: + Male: no |
| ***11-Beta Hydroxylase*** | Aldosterone | Cortisol | - | Deoxycorti-costerone (DOC) | 11-Deoxy-cortisol (Comp. S) | DHEA; Androstene-dione; Testos-terone | Rarely | Female: + Male: no |
| ***3-Beta Hydroxysteroid Dehydrogenase*** | Aldosterone | Cortisol | Androstene-dione; Testos-terone | Pregnelo-lone | 17-OH Pregnelo-lone | DHEA | Yes | Female: mild + Male: - |

As a result, when you have 3-beta deficiency, you can have problems with *under-*, rather than *over-*, masculinization. This relatively rare type of CAH accounts for less than 3 percent of all cases.

## OTHER DISORDERS OF THE ADRENAL GLANDS

CAH results in the inability to properly produce cortisol and aldosterone. The inability to produce these hormones can also be seen in a few other medical conditions.

"Addison's disease" is a condition in which the adrenal glands cease to function over time. When you have Addison's disease, you have impaired production of *all* the major adrenal hormones, including cortisol, aldosterone, *and* androgens. The inability to produce androgens is an important distinction between Addison's and 21-OH and 11-OH CAH.

Also unlike CAH, Addison's disease usually develops after birth, rather than being present when you are born. Addison's can occur as a result of infections that destroy adrenal tissue, such as tuberculosis. It can also result from autoimmune processes, in which the body "attacks" its own adrenal glands, resulting in their destruction. Though Addison's disease can affect both males and females, some causes of Addison's, such as adrenal leukodystrophy (ALD), tend to affect only males.

Hypoadrenalism (underactive adrenal glands) can also be seen in a condition referred to as "Congenital Adrenal *Hypo*plasia." Like Addison's disease, this disorder results in deficiencies of all the adrenal cortex hormones, causing adrenal "*hypo*plasia" (*under*developed adrenal glands), rather than "*hyper*plasia" (*over*developed adrenal glands).

Congenital Adrenal Hypoplasia is caused by a problem with the protein called "STAR." Problems with this enzyme prevent the conversion of cholesterol to the hormone "pregnenolone." Problems with proteins called "DAX" and "SFI" can also result in adrenal hypoplasia.

## LONG-TERM PROGNOSIS FOR THOSE WITH CAH

CAH can have a variable impact on your life. A lot depends on the type of CAH that you have and the age at which you are diagnosed. The treatment prescribed, as well as your ability to comply with treatment, will also influence how you fare.

If you have a severe form of CAH, and especially if you are a salt-waster, you are at risk for developing life-threatening adrenal crisis with illnesses, surgery, or trauma. Extra care must be taken to safeguard health during those times.

Long-term problems are usually related to the effects of increased androgen production. These include the problems of girls born with masculinized genitalia; growth and precocious puberty problems in children; and, in adults, problems with infertility.

The medications used to treat CAH can also impact how you do. Under-medication can result in the worsening of symptoms, while over-medication can also produce undesirable effects. As a result, careful monitoring of treatment is required.

Treatment of CAH is a life-long proposition. Vigilance is needed to achieve good results and minimize potential problems, but—with a good understanding of the condition, as well as how it's treated—you can lead a relatively normal life, even with CAH.

♦♦♦

## WHAT YOU MAY BE CONCERNED ABOUT: FREQUENTLY ASKED QUESTIONS

♦ ***Is there a cure for CAH?***

At present, no, though there are studies being done looking for a cure. Once a cure is found in a laboratory, however, it must still await rigorous testing and approval by the Federal Drug Administration, before it is made available to the public. This can mean another 5-10 years of waiting time. Thus—because current studies are still in the early experimental stages—it is unlikely that a cure for CAH will be available for at least another decade, likely, much longer.

♦ ***What about re-creating the missing enzyme and ingesting (eating) it? Hasn't this been done before with other disorders?***

To cure CAH, you must deliver the missing enzyme into the adrenal cells. This is not possible through ingestion. For medical conditions, which involve missing digestive enzymes—which exist *outside* of your cells—it might be possible to replace the missing enzymes by mouth. Treating CAH with replacement hormone therapy is similar to "curing" those conditions, with replacement oral enzymes.

♦ ***Is life expectancy affected by CAH?***

Long-term studies of this issue are not available. If diagnosed early and properly treated, life expectancy should not be affected by CAH. However, serious consequences, including death, can occur if CAH is undiagnosed or untreated, or if proper precautions are not taken during times of stress and illness.

♦ ***Does CAH impact intelligence?***

Intellectual development is normal if you have CAH. However, if there are severe episodes of shock or hypoglycemia, brain injury can occur which may compromise intelligence.

♦ ***Does exposure to excess androgens in the womb affect the development of the female brain?***

The effect of excess androgens on the female brain is not completely known. Until large numbers of CAH girls are studied in a very systematic fashion, it will be difficult to make a conclusive assessment of this issue. This is an area that is currently being studied by several groups of scientists.

♦ ***Will having CAH limit my child's ability to participate in sports or other physical activity?***

No. Your child should be able to participate in all normal physical activity including sports and athletics. However, you should be sure that he or she is up-to-date with all medications, and has access to quick sources of energy and plenty of fluids, before undergoing strenuous physical exercise.

♦ ***Is there a relationship between high and low cholesterol levels in those with CAH?***

No. There are many enzyme systems involved in cholesterol processing. If you have CAH, problems exist with cholesterol metabolism in your adrenal glands. However, the ability to process cholesterol in other tissue is normal. Thus, overall cholesterol levels are not affected by CAH.

♦ ***Is CAH known by any other names?***

Previously, CAH was referred to in the medical community as "adreno-genital syndrome" (AGS). It can also be referred to as "Adrenal Hyperplasia" or "Congenital Adrenocortical Hyperplasia."

♦ ***Can you serve in the military, if you have CAH?***

Most likely, no. When you have CAH, or another form of adrenal insufficiency, you are at risk of suffering an adrenal crisis, if injured or ill. This would generally preclude you from serving in the armed forces. However, eligibility criteria may be different if you have a very mild form of the disorder. In that case, you may wish to talk to a recruiting officer, who will be better able to evaluate your specific situation.

♦ ***I feel so guilty and depressed that I have given this condition to my child. Is it normal to feel this way?***

It is normal to feel sad, depressed, angry, and guilty when told that your child has a serious medical condition. For some, it can take months—even years—to regain a sense of equilibrium. For most, things generally *do* get better with time.

If you feel completely overwhelmed, you may wish to speak to a counselor or psychotherapist. You may also find it helpful to talk to others who have been in the same situation. A list of CAH support organizations is included in the appendix of this book. Your doctor may also be able to connect you with other CAH families in your area.

♦♦♦

# 2

# The Inheritance of Congenital Adrenal Hyperplasia

*Until they have a child diagnosed with CAH, most parents are not aware that they carry a defective gene for this condition. Thus, parents of a newly diagnosed child often find that their worries extend beyond the health of the affected child to the health of other children in the family.*

*In this second chapter, we explain the genetics of CAH. By knowing how CAH is passed on from parent to child, you can better evaluate the need to test other children in your family. You can also better understand the chance of having another child with CAH.*

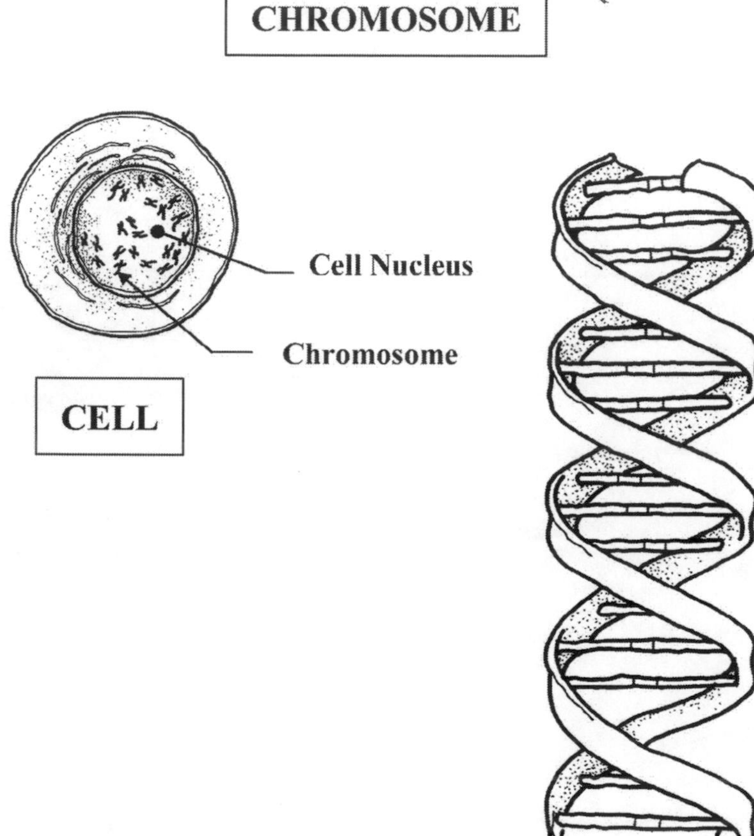


DNA DOUBLE HELIX

CONgenital Adrenal Hyperplasia is an inherited condition. This means that you are born with CAH, even if symptoms do not show up until later in life.

CAH is passed down from both the mother and father. For someone to be born with CAH, each parent must have a problem with an adrenal gland gene and pass this problem down to the child.

## CHROMOSOMES, GENES, AND DNA

Every cell in the body contains structures called "chromosomes." Chromosomes contain your genetic "blueprint."

Humans have twenty-three pairs of chromosomes. Normally, you have two copies of each chromosome—one from your father and one from your mother. Thus, there are forty-six *total* chromosomes in each cell in your body.

Chromosomes are made of chemical material called DNA ("Deoxyribonucleic Acid"). DNA is then arranged into large fragments called "genes." The inheritance of traits is passed down from parent to child via your genes. Genes regulate the production of proteins and enzymes, including those made by the adrenal glands.

A chromosome is made up of two strands of DNA that intertwine in a double-helix shape, like a spiral staircase. The "steps" of the staircase are formed of chemicals called "bases."

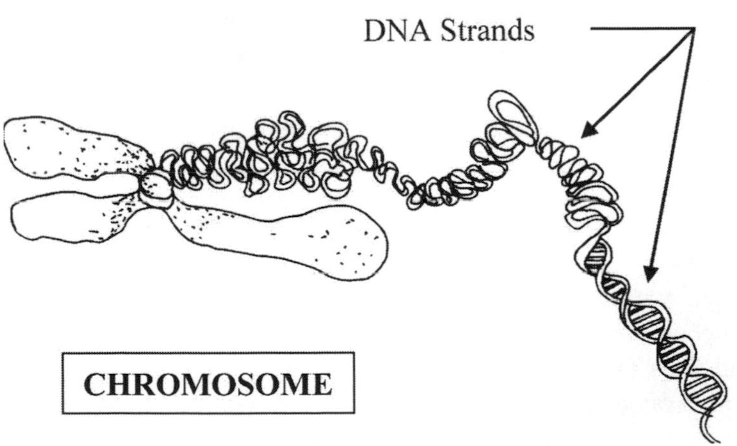


Bases can be one of four chemicals—"adenine" (A), thymine" (T), "guanine" (G), or "cytosine" (C). These four chemicals are the building blocks from which all proteins and enzymes are made.

Each base on one strand of DNA is paired with a base on the opposite strand of DNA. Adenine is always paired with thymine, while guanine is always paired with cytosine. Thus, each "step" of a DNA molecule—either an A-T combination or a C-G combination—is known as a "base pair." The size of a gene or chromosome is often expressed in numbers of base pairs.

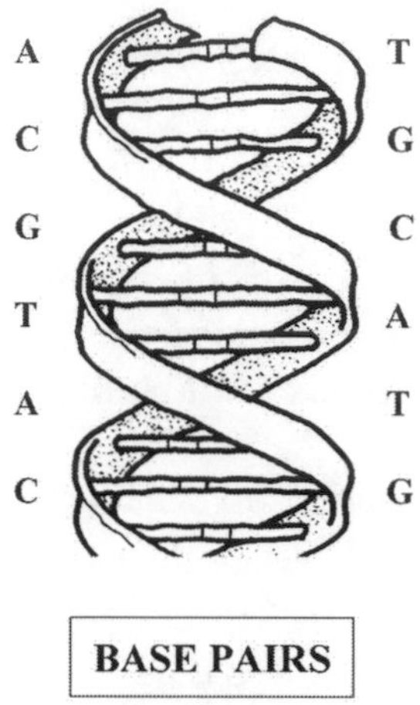


**BASE PAIRS**

Within each strand of DNA are the genes. Humans have approximately 30,000 genes, each ranging in size from a few hundred to several million base pairs.

A gene is a specific arrangement of DNA and bases. The sequence of the bases—that is, the order of the As, Ts, Cs, and Gs—forms a "genetic code" that tells your cells how to produce a particular protein. Protein is the essential component of human tissue, such as muscle, skin, hair, and nail.

Proteins are made of simple molecules called "amino acids." Humans make twenty different amino acids, each coded by a different sequence of three bases. The sequence "TTA," for example, tells the cell to make "leucine," while the sequence "GTA" codes for "valine." By following the genetic code, cells are able to know what amino acid to make at which step, in order to produce a particular protein.

The arrangement of DNA and bases is very similar from person to person; however, minor variations do exist. While these differences (called "polymorphisms") account for less than 0.1 percent (one tenth of one percent) of your total store of DNA, they are responsible for the features that distinguish one person from another. For example, the substitution of an A in the place of a G in a gene might result in you having brown eyes instead of blue, or blonde hair instead of black. Thus, these slight variations in DNA sequencing are what make all human beings unique.

## MUTATIONS: WHEN GENES GO WRONG

While most DNA variation is normal, some can have harmful consequences. Normally, genes are always being damaged and repaired. When damage is done and repair is incomplete, problems can occur with how the genes work.

Abnormal base sequences, resulting in structural changes to your genes, are called "mutations." Mutations can lead to illness and disease.

### The Different Ways That Your Genes Can Mutate

There are several ways that genes can mutate. Sometimes, part of the DNA on a gene can be lost. This results in a "deletion." Other times, extra DNA is added. This is called an "insertion." Deletions and insertions can involve a single base pair or large fragments of DNA.

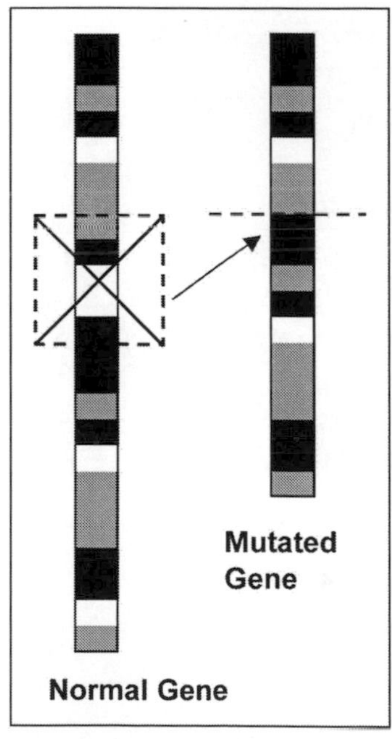


DELETION

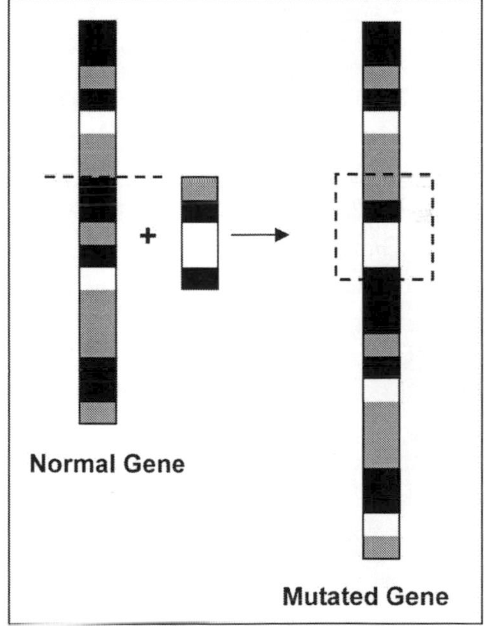


INSERTION

Other times, a single base on an element of DNA might be altered, leading to the production of an erroneous amino acid. This is called a "point-mutation." DNA can also be swapped among different genes. This is called "recombination."

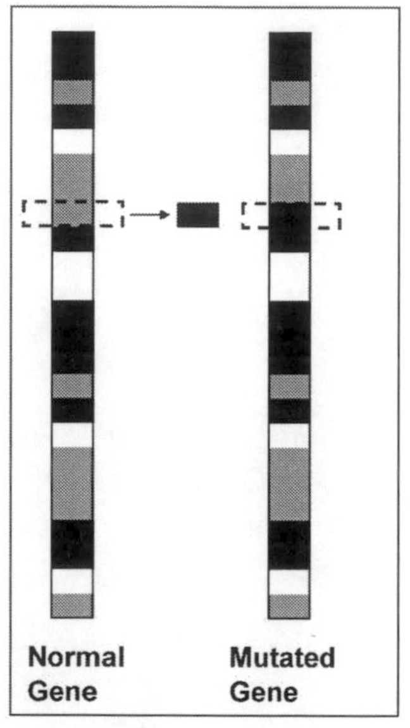


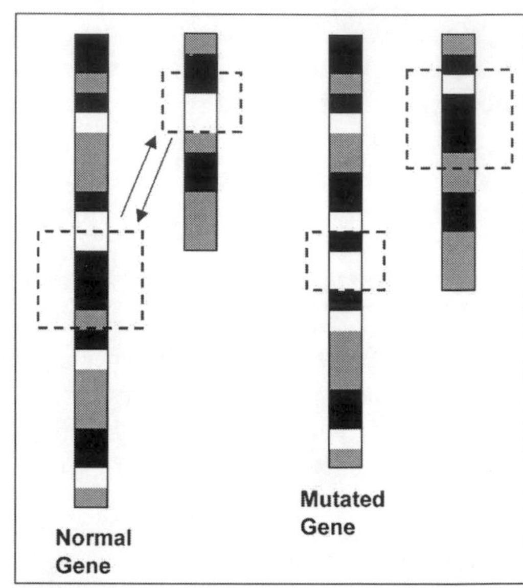


**POINT MUTATION** **RECOMBINATION**

Chromosomes are not continuous strings of genes. Interspersed among the genes on each chromosome are millions of bases of "non-coding" DNA, whose functions are largely unknown. Sequence variations can also occur in these "filler" stretches of DNA, though these abnormalities are not thought to be harmful.

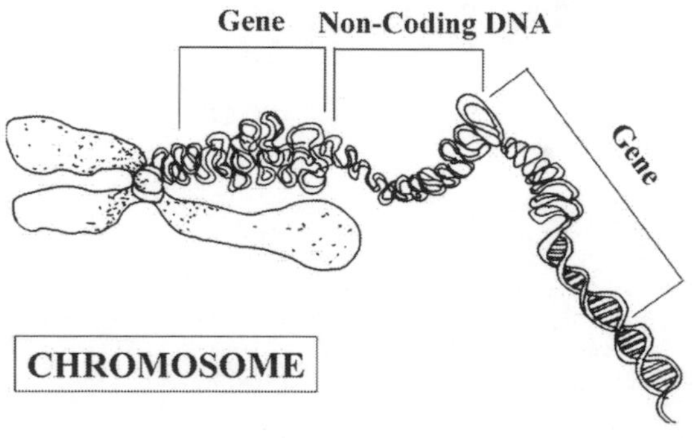

## GENE DEFECTS FOUND IN CAH

CAH occurs when there are mutations in the genes that code for production of the adrenal enzymes. These mutations can be caused by deletions, insertions, point mutations, or recombinations. Each type of CAH is caused by the deficiency of a different enzyme. Thus, each type of CAH involves mutations of a different gene.

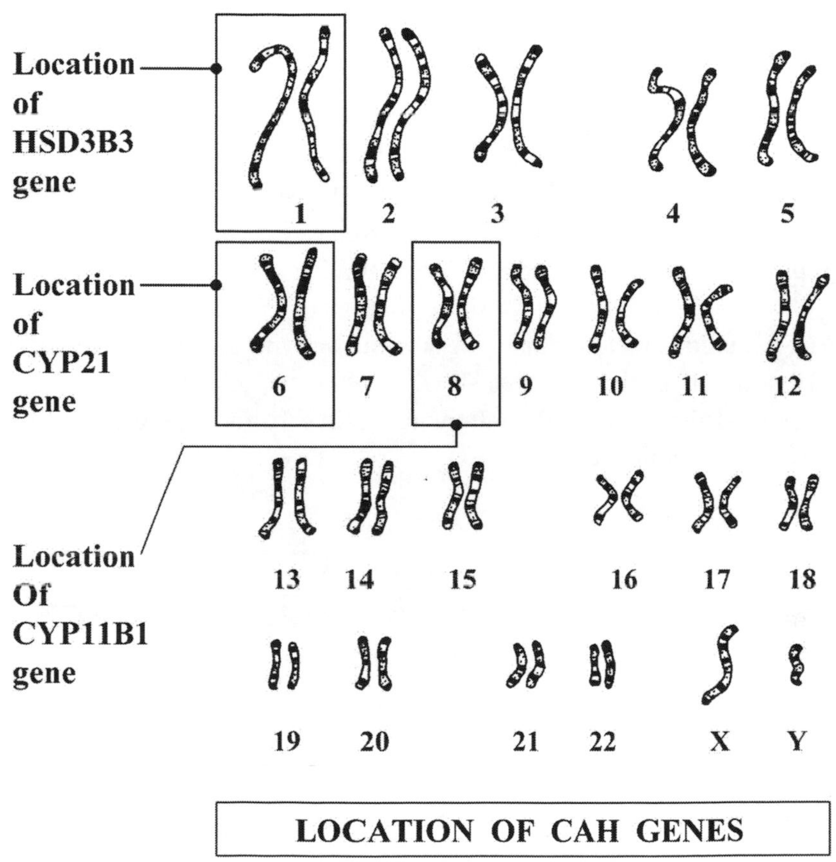


LOCATION OF CAH GENES

### Defects Found in 21-Hydroxylase Deficiency

The gene that codes for the 21-hydroxylase enzyme is called "CYP21" (also known as "21-OH" or "P450C21B.") CYP21 is located on chromosome number 6.

CYP21 is located close to another gene called "CYP21P." CYP21P is a false (or "pseudo") gene that does not code for the 21-hydroxylase enzyme. Sometimes, there is exchange of DNA material between CYP21 and CYP21P (recombination). When parts of CYP21 are replaced by parts of CYP21P, the result is a CYP21 gene that does not work.

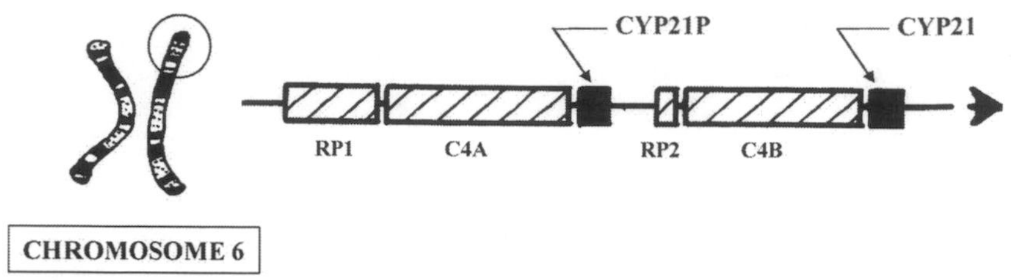


More than fifty mutations of the CYP21 gene have been discovered, though 95 percent of diagnosed CAH cases can be traced to nine or ten common mutations. By studying large numbers of patients, researchers have been able to link each of these mutations to a different severity of CAH. Mutations that eliminate all enzyme activity result in salt-wasting CAH, while those that preserve about 2 percent of enzyme activity result in simple-virilizing CAH. Mutations that allow 10 to 75 percent function are associated with late-onset CAH.

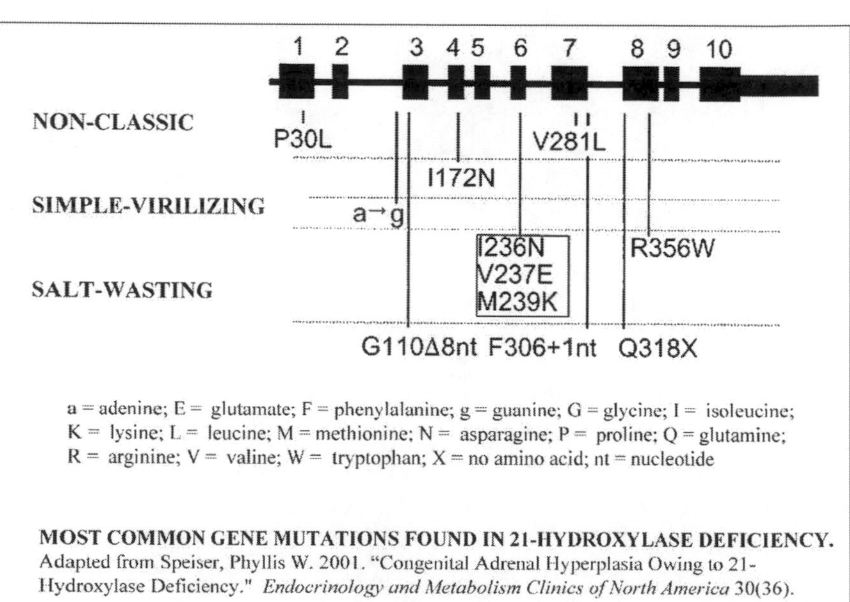


**MOST COMMON GENE MUTATIONS FOUND IN 21-HYDROXYLASE DEFICIENCY.** Adapted from Speiser, Phyllis W. 2001. "Congenital Adrenal Hyperplasia Owing to 21-Hydroxylase Deficiency." *Endocrinology and Metabolism Clinics of North America* 30(36).

Much like there are stretches of DNA on a chromosome that code for a protein, and stretches of DNA that do not, so there are "active" and "inactive" sequences on a gene. The active regions on a gene are called "exons," while the filler sequences are called "introns." Mutations of the CYP21 gene are often identified by their location on the gene, e.g., "exon 1" or "exon 8."

There are ten exons and nine introns on the CYP21 gene. Each exon normally codes for a different piece of the complete 21-hydroxylase enzyme.

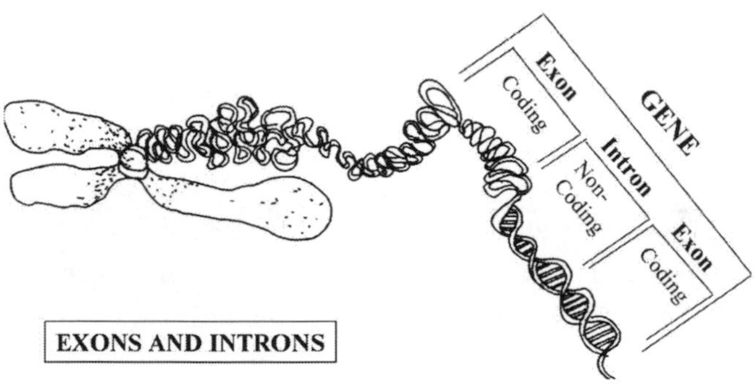

EXONS AND INTRONS

## Defects Found in Other Types of CAH

The gene that codes for the 11-beta hydroxylase enzyme is called "CYP11B1." CYP11B1 is located on chromosome number 8. As in 21-hydroxylase deficiency, many different mutations have been found in the CYP11B1 gene. Most of these problems are point mutations.

The CYP11B1 gene is located close to another gene called "CYP11B2." The CYP11B2 gene is important for producing aldosterone. Mutations in CYP11B2 result in a condition called "Aldosterone Synthase Deficiency." While this condition also results in salt-wasting, it is not considered a form of CAH, because cortisol production is not impaired. Aldosterone Synthase Deficiency is extremely rare.

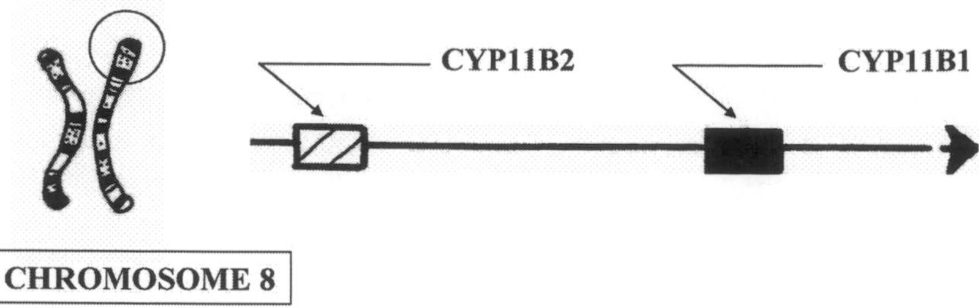


Three-beta hydroxysteroid dehydrogenase deficiency results when there is an abnormality in the gene known as "HSD3B3." This gene is located on chromosome number 1. Similar to 21-hydroxylase and 11-hydroxylase deficiencies, different point mutations have been identified in the HSD3B3 gene.

## HOW CAH IS INHERITED

CAH is classified as an "autosomal recessive" condition. "Autosomal" means that CAH can affect both sexes equally, while "recessive" means that problems must exist in *both* copies of your adrenal gland genes.

### Sex Chromosomes vs. Autosomes

Of the twenty-three pairs of chromosomes in the body, one pair is known as the "sex chromosomes." The other twenty-two pairs are called "autosomes." The letters X and Y designate the sex chromosomes, while the autosomes are numbered from one to twenty-two.

The X and Y chromosomes help to determine gender. Females normally have two X chromosomes, while males have one X and one Y chromosome, though there are exceptions to this general rule.

The sex chromosomes also pass on other traits. When traits are carried on a sex chromosome, they may be more prevalent in one gender. For example, color-blindedness, which is carried on the X chromosome, generally affects only males. In contrast, traits carried on autosomes are not sex-linked and can affect both genders equally.

The chromosomes affected by CAH—numbers 1, 6, and 8—are all autosomes. Thus, CAH is termed an "autosomal" condition and has equal chance of affecting males and females.

**Dominant vs. Recessive Traits**

All people carry two genes for a given trait, one inherited from the mother and one from the father. The two alternate copies of a gene are called "alleles."

Sometimes, the same variation of a gene will be carried on each allele. For example, you can inherit genes for blue eyes from both your mother and father. When this is the case, you are known as a "homozygote."

Other times, the two alleles may carry different variations of the gene. For example, you may get a "blue" gene from your mother, but a "brown" gene from your father. In that case, you would be a "heterozygote."

Your genetic makeup (i.e., "blue/blue" or "blue/brown") is referred to as your "genotype." In contrast, your visible physical characteristic—whether your eyes are actually brown or blue—is termed "phenotype." When each allele carries a different variation of a gene, your phenotype will depend on which trait is "dominant" (stronger) and which is "recessive" (weaker).

A dominant trait will show up, even if it is carried on only one allele. In contrast, a recessive trait will only show if it is carried on *both* alleles. For example, brown eyes are dominant, while blue eyes are recessive. Thus, if you have one "brown" gene and one "blue" gene, you will end up with brown eyes, because "brown" is the dominant trait. For you to have blue eyes, both of your genes must be "blue."

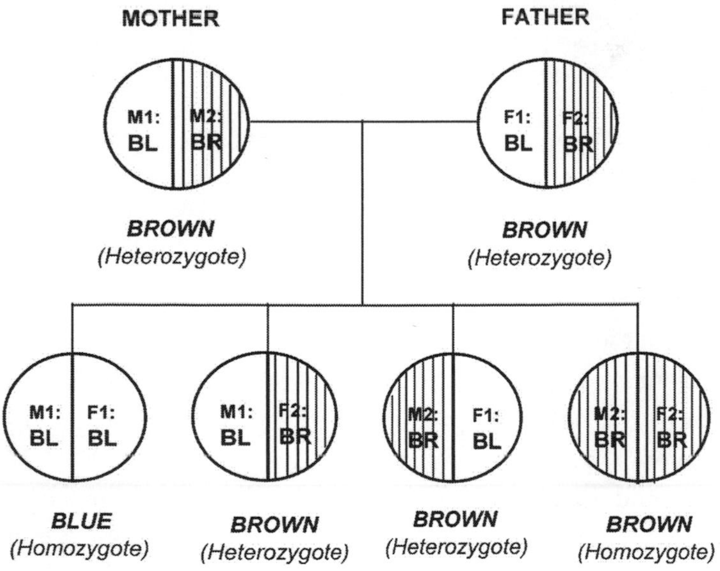

## Affected, Carrier, and Unaffected Status in CAH

CAH is passed on as a recessive condition. For you to be born with CAH, *both* copies of your adrenal enzyme genes must have abnormalities. Thus, you are an *affected* person—someone who actually *has* CAH—if you have inherited a mutated gene from *both* your parents.

If you receive an abnormal gene from one parent, but a normal gene from the other parent, then you are called a *carrier.* Carriers of CAH are considered heterozygotes. Because only one working gene is needed for normal adrenal function, carriers do not actually have CAH, though they can pass it on to their children. Carriers do not generally exhibit any symptoms of CAH.

If you have normal copies of *both* adrenal enzyme genes, then you are *unaffected.* Those who are unaffected do not have CAH and cannot pass it on to their children.

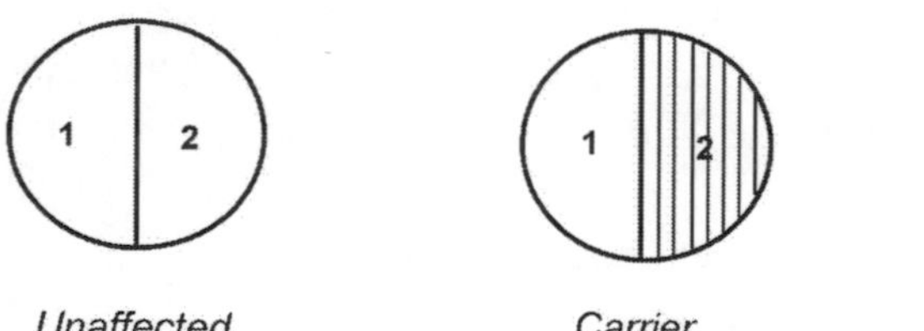

*Unaffected* *Carrier* *Affected*

## Genotype/Phenotype Correlations in CAH

Depending on the nature of the abnormalities, an affected person can be further classified as a "homozygote" or "compound heterozygote." You are a homozygote if you receive the same mutation from both parents, e.g., an exon 1 mutation from your father, and the same exon 1 mutation from your mother. In contrast, you are a compound heterozygote if you receive different mutations from each parent, e.g., an exon 1 mutation from your father, but an exon 8 mutation from your mother. Because it is more likely that each parent will pass on a different gene defect, most people with CAH are compound heterozygotes.

Compound heterozygotes will usually show the characteristics of the less severe ("better") gene copy. For example, if you have an exon 7 mutation on one allele (associated with late-onset CAH) and an exon

8 mutation on your other allele (associated with salt-wasting CAH), you would be expected to have late-onset CAH. In that way, the less severe defect is considered the dominant trait.

With CAH, however, genotype does not always predict phenotype. Sometimes, you can have a mild form of the disorder, if you carry salt-wasting mutations. Likewise, you can appear to have salt-wasting CAH, even if you carry a mild defect.

Affected sisters, who possess the same gene mutations, may also have different degrees of masculinization. Thus, while there is generally good correlation between genotype and phenotype, knowing the gene problem does not always predict the degree of the problem.

**Chances That Your Child Will Have CAH**

Most carriers do not realize that they have a defective adrenal gland gene, until they have a child with CAH. As a result, many parents are faced with uncertainty when considering future pregnancies.

However, once you know the affected status of both parents, it is relatively simple to figure out the chances of the next child being affected, unaffected, or a carrier of CAH. This can make family planning much easier for parents who desire more children.

The probability of a particular outcome applies to *each* pregnancy. Thus, when both parents are carriers of a defective gene, a 1 in 4 chance of having an affected child means that *each* child has a 1 in 4 chance of being born with CAH. It does *not* mean that one-quarter of the total number of children in the family will be affected.

With each new pregnancy, the same odds are repeated. Thus, in a family of four children, it is possible that *all four* children will be affected, just as it is possible that *none* of the children will be affected.

### *When Both Parents are Carriers*

There is a 1 in 4 (25 percent) chance that the child will have CAH; a 2 in 4 (50 percent) chance that the child will be a carrier; and a 1 in 4 (25 percent) chance that the child will be unaffected.

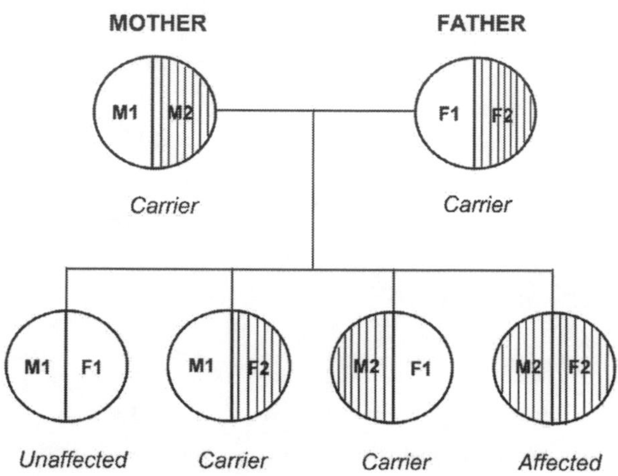


### *When One Parent Has CAH and the Other is a Carrier*

There is a 2 in 4 (50 percent) chance that the child will have CAH, and a 2 in 4 (50 percent) chance that the child will be a carrier. There is no (0 percent) chance that the child will be completely unaffected.

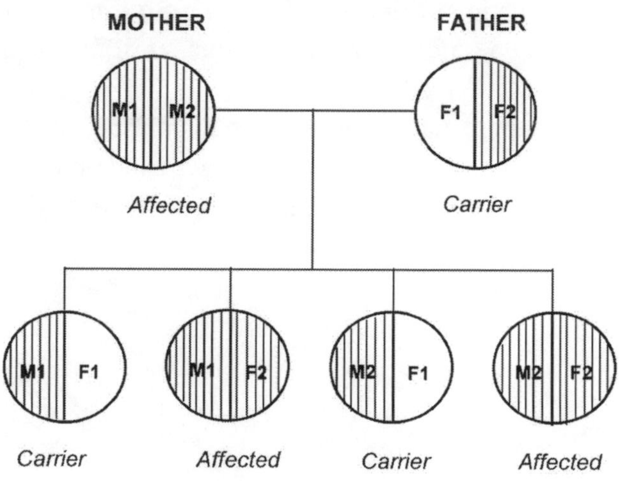

### *When One Parent Has CAH and the Other is Unaffected*

There is a 4 in 4 (100 percent) chance that the child will be a carrier. There is no (0 percent) chance that the child will have CAH, and no (0 percent) chance that the child will be completely unaffected.

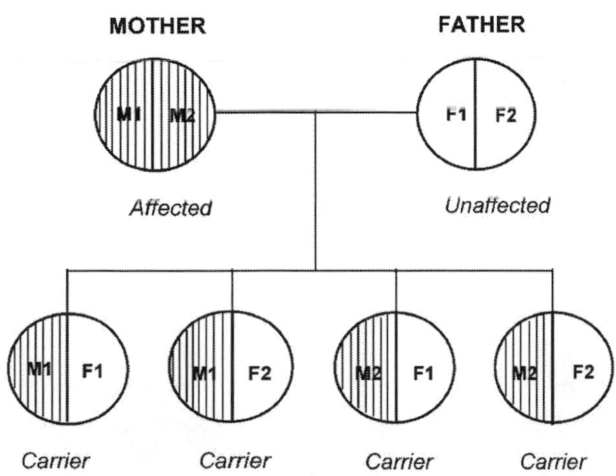


### *When Both Parents Have CAH*

There is a 4 in 4 (100 percent) chance that the child will have CAH. There is no (0 percent) chance that the child will be a carrier, and no (0 percent) chance that the child will be completely unaffected.

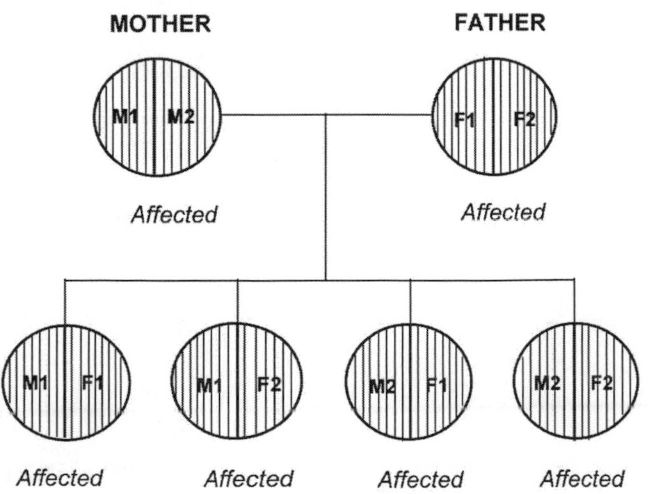

## GENE TESTING FOR CAH

While not routinely used to establish a diagnosis of CAH, gene testing can be very useful for family-planning purposes. Thus, affected individuals and their family members—including prospective spouses—may wish to undergo genetic counseling and testing prior to undertaking a new pregnancy.

The advantage of genetic testing is that specific mutations can be identified, which can be associated with salt-wasting, simple-virilizing, or late-onset CAH. As a result, you can be prepared, not only for the possibility of having a child with CAH, but also for the degree to which your child might be affected.

### How Gene Testing is Accomplished

Gene testing for illness and disease essentially involves searching through your DNA for abnormal base sequences. With over three billion base pairs (six billion total bases) of DNA on forty-six chromosomes (known as your *genome*), this is not an easy task. Fortunately, rapid advances in research and technology have enabled scientists to pinpoint the chromosomal abnormalities that cause many serious medical conditions, including CAH.

Gene testing for CAH is performed by comparing one's adrenal gland genes to those of a normally functioning adrenal gland gene. If differences exist in the size (total number of base pairs) of your adrenal gland genes, or the sequence of the bases, then the presence of mutations is indicated.

There are several tools that scientists have developed to help them detect these abnormalities. "Southern Blot Analysis" and "Polymerase Chain Reaction" (PCR) are two that are often used. Because each has limitations, the two are often used in conjunction, as complementary methods of testing.

Southern Blot Analysis uses specially designed pieces of DNA called "probes." Probes are short segments of DNA that contain bases complementary to those in known mutated sequences. If a mutation is present, the probe will bind to its complement, thus flagging the abnormality.

PCR is another technique that is often used in genetic testing. Sometimes referred to as "molecular photocopying," PCR allows scientists to quickly and inexpensively enlarge and copy small pieces of DNA. Using

PCR, scientists can examine samples of DNA in minute detail to detect abnormalities.

### Limitations of Gene Analysis

Because 21-hydroxylase deficiency is the most common form of CAH, many labs that perform DNA analysis for CAH test only for mutations of the CYP21 gene. Further, because gene testing is accomplished by looking for specific known abnormalities, labs will usually test first for the nine or ten mutations most commonly associated with CYP21.

Sometimes mutations are not found, even if you have been diagnosed with CAH. This usually does not mean that the diagnosis is wrong, only that the defects may occur in the less-charted regions of your genes. Further testing may then be necessary to confirm the presence of an abnormality.

### HLA Linkage

Though a complete copy of your genome is contained in nearly every cell in your body, genetic testing for CAH is usually accomplished via examination of blood. This is because the white cells in your blood contain a copy of your DNA. Red blood cells have lost their nuclei and thus are not useful.

Blood can also be used to identify certain people with 21-OH CAH. This is done via analysis of proteins called "Human Leukocyte Antigens" (HLA), which can be found on the surface of your white blood cells. These proteins are important in regulating your immune function. Much like you can be typed for different types of red blood cells (A, B, O), so you can be typed for different kinds of HLA.

The CYP21 gene and the genes that pass on the inheritance of HLA are both located in an area of chromosome 6, known as the "Major Histocompatibility Complex" (MHC). Because of their proximity, the genes for the adrenal enzymes are often passed on together with the genes for the HLA. Thus, certain CYP21 mutations are linked with certain types of HLA. By typing your blood for HLA, it can also be established if you are affected with CAH.

♦♦♦

## WHAT YOU MAY BE CONCERNED ABOUT: FREQUENTLY ASKED QUESTIONS:

♦ ***Is CAH more prevalent in certain ethnic groups?***

Yes. For example, in North America, the incidence of 21-hydroxylase deficiency is between 1:10,000 and 1:40,000 in the general population (one case for every 10,000-40,000 infants born). However, in Yupik Eskimos, it occurs at a rate of 1 in 400.

Specific types of CAH can also be more prevalent in certain ethnic groups. For example, late-onset CAH has a high incidence in individuals of Ashkenazi Jewish descent, where it is thought to occur at a rate of 1 in 200 persons.

♦ ***What is meant by the different "types" of CAH? There are the "21-hydroxylase," "11- hydroxylase," and "3-beta" types of CAH; but there are also the "salt-wasting," "simple-virilizing," and "late-onset" types of CAH. Can you clarify the differences in these terms?***

In a nutshell, the former terms refer to genotype, while the latter terms refer to phenotype. Thus, "21-hydroxylase," "11-hydroxylase," and "3-beta dehydrogenase" refer to the different enzyme problems that can lead to CAH, while "salt-wasting," "simple-virilizing," and "late-onset" refer to the different ways that you can present with symptoms, irregardless of the specific enzyme problem.

Because most people have 21-hydroxylase deficiency, it is usually assumed that you are talking about someone with 21-hydroxylase deficiency when you use the terms "salt-wasting," "simple-virilizing," or "late-onset." However, these terms can also be used to describe someone with a different enzyme deficiency. For example, if you had a severe deficiency of the 3-beta enzyme, you would also be a "salt-waster" while a mild deficiency of the 3-beta enzyme would characterize you as being "late-onset."

♦ ***Will children in the same family usually have the same form of CAH?***

Generally, yes. Affected children who share the same parents will usually be of the same genotype. However, because genotype does not always predict phenotype, siblings may not always present with the same severity of CAH, even if they possess the exact same mutations.

♦ ***What if one parent has CAH? Will the child end up with the same form of CAH as the parent?***

Not necessarily. An affected child will have the same mutations as the affected parent on only one allele. The severity of CAH may be significantly modified by the mutations inherited from the other parent, on the other allele. Thus, while siblings are likely to have the same mutations, because they have the same two parents, family members of different generations are more likely not to.

♦ ***If parents are each carriers of different types of CAH—for example, one parent is a carrier of a 21-OH defect, while the other parent is a carrier of an 11-OH defect—can their children end up with CAH?***

Probably not. Generally, two parents would have to have problems with the same chromosome in order for their child to end up with CAH. However, DNA can be exchanged between different chromosomes, resulting in gene mutations and disease. At the same time, while theoretically possible, such a case of CAH has probably never been identified.

♦ ***The "better" gene is dominant when someone has only one mutation on each allele. What if there is more than one mutation on each allele?***

The picture is more complicated when you have multiple mutations on one or both alleles (e.g., an "exon 1" and "exon 7" mutation on one allele, and an "exon 2" mutation on the other allele). When there is more than one mutation on each allele, the severity of CAH will depend on the particular combination of gene defects. Thus, each case will be slightly different and the "better" gene rule may not necessarily apply.

♦ ***Is DNA testing for CAH 100 percent accurate?***

DNA testing picks up 90 to 95 percent of cases of 21-hydroxylase CAH, so it is not 100 percent accurate. However, accuracy has more to do with whether it is possible to identify all the possible mutations, rather than whether a mistake was made. In other words, if you get a positive result, chances are likely that you have CAH. If you get a negative result, it is possible that you may still havc CAII, but just happen to have a less common mutation.

♦ ***Where can I go to get genetic testing done? How expensive is it? Is testing covered by insurance?***

There are a limited number of laboratories in the U.S. that will perform testing for 21-hydroxylase deficiency. Most will accept mailed blood samples, prepared as instructed. Results are usually available in two to six weeks.

The cost of testing can be highly variable. Depending on the lab, costs can range from several hundred dollars per family, to over six hundred dollars per person. Insurance reimbursement can also be highly variable. Some policies will pay in full, while others will reimburse little to nothing. In order to avoid unpleasant "sticker shock," you may want to fully understand the charges that might be incurred, prior to undergoing any actual testing.

A partial listing of labs is included in the appendix of this book. You may also want to ask your endocrinologist for a recommendation.

♦ ***I got our DNA report back and can't understand what it says. What are all these mysterious "codes" and who can help me interpret what they mean?***

A DNA report for CAH will usually list the specific mutations that have been found, as well as their locations on the gene. For example, "Exon 1, P30L" indicates that the mutation called "P30L" was found on exon 1 of your 21-hydroxylase gene. "P30L" means that at position 30, on exon 1, the amino acid "proline" (P) was supposed to have been made, but instead became "leucine" (L). (This would be an example of a point mutation.)

Practically speaking, the usefulness of a DNA report lies in understanding the severity of CAH that is normally associated with the detected mutations. If you have trouble understanding how to use the information in the report, ask the lab for help. Usually, they will have a genetic counselor available that can help explain the results and their significance. You can also ask the lab for an accompanying letter of explanation.

♦♦♦

# 3

# Recognizing the Symptoms of Congenital Adrenal Hyperplasia

*The symptoms of CAH can be quite variable. The age at which symptoms appear can also be quite wide ranging. Much depends on the type of CAH and its severity.*

*In states with newborn screening for CAH, many affected infants are now identified before the onset of any symptoms. If these children are promptly treated (within seven days of birth), many early symptoms of CAH may be averted altogether.*

**COMPARING SEVERITIES OF CONGENITAL ADRENAL HYPERPLASIA**

| Phenotype | Percent Enzyme Activity | Aldosterone Production | Cortisol Production | Androgen Production | Plasma Renin (PRA) | 17 OHP after ACTH Stim. | Typical Age at Diagnosis | Genitalia at Birth |
|---|---|---|---|---|---|---|---|---|
| **Salt-Wasting** | None | Decreased | Decreased | Elevated | Elevated | >20,000 ng/dl | Infancy | Female: masculinized<br>Male: normal |
| **Simple-Virilizing** | Low | Normal | Decreased | Elevated | Possibly Elevated | >10,000-20,000 ng/dl | Female/Male Infancy to adolescence | Female: masculinized<br>Male: normal |
| **Late-Onset** | Moderate | Normal | Normal | Elevated | Normal | 1500-10,000 ng/dl | Female/Male: late childhood to adulthood | Female: poss. mild masculinization<br>Male: normal |

**MOST** cases of CAH are due to 21-OH deficiency. With 21-OH deficiency, symptoms will be related to the effects of impaired cortisol and aldosterone production, and the overproduction of androgens. CAH due to a different enzyme deficiency may produce slightly different symptoms.

There are generally three recognized severities of 21-OH CAH. These are known as "salt-wasting," "simple-virilizing," and "late-onset" CAH. Each involves a different degree of enzyme impairment. While the severity of CAH may be clear in many people, others may appear intermediate between two different types.

## SALT-WASTING CAH

Salt-wasters have the most severe enzyme impairment. If you are a salt-waster, you produce little cortisol and aldosterone. As a result, you are at risk of suffering an early life-threatening adrenal crisis if not promptly diagnosed and treated. Adrenal crisis can occur within the first week of life, but—more commonly—occurs two to four weeks after birth.

Salt-wasting can also occur with severe 3-beta dehydrogenase deficiency. It does not normally occur with 11-beta hydroxylase deficiency.

### The Danger of Early Adrenal Crisis

Adrenal crisis is a life-threatening condition in which there are electrolyte abnormalities, poor circulation of blood, or low blood sugar levels (hypoglycemia). Each of these problems can cause you to go into "shock," a situation that occurs when blood circulation stops altogether. When you are in shock, unconsciousness and sudden death can occur.

In early infancy, adrenal crisis is not usually triggered by a specific event or illness. Rather, the lack of cortisol and aldosterone leads to a progressive decline in health.

### Symptoms in Newborns and Infants

There are several warning signs of developing adrenal insufficiency in newborns. These include dehydration, vomiting, reflux, irritability, and lethargy.

Before the onset of shock, an infant will show signs of dehydration. Moisture will be lost from the lips, and the skin will start to lose its normal tone. Urination may become less frequent. An infant should have a wet diaper every three hours or so. When dry diapers become more common than wet ones, the child may be becoming dehydrated. As dehydration becomes more severe, body temperature can drop and hypothermia—a dangerous situation in which body temperature drops below 95 °F—can develop.

Vomiting and irritability are also signs of developing adrenal insufficiency. It is not uncommon for infants with CAH to visit the pediatrician for evaluation of vomiting or reflux, only to have the formula changed, but the condition still not detected. Some infants may lose interest in feeding altogether and become lethargic. Weight loss may occur. At the end of the first month of life, a CAH child may weigh less than at birth.

**SIGNS AND SYMPTOMS OF SALT-WASTING CAH**

- Ambiguous genitalia in female infants
- Salt-wasting crises in boys or girls
- Poor feeding
- Poor weight gain
- Vomiting/reflux
- Weight loss
- More dry diapers than wet
- Low body temperature
- Lethargy
- Prolonged newborn jaundice

## Ambiguous Genitalia

CAH is the most common cause of "ambiguous genitalia" in infants. The term "ambiguous genitalia" is used to describe genitals that do not look typically male or female. Because most CAH cases are due to 21-hydroxylase or 11-hydroxylase deficiency—both of which result in an overproduction of male hormones—ambiguity in CAH generally involves girls with genitals that have male-like characteristics. Excess male hormones do not affect the proper formation of male genitalia.

Masculinization of the female genitalia can be either mild or severe. For comparative purposes, many doctors use a scoring system called the "Prader scale." Named after the physician who developed this tool, the Prader scale differentiates between five levels of masculinization. Those who are considered "Prader 1" are only mildly masculinized, while those who are a "Prader 5" appear like boys.

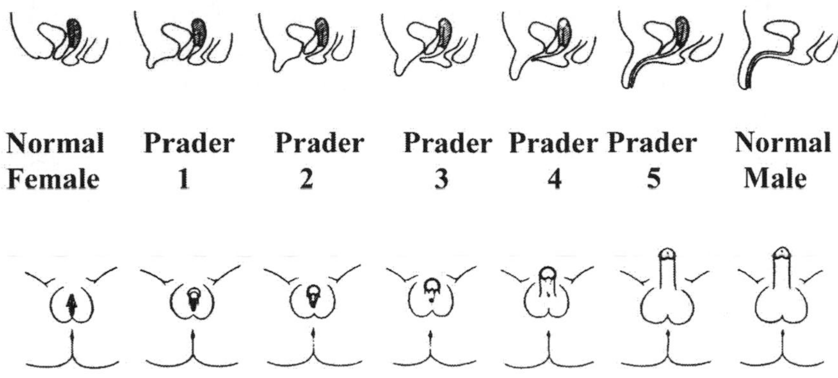


**COMPARISON OF PRADER LEVELS.** Adapted from *Pediatric Endocrinology*, Eds. Colu R. et al. (Raven Press, N.Y., 1981) p. 491.

The most common effect of excess androgens is an enlarged clitoris. When masculinization is pronounced, the clitoris may be so enlarged as to look like a small penis. The labia may also be partly, or completely, joined or fused together. In severe cases, the fused labia can take on the appearance of male scrotum, though there will be no testicles.

Excess androgens can cause incorrect formation and positioning of the vagina and urethra (the tube through which the bladder empties.) Normally, the vagina and urethra are separate from each other. In cases where masculinization is severe, the two may end up as a single structure. Sometimes, the tip of the urethra may end within, or at the tip of, the clitoris.

Abnormalities of the ureters (the tubes connecting the kidneys to the bladder) may also be present. This can interfere with the draining of urine from the kidneys to the bladder and increase the risk of urinary tract infections (UTIs).

To assess the degree of ambiguity, your doctor may refer you to another specialist called a pediatric urologist. This type of physician specializes in the care and treatment of the urinary and reproductive tracts in children.

The internal female reproductive structures—i.e., the uterus, Fallopian tubes, cervix, and ovaries—are unaffected by excess androgens. Thus, though some CAH girls may have an outwardly male appearance, it is important to realize that they do not possess both male and female sex organs and are biologically female.

If ambiguity of the genitals is present at birth, a physician may suspect CAH, leading to early diagnosis and prevention of an adrenal crisis. However, some girls may be so masculinized that they are initially misidentified as boys. Like boys, severely masculinized girls may escape detection until they become seriously ill with adrenal crisis.

In a small minority of CAH cases, ambiguous genitalia can also affect males. Where the enzyme impairment—such as with 3-beta dehydrogenase deficiency—results in a *deficiency* in androgen production, ambiguity can result in *under*-masculinized male genitalia. In some cases, this can result in the misidentification of infant boys as girls.

## SIMPLE-VIRILIZING CAH

When you are a simple-virilizer, the ability to make cortisol is impaired, but the ability to make aldosterone—while also impaired—is close to normal. As a result, diagnosis is usually related to signs of increased adrenal androgen production, rather than early adrenal crisis. (The term "simple," in this case, might be thought of as meaning "only." Thus, "*simple*-virilizing" refers to a still-severe form of CAH characterized "*only*" by signs of virilization, rather than salt-wasting.)

Though aldosterone production is near normal, some simple-virilizers can have a problem with elevated renin. Renin is a hormone that is produced by the kidneys. High renin signifies that blood volume may be too low. To restore blood volume, mineralocorticoid replacement may be necessary, making treatment of these simple-virilizers similar to treatment of those with salt-wasting CAH.

### Symptoms in Newborns and Infants

Excess androgen production can be as severe in simple-virilizers, as in salt-wasters. As a result, girls with simple-virilizing CAH may have masculinization of the genitalia to as great a degree as girls with salt-wasting CAH. For those female infants, atypical genitalia may lead to a diagnosis in infancy.

In contrast, the lack of obvious symptoms at birth will prevent boys—as well as girls with a milder defect—from being diagnosed in infancy. These children will often escape detection until they are evaluated for excessive growth or early signs of puberty, later in childhood. In some cases, CAH may be discovered when an otherwise healthy child suffers an adrenal crisis, or has trouble getting well, after a routine illness.

| COMMON SYMPTOMS OF SIMPLE-VIRILIZING CAH |
|---|
| • Masculinized genitalia in girls<br>• Enlarged genitalia in boys<br>• Signs of early puberty<br>• Acne<br>• Adult type body odor<br>• Axillary hair<br>• Early development of pubic hair<br>• Accelerated growth |

## Signs in Older Children

Excessive androgen production will produce signs of masculinization in both boys and girls. Without treatment, girls may develop progressive clitoral enlargement. Boys may have progressive penis enlargement. Some undiagnosed CAH boys may achieve an adult-size phallus during the toddler years.

Increased androgen production can also lead to accelerated statural growth. An abnormal growth pattern may be suspected in the child who reaches a higher curve on the growth charts each year. For example, a child with unrecognized CAH may grow at the 50th percentile line for height at one year of age; reach the $75^{th}$ percentile by three years of age; and be significantly taller than the $95^{th}$ percentile at five years of age. This is in contrast to the child who starts, and stays, at the $95^{th}$ percentile line each year.

Growing too quickly is of concern because linear growth may stop prematurely. Excess androgens cause early closure of the growth plates in the skeleton. When the growth plates close, no more height is possible. Thus, though tall as children, some children with CAH do not achieve their genetic height potential and can end up as short adults.

High androgen levels can also lead to signs of puberty at a very young age. These symptoms include development of adult-type body odor, which is detectable in the armpits; acne; and pubic and underarm (axillary) hair. In children with CAH, these symptoms can start to appear around the age of three or four, though in infrequent cases, they may be present even in infancy.

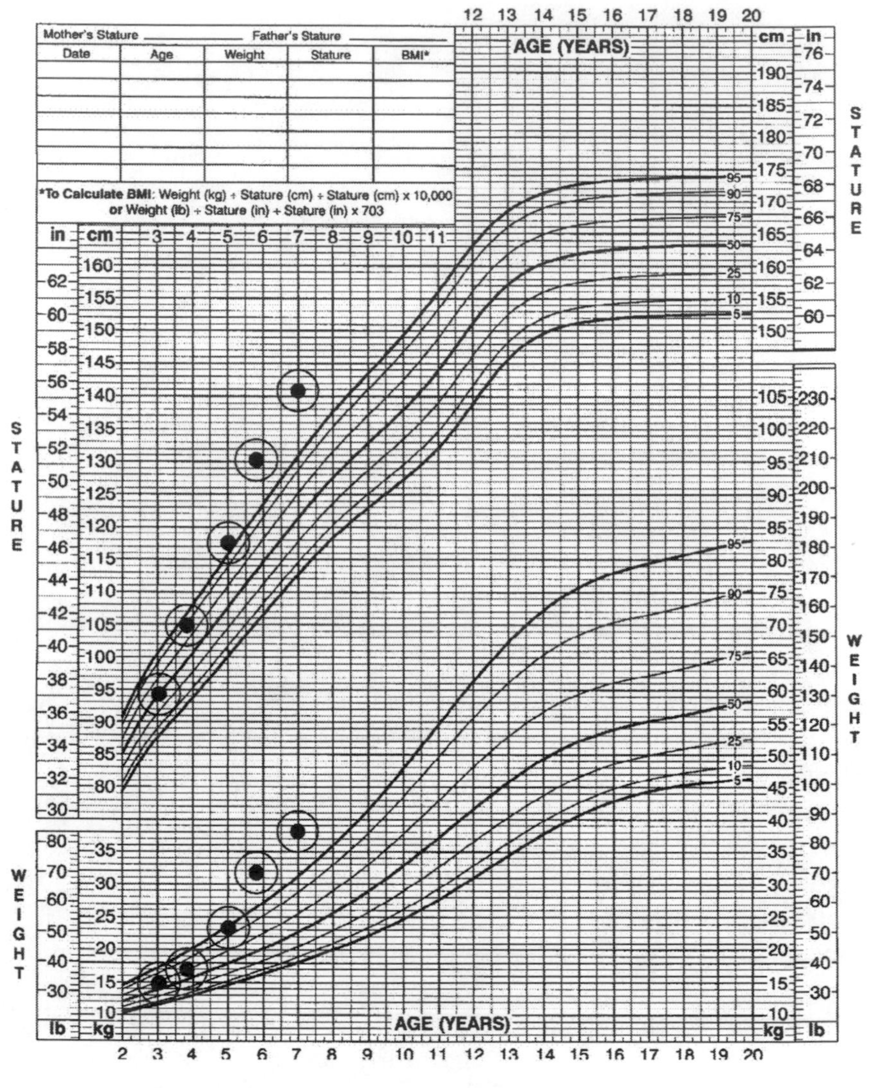


**EXAMPLE OF ACCLERATED GROWTH.**

## LATE-ONSET CAH

The mildest form of 21-hydroxylase deficiency is known as "late-onset" CAH (LOCAH). Late-onset CAH is sometimes referred to as "adult-onset" CAH or the "attenuated" form of CAH. When you have late-onset CAH, you may not be diagnosed until adolescence or young adulthood, when there are problems of infertility or menstrual irregularity.

Not normally life threatening, because aldosterone and cortisol production is near normal, late-onset CAH is also characterized by problems resulting from high androgen levels, rather than salt-wasting. These tend to manifest themselves as problems of hormonal imbalance and infertility, though some symptoms may overlap with those seen in simple-virilizing CAH.

Symptoms of LOCAH can first appear during adolescence or even into adulthood. Because problems resulting from excess male hormones tend to be more obvious in females, LOCAH is more often diagnosed in women than men.

### Signs in Childhood

If LOCAH is detected in childhood, symptoms may be similar to those seen in simple-virilizing CAH. Girls may have progressive clitoral enlargement, while boys *and* girls may show signs of precocious puberty. Children may have oily hair and oily skin, and moderate or severe acne may be present.

### Signs in Adolescents and Adults

LOCAH is often not detected until signs of hormone imbalance or infertility are discovered in adolescent girls and young women. Problems may include excessive hair (known as "hirsutism"), which develops in a male pattern; premature balding; and development of a muscular build and low voice. Acne problems may persist into adulthood.

In some cases, hirsutism may cause a woman to develop hair on the chest, back, or abdomen. Others may have facial hair that necessitates daily removal or shaving. While not life threatening, these cosmetic problems can still present challenging quality of life issues for women with late-onset CAH.

Infertility is also often a problem for those with LOCAH. Because androgens interfere with the normal female reproductive cycle, women may have irregular menstrual periods, or no periods at all ("amenorrhea.") While problems of infertility are not limited to those with this type of CAH, it can be particularly prevalent in women with LOCAH who—by definition—are diagnosed later in life and have been exposed to excess androgens for long periods of time.

**COMMON SYMPTOMS OF LATE-ONSET CAH**

- Signs of genital virilization, early puberty, and accelerated growth, as occurs with simple-virilizing CAH
- Signs of hormone imbalance in girls/women, including:
  - hirsutism
  - premature balding
  - low voice
  - muscular build
- Menstrual irregularities in women
- Infertility in men and women

## LOCAH and Polycystic Ovary Syndrome (PCOS)

Late diagnosis and delayed treatment can cause a LOCAH woman to develop another condition called Polycystic Ovary Syndrome (commonly known as PCOS.) Like LOCAH, PCOS also results in an excess production of male hormones; however, with PCOS, the sources of the excess androgens are the ovaries, rather than the adrenal glands.

PCOS occurs when the pituitary gland releases high levels of a hormone called "Luteinizing Hormone" (LH). High levels of LH can cause the ovaries to enlarge and develop fluid-filled cysts. Like the adrenal glands, these cysts produce excess androgens, including testosterone.

In LOCAH, delayed initiation of treatment can stimulate the pituitary gland to release excess LH, triggering PCOS. Therefore—while PCOS can occur independently of CAH—having late-onset CAH can predispose you to developing PCOS. Thus, if you are a woman with LOCAH, symptoms can be particularly difficult to treat, because excess androgens can come from two different sources—the ovaries, as well as the adrenal glands.

While infertility appears to be more prevalent in women with CAH, it can also be a problem for CAH men. If androgen secretion is high, even in the face of proper therapy, a physician may suspect the presence of "adrenal rests." Rests are pieces of adrenal tissue—like benign tumors—which develop in the testicles and produce steroid hormones. They can be associated with a low sperm count which, in turn, can result in reduced fertility. Most CAH men, however, have normal sperm counts and are able to father children.

Adrenal rests are usually detected via ultrasound, though some are large enough to be palpable. Often, they will diminish in size after proper therapy. In rare instances, they may need to be surgically removed.

While adrenal rests can occur even with good control, the possibility that they will occur increases with poor control. Typically, they do not appear until adolescence or adulthood.

♦♦♦

## WHAT YOU MAY BE CONCERNED ABOUT: FREQUENTLY ASKED QUESTIONS

♦ ***What is meant by the terms "classical" and "non-classical" CAH?***

The terms "classical" and "non-classical" are used to differentiate between the relative severities of 21-OH CAH. Usually, salt-wasting and simple-virilizing CAH are considered "classical" forms of CAH, while late-onset CAH is considered "non-classical;" however, the use of these terms does not appear to be entirely consistent in either the medical or lay communities. Simple-virilizing CAH is often referred to as "non salt-losing" or "non salt-wasting" CAH, terms which can easily be confused with "non-classical" CAH. Other times, "non salt-losing" or "non salt-wasting" is used to mean late-onset CAH. Because it is easy to confuse meaning with terminology, only "salt-wasting," "simple-virilizing," and "late-onset" will be used in this book. (Where figures or diagrams are adapted from other sources, other terms might be used.)

♦ ***Why is CAH sometimes referred to as an "intersex" condition? I find this misleading and upsetting.***

The term "intersex" is used to describe a number of different medical conditions that can result in atypical sexual anatomy. Some use it to describe any condition that can produce ambiguous genitalia in infants. Others use it to describe conditions in which both male and female sex organs and characteristics are present at birth. Still others use it to describe conditions in which there are problems with the sex chromosomes, even when there are no genital abnormalities.

Because of the wide range of interpretations, there is active discussion in the medical community and public about whether this term should be applied to masculinized girls with CAH. Regardless of interpretation, it is important to realize that—while masculinized girls with CAH may appear like boys on the outside—they possess XX chromosomes and have female internal reproductive organs.

♦ ***Can ambiguous genitalia be corrected through surgery?***

Yes, though this may not be without complications. While surgery can result in normal-appearing female genitalia and normal sexual function, some women who have undergone surgery in childhood have reported sexual dysfunction in adulthood. Problems include the inability to achieve orgasm and pain during intercourse.

When considering surgery, families should have a thorough discussion with their endocrinologist and surgeon, in order to fully understand the procedures and risks involved. Most importantly, surgery—if elected—should be performed by an expert in the field (see chapter 10.)

♦ ***Is there a relationship between CAH and neonatal jaundice?***

It is not clear that there is a relationship between CAH and neonatal jaundice. However, stressed infants can have prolonged jaundice. Thus, if an infant with CAH is ill, there may be jaundice.

♦ ***How can the doctor know that this is CAH and not something else?***

The symptoms seen in CAH can sometimes be found in other medical conditions. Salt-wasting can result from other adrenal gland disorders, while excess androgens can be caused by a pituitary gland problem, or cysts or tumors in the adrenal glands or gonads.

However, while there are often overlaps in symptoms between different medical conditions, there are usually also important key differences. By looking at the complete picture—physical symptoms; age at which symptoms appear; biochemical markers, as indicated on laboratory tests, etc.—doctors can usually pinpoint a diagnosis.

♦ ***Aren't children reaching puberty at an earlier age than in the past? Maybe my child's signs of puberty—odor, hair, acne, etc.—just mean that he or she is an "early bloomer," not that he has CAH.***

Some researchers have suggested that puberty is occurring at earlier ages in children. However, a distinction must be made between true puberty and symptoms of androgen excess.

The first sign of true puberty is the appearance of breast buds in girls and the enlargement of testicles in boys. When there is no breast bud development or testicular enlargement, in the presence of other sexual characteristics—such as pubic hair, axillary hair, and body odor—the cause is usually excess androgen production by the adrenal glands, rather than true puberty. In that case, a physician may suspect CAH, or another adrenal gland problem, rather than true puberty.

♦ ***Does late-onset mean that you are born with the condition, and symptoms just appear later in life? Or does it mean that the condition is acquired after birth?***

CAH is an inherited condition, meaning that you are born with it. If you have a mild form of the disorder, symptoms may not appear, or be detected, until late childhood or even early adulthood. However, the problem that causes you to have CAH is still present at birth.

♦ ***How does early, rapid growth affect the development of vital organs, such as the heart, kidneys, and lungs?***

Organ growth keeps up with the rate of skeletal growth. Therefore, early, rapid growth does not have a detrimental effect on the development of the vital organs.

♦ ***I am worried about my other children. How do I know they don't also have CAH?***

Without running the proper diagnostic tests, you won't know for sure. However, because affected children in the same family will usually have the same type of CAH, you may be able to make some educated guesses by looking at the sex and ages of your other children.

For example, if your CAH child is a salt-waster, your other children will likely also be salt-wasters. Thus, if they are older and appear to be healthy, chances are good that they probably do not have CAH. However, if your affected child is a simple-virilizer, and your other children are younger or of a different sex, it is possible that symptoms have not yet appeared. In that case, the possibility of CAH increases.

If you are very worried, talk to your endocrinologist. He or she may help to set your mind at ease, by suggesting the appropriate tests to run.

### ♦ *Should I have my other children tested for CAH? When?*

If you and your doctor believe there is a good possibility that your other children might have CAH, you should run the appropriate tests as soon as you feel comfortable. However, if you both agree that they probably don't, testing can probably wait.

Before they reach childbearing age, you may want to have all your children genetically tested for CAH. This will establish whether they are carriers of the defective gene, and prepare them for the possibility of having a CAH child of their own.

♦♦♦

# 4

# The Tests Used to Diagnose Congenital Adrenal Hyperplasia

*In this fourth chapter, we explain the biochemistry of CAH. By understanding the hormone imbalances that occur in CAH, you can better understand how doctors come by their diagnoses. You can also better understand the goals of CAH treatment and monitoring, which are discussed next in chapters 5 and 6.*

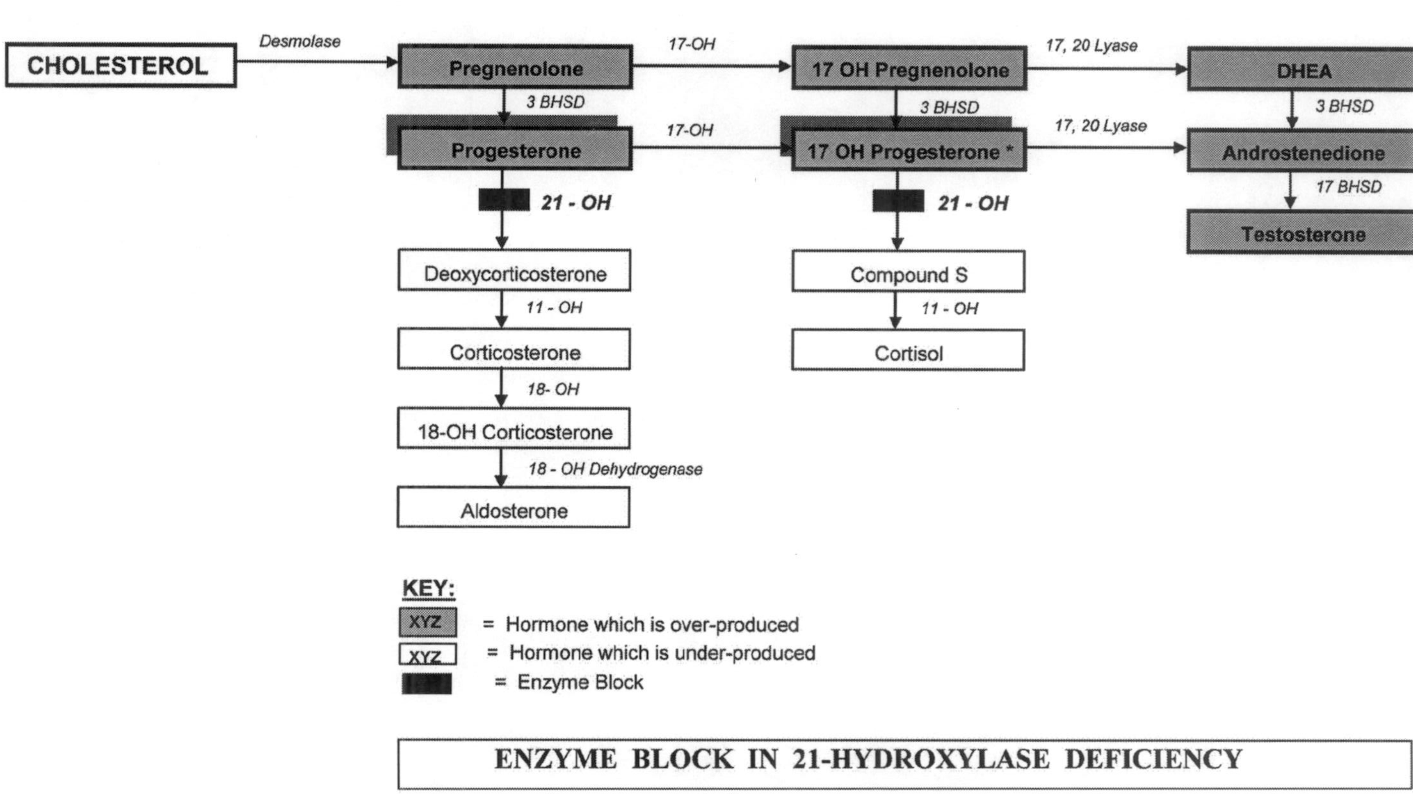
MINERALOCORTICOIDS
GLUCOCORTICOIDS
ANDROGENS
CHOLESTEROL
Desmolase
Pregnenolone
17-OH
17 OH Pregnenolone
17, 20 Lyase
DHEA
3 BHSD
3 BHSD
3 BHSD
Progesterone
17-OH
17 OH Progesterone *
17, 20 Lyase
Androstenedione
17 BHSD
Testosterone
21 - OH
21 - OH
Deoxycorticosterone
Compound S
11 - OH
11 - OH
Corticosterone
Cortisol
18- OH
18-OH Corticosterone
18 - OH Dehydrogenase
Aldosterone
KEY:
XYZ = Hormone which is over-produced
XYZ = Hormone which is under-produced
= Enzyme Block
ENZYME BLOCK IN 21-HYDROXYLASE DEFICIENCY

PHYsical symptoms can lead a physician to suspect CAH. Follow-up laboratory tests are necessary to confirm the diagnosis.

In states with newborn screening programs for CAH, affected infants may be identified prior to the development of any physical symptoms. Screening is done by testing drops of blood taken from a baby's heel, a few days of birth.

## MAKING THE DIAGNOSIS OF CAH

The diagnosis of CAH can be made by analyzing levels of the different adrenal hormones in the blood. If you are deficient in a particular enzyme (resulting in CAH), there will be a block (or dam) in the adrenal cortex, where that enzyme is needed to convert one hormone to another. As a result, you will have high levels of the hormones produced *before* the block, and low levels of the hormones produced *after* the block. Hormone production will then be shifted to a pathway where there is no enzyme block. As a result, hormone levels in the unobstructed pathway will rise.

By comparing your adrenal hormone levels to "normal" numbers, doctors can determine if there is an enzyme block indicative of CAH. By identifying the particular hormones that are lacking or elevated, they should also be able to pinpoint the specific type of CAH.

### Recognizing 21-Hydroxylase Deficiency

21-hydroxylase deficiency is the most common type of CAH, accounting for more than 90 percent of all cases. Because the 21-hydroxylase enzyme is needed in both the mineralocorticoid and glucocorticoid pathways of the adrenal cortex, a deficiency of 21-OH will cause impaired production of both aldosterone and cortisol. When the enzyme deficiency is severe, salt-wasting will occur.

In the mineralocorticoid pathway, 21-OH is needed to convert progesterone to deoxycorticosterone (DOC). A deficiency of 21-OH will, therefore, result in high levels of progesterone and pregnelolone, but low levels of DOC and the hormones that follow it, most notably aldosterone.

In the glucocorticoid pathway, 21-OH is needed to convert 17-hydroxyprogesterone (17-OHP) to 11-deoxycortisol (Compound S). A deficiency of 21-hydroxylase will, therefore, cause a buildup of 17-OHP and 17-hydroxypregnelolone, but low levels of Compound S and cortisol.

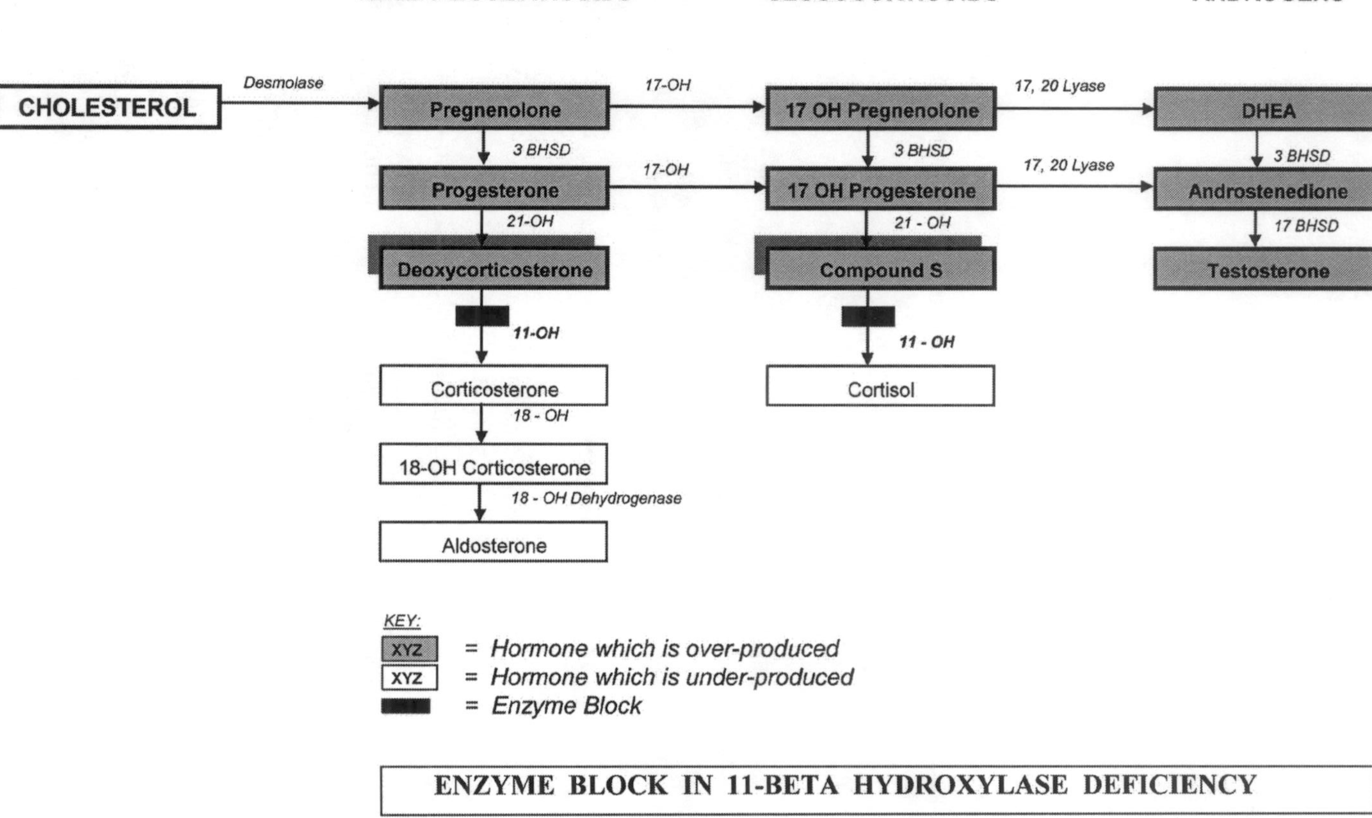


ENZYME BLOCK IN 11-BETA HYDROXYLASE DEFICIENCY

The inability to properly produce aldosterone and cortisol will cause adrenal hormone production to be shifted into the androgen pathway. As a result, when you have 21-OH deficiency, you will have high levels of DHEA, androstenedione, and testosterone. High levels of these androgens can cause masculinization of female infants.

## Recognizing 11-Beta Hydroxylase Deficiency

The second most common type of CAH, accounting for about 5 percent of all cases, is 11-beta hydroxylase deficiency. Like 21-hydroxylase, the 11-OH enzyme is needed in the mineralocorticoid and glucocorticoid pathways of the adrenal cortex. Thus, a deficiency of 11-OH causes impaired production of both aldosterone and cortisol.

In the mineralocorticoid pathway, 11-OH is needed to convert deoxycorticosterone to corticosterone, a precursor of aldosterone. Lack of 11-OH will result in a buildup of DOC, but impaired aldosterone production.

In the glucocorticoid pathway, 11-OH is needed to convert Compound S to cortisol. Lack of 11-OH will result in a buildup of both 17-OHP and Compound S, but low levels of cortisol.

In contrast to 21-OH deficiency, the lack of aldosterone does not generally produce salt-wasting with 11-OH deficiency. This is because DOC and Compound S each have mineralocorticoid properties and act like aldosterone to help retain salt. High levels of these hormones can produce problems with hypertension (high blood pressure), the opposite of what is normally associated with low aldosterone. Thus, measuring levels of DOC and Compound S can help distinguish between 21-OH and 11-OH CAH.

Similar to 21-OH deficiency, the inability to produce cortisol and aldosterone will result in the overproduction of androgens. High levels of DHEA, androstenedione, and testosterone can cause girls with 11-OH deficiency to have masculinization of the genitalia to as severe a degree as girls with 21-OH deficiency.

## Recognizing 3-Beta Hydroxysteroid Dehydrogenase Deficiency

The enzyme 3-beta dehydrogenase is found in all three major pathways of the adrenal cortex. As a result, when 3-beta dehydrogenase is defective, there may be low production of aldosterone, cortisol, *and* testosterone. Poor testosterone production is an important distinction between 3-beta deficiency and the more common 21-OH or 11-OH types CAH.

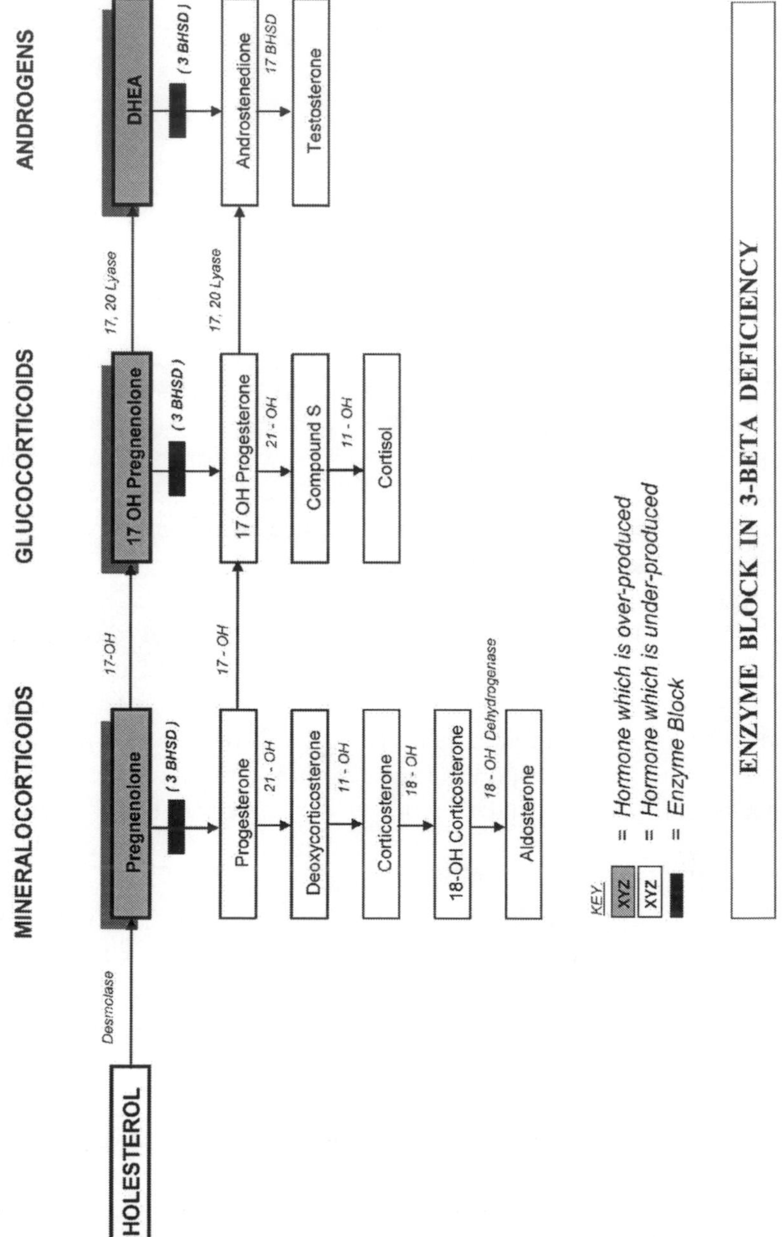
MINERALOCORTICOIDS
GLUCOCORTICOIDS
ANDROGENS
CHOLESTEROL
Desmolase
Pregnenolone
( 3 BHSD )
17-OH
17 OH Pregnenolone
( 3 BHSD )
17, 20 Lyase
DHEA
( 3 BHSD )
Progesterone
21 - OH
Deoxycorticosterone
11 - OH
Corticosterone
18 - OH
18-OH Corticosterone
18 - OH Dehydrogenase
Aldosterone
17 - OH
17 OH Progesterone
21 - OH
Compound S
11 - OH
Cortisol
17, 20 Lyase
Androstenedione
17 BHSD
Testosterone
KEY:
XYZ = Hormone which is over-produced
XYZ = Hormone which is under-produced
= Enzyme Block
ENZYME BLOCK IN 3-BETA DEFICIENCY

In the mineralocorticoid pathway, 3-beta dehydrogenase is needed to convert pregnenolone to progesterone. A deficiency of 3-beta dehydrogenase, therefore, results in a buildup of pregnenolone, but a deficiency of all other mineralocorticoids, including aldosterone. If the enzyme defect is severe, the lack of aldosterone will result in salt-wasting.

In the glucocorticoid pathway, 3-beta dehydrogenase is needed to convert 17 OH Pregnenolone to 17- hydroxyprogesterone. A deficiency of 3-beta dehydrogenase will result in a buildup of 17 OH Pregnenolone, but a deficiency of all other glucocorticoids, including cortisol.

In the androgen pathway, 3-beta dehydrogenase is needed to convert DHEA to androstenedione. Lack of 3-beta dehydrogenase will result in high levels of DHEA, but low levels of androstenedione and testosterone.

Testosterone is the most potent androgen. As a result, those with 3-beta deficiency will more often have problems associated with low, rather than high, androgen levels. Because testosterone is important for the formation of the penis and scrotum in boys, some males with 3-beta deficiency may have underdeveloped genitals. Sometimes, the urethra will not end at the tip of the penis, instead opening at the penis base. This condition is called "hypospadias."

Low levels of testosterone will also prevent severe masculinization of the genitalia in girls with 3-beta deficiency. Masculinization—if it happens at all—is generally mild, and occurs as a result of the buildup of DHEA.

## ACTH STIMULATION TEST

In situations where the hormone levels are borderline or inconclusive, a physician may suggest doing an ACTH stimulation test. With this test, a synthetic form of ACTH called "Cortrysn" is used to stimulate the adrenal glands to produce cortisol. If you *do not* have CAH, cortisol levels should rise. If you *do* have CAH, the rise in cortisol may be low and other hormone levels will increase excessively.

An ACTH test is performed by first drawing blood to measure baseline adrenal hormone levels. Cortrysn is then injected into the bloodstream to stimulate adrenal gland activity. A second blood sample is taken sixty minutes later.

When you have 21-OH deficiency, the hormone that will rise most significantly is 17-OHP. Whereas other hormones might double or triple, 17-OHP can easily increase by more than ten-fold, after ACTH stimulation.

The size of the rise in 17-OHP may make it possible to distinguish between different severities of 21-OH CAH. In general, a more severe enzyme impairment results in a larger buildup of 17-OHP, while a less severe defect will result in lower increases. Salt-wasters and simple-virilizers will generally have higher stimulated 17-OHP levels than someone with late-onset CAH.

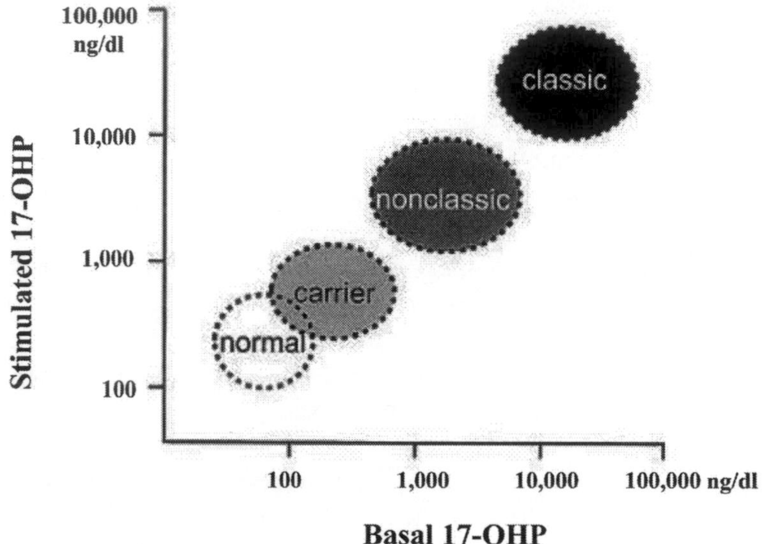


**COMPARISON OF 17-OHP LEVELS WITH DIFFERENT SEVERITIES OF CAH.**
Adapted from Speiser, PW. 2001. "Congenital Adrenal Hyperplasia Owing to 21-Hydroxylase Deficiency." Endocrinology and Metabolism Clinics of North America 30(47).

## NEWBORN SCREENING

In all states, before a newborn baby is sent home from the hospital, a few drops of blood are obtained by pricking the baby's heel. These drops of blood are then placed on small pieces of paper, and the "blood-spot" samples sent to state laboratories where they are tested for serious medical problems.

The conditions that are tested for vary from state to state, but commonly include Congenital Hyperthyroidism, Phenylketonuria (PKU), Galactosemia, Maple Syrup Urine Disease (MSUD), Biotinidase Deficiency, and Homocystinuria. Early diagnosis and treatment of these conditions can prevent irreversible and catastrophic consequences, including mental retardation, brain damage, and death. Although all states have newborn screening programs, not all states test for CAH.

## Screening For CAH

More than a decade ago, it was found that the most severe forms of CAH could be detected shortly after birth through newborn screening. Because most babies with severe CAH have high levels of 17-OHP, measurement of 17-OHP can be used to identify newborns with CAH.

More than thirty-five states perform newborn screening for CAH. The National Newborn Screening/Genetic Resource Center (NNSGRC), based at the University of Texas Health Science Center in San Antonio, Texas, serves as a national resource center for information and education on newborn screening and genetics. Information on individual state programs can be found by visiting the Center's website at *<http://genes-r-us.uthscsa.edu/>* (see appendix.)

## The Purpose of Newborn Screening For CAH

The primary goal of most state newborn screening programs is to prevent death due to early adrenal crisis. Typically, blood-spot samples are obtained in the hospital within forty-eight hours after birth, prior to discharge.

Because it can take one to two weeks to gather results, most babies with CAH are still sent home from the hospital before diagnosis. Consequently—in order to effectively avert crises in those children who are at greatest risk—it is crucial that screening programs have an efficient system in place to process samples, interpret results, and inform affected patients. This requires careful coordination between hospitals, labs, healthcare professionals, and families.

## Interpreting Screening Results

Because newborn screening for CAH is based on measuring levels of 17-OHP, most detected children will have 21-hydroxylase deficiency. However, some babies with 11-beta hydroxylase or 3-beta dehydrogenase CAH may also have elevated 17-OHP. If so, these children may be detected through newborn screening, as well.

When interpreting results, the duration of pregnancy (gestational age) and birth weight of the child must be considered. Because the adrenal glands of a developing fetus are quite large, infants who are born early (premature) will often have elevated 17-OHP. This does not usually indicate the presence of CAH, but rather reflects the immaturity of the adrenal glands. (Any infant born less than thirty-five weeks after conception is considered premature.)

As a child becomes older and the adrenal glands mature, 17-OHP levels will fall. Thus, though there may be the occasional exception, most premature infants with elevated 17-OHP do not have CAH.

Some states will utilize one cutoff level for 17-OHP for full-term babies (>35 weeks gestational age), and a much higher cutoff for those who are born premature (<35 weeks gestation). Cutoffs are also adjusted to infant birth weight. While some states may distinguish between two different levels of patients, others may distinguish between three or four.

The specific numbers that are used to indicate an abnormal newborn screening result are set by the individual state. Differences in cutoff levels, from one state to another, do not necessarily indicate flaws in the screening system, but rather the fact that different equipment and testing methods are used.

## When There Is an Abnormal Result

A baby with an abnormal newborn screening result requires immediate medical attention. Thus, an efficient communication system is an important component of any newborn screening program for CAH.

In some states, when an abnormal 17-OHP level is detected by newborn screening laboratories, the child's pediatrician and local pediatric subspecialists are immediately notified. Public health workers may also contact the family. This is a "three-pronged" approach that helps to ensure that the severely affected child, who is in danger of suffering a salt-wasting crisis, is promptly evaluated and treated as soon as possible after an abnormal test result is obtained.

Following a "positive," or abnormal, newborn screening result, doctors will run additional tests to confirm the diagnosis of CAH. These generally include measurement of adrenal hormone levels (including 17-OHP, Compound S, DHEA, androstenedione, and 17-hydroxypregnelolone), as well as tests for sodium, potassium, and renin. A positive test on a newborn screen should also alert doctors to check the genitalia of infants for problems.

◆◆◆

## WHAT YOU MAY BE CONCERNED ABOUT: FREQUENTLY ASKED QUESTIONS

♦ ***In addition to a blood test to assess the levels of the different adrenal hormones, are any other tests recommended, if there is a suspicion of CAH?***

A physician who suspects CAH will test electrolyte levels—including sodium, potassium, and bicarbonate (total $CO_2$)—and renin. Depending on the age of the child, a bone-age x-ray may also be done to assess the effects of excess androgens on bone maturation. In addition, the physician may elect to perform ultrasounds of the adrenal glands or gonads to look for tumors that produce androgens.

♦ ***Should we get an ACTH stimulation test, just to be sure?***

By measuring adrenal hormone levels, the diagnosis of CAH can often be made with certainty, even without ACTH stimulation. However, in borderline cases or uncertain situations, an ACTH stimulation test or genetic test can be performed. (See chapter 2 for details on genetic testing.)

♦ ***Should an ACTH test be performed at a certain time of day, or under certain conditions, e.g., after fasting?***

An ACTH stimulation test can be performed at any time of the day. No dietary restrictions are necessary. If you are already taking glucocorticoid medications, you may need to discontinue your medication before undergoing this test.

♦ ***Won't an ACTH test performed at a different time of the day—or on a different day—produce different 17-OHP numbers? Couldn't this lead you to a slightly different diagnosis, e.g., simple-virilizing, instead of salt-wasting?***

In general, no. Though levels of 17-OHP are typically higher if you are a salt-waster, the diagnosis of salt-wasting is not based on 17-OHP numbers. Rather, it is based on renin and electrolyte levels, which do not have these same types of daily fluctuations. Thus, if your overall profile is properly taken into account, the time of day that the ACTH test is given should not affect the diagnosis.

♦ ***Will you feel any side effects after taking an ACTH stimulation test?***

Generally, no. However, some people have reported slight irritability, excitability, and headache after undergoing an ACTH test. These symptoms are uncommon.

♦ ***Can carriers of CAH be diagnosed via ACTH testing?***

Some carriers of CAH may have enough of an elevated response to be diagnosed via ACTH stimulation; however, not all will. Thus, genetic testing can be more accurate than ACTH testing, if you are a carrier.

♦ ***Is it possible to have my newborn child screened for CAH, even if it is not required by my home state?***

In some states, it may be possible to request testing for disorders other than those normally mandated by that state. The National Newborn Screening Center (NNSGRC) keeps a list of the states, which offer this option. Usually, a small fee is charged.

You can also pay to have elective testing done by a commercial laboratory. Pediatrix Screening, a company in Pennsylvania, will test for a variety of newborn disorders, including CAH. The Baylor University Medical Center in Houston, Texas, also offers commercial newborn testing; however, at present, they do not test for CAH. Additional information on these laboratories is available in the appendix.

♦ ***What is the likelihood of getting a false-positive newborn screening result?***

A false-positive result means that the 17-OHP level is abnormally high, but the child does not have CAH. False-positive test results can occur in full term infants, although they are uncommon. In comparison, there is a higher rate of false-positives in premature infants because their adrenal glands are large and produce high levels of 17-OHP.

♦ ***What about a false-negative?***

A false-negative result means that the 17-OHP level is not elevated, even though the child has CAH. The primary goal of newborn screening for CAH is to prevent death due to early adrenal crisis. Thus, while babies with severe forms of CAH should be identified through newborn screening, children with mild forms of the disorder may not be.

A test result may also be inaccurate if a sample is not properly collected, shipped or tested. Thus it is important that samples be properly obtained and processed.

♦ ***Are high 17-OHP levels in infancy associated with any other disorders besides CAH?***

Usually not. Because 17-OHP is a hormone produced in the adrenal glands, persistently high levels would generally point to the presence of overactive adrenals. This is usually seen in CAH, but in some babies—especially those who are ill or under some kind of physical stress—the adrenal glands can remain large after birth, sometimes up to one year. This is called "Persistence of the Fetal Adrenal Gland."

♦♦♦

# 5

# Glucocorticoid Treatment for Congenital Adrenal Hyperplasia

*Whether they are salt-wasting or not, children with CAH are treated with glucocorticoid medications. In this chapter, we give you the nuts-and-bolts information you need to understand the primary medication that your child takes for treatment of CAH. We also discuss the basic goals of glucocorticoid treatment and outline the side effects that can sometimes accompany steroid use.*

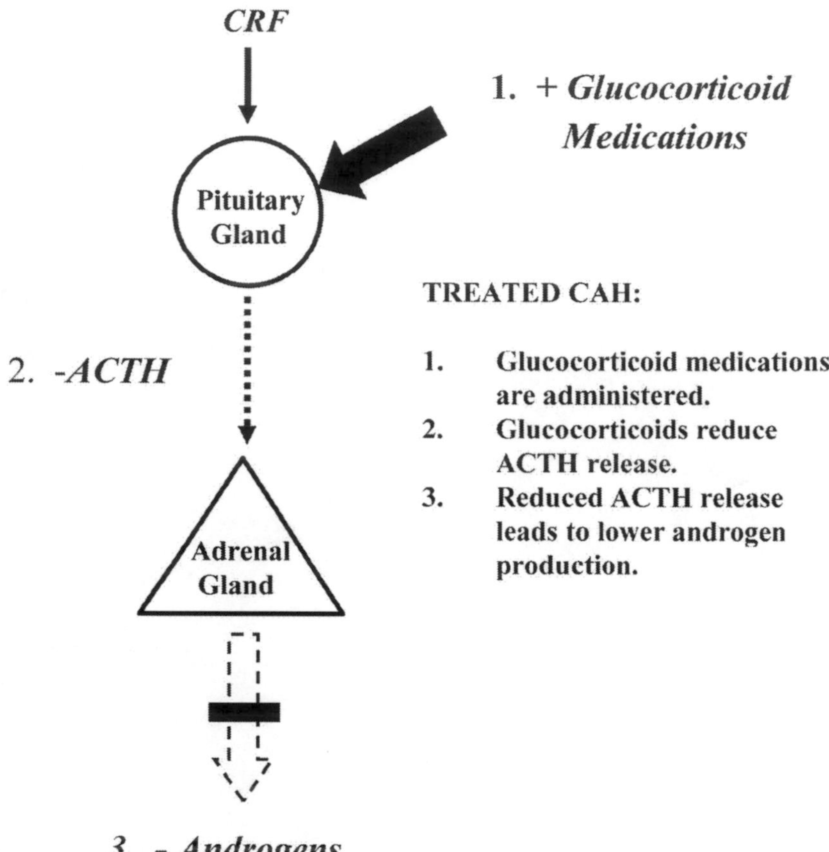


**GLUCOCORTICOID TREATMENT OF CAH**

**WHEN** you have CAH, you cannot produce cortisol and, instead, overproduce androgens. If you are a salt-waster, you cannot produce aldosterone, either. The goal of CAH treatment is therefore: 1) to replace deficient cortisol and aldosterone, and 2) to prevent androgen over-secretion.

To provide cortisol replacement and suppress adrenal androgen production, synthetic glucocorticoids are used. To provide aldosterone replacement, a synthetic aldosterone (known as "fludrocortisone") is given. If you are a salt-waster, you need treatment with both glucocorticoids and fludrocortisone. If you are not a salt-waster, you need treatment with only glucocorticoids.

## BASICS OF GLUCOCORTICOID TREATMENT FOR CAH

Glucocorticoid treatment for CAH serves the dual purpose of replacing deficient cortisol and preventing androgen overproduction. Giving enough medication to sustain normal body function is generally straightforward. Preventing androgen overproduction, while avoiding the side effects of the medication, is a much more difficult task.

### Challenges of Glucocorticoid Treatment

Glucocorticoids can result in a number of undesirable side effects, when given at too high doses. Yet, if not *enough* medication is given, negative effects can be seen, as well. To successfully treat CAH, a physician must walk a fine line between giving *too much* or *too little* glucocorticoid medication.

A particular challenge of glucocorticoid treatment is the ability to maintain normal growth rates in children. At high doses, glucocorticoids can inhibit a child's growth. Once medication is adjusted, a child who has been growing slowly may "catch up," but delayed growth over prolonged periods may not be completely recovered.

Glucocorticoids can also cause excessive weight gain. If a lot of weight is gained in a short period of time, reddish stretch marks (called "striae") may develop along the abdomen, upper thighs, and elsewhere. Weight can be lost, once doses are lowered, but skin discoloration from stretch marks may never completely disappear. Likewise, other problems from persistent overtreatment may be irreversible.

Too *little* glucocorticoid medication, resulting in high levels of androgens, can also cause problems with growth. When there are high levels of androgens, the growth plates in your skeleton can close early. When the growth plates close, no increase in height is possible.

In a child, who has never been treated for CAH, the growth plates can close by the time a child is eight or nine years old. Thus, though tall initially, these children can end up as small adults, sometimes under five feet tall.

Under-treatment can also put you at risk for developing problems such as infertility and adrenal rests. It can also make you more vulnerable to illness and adrenal crisis.

The challenge of glucocorticoid treatment for CAH is thus to safeguard health and prevent androgen over-secretion, while avoiding the side effects of the medication. Finding the smallest effective dose allows for normal growth and development. It also minimizes the side effects that can accompany steroid use.

## Suppressing ACTH Secretion

When you have CAH, you produce excess androgens when ACTH levels rise. To prevent androgen overproduction, it is therefore necessary to prevent the overproduction of ACTH.

Normally, ACTH levels are high during the day and low at night, following a day-night, or "circadian," rhythm. This circadian rhythm is regulated by approximately twenty-four-hour cycles of light and dark.

ACTH starts to increase gradually in the early morning hours, around 3 a.m. Around 8 a.m., shortly after you wake, levels reach a sharp peak. After this peak, ACTH then slowly declines, reaching lowest levels during the nighttime.

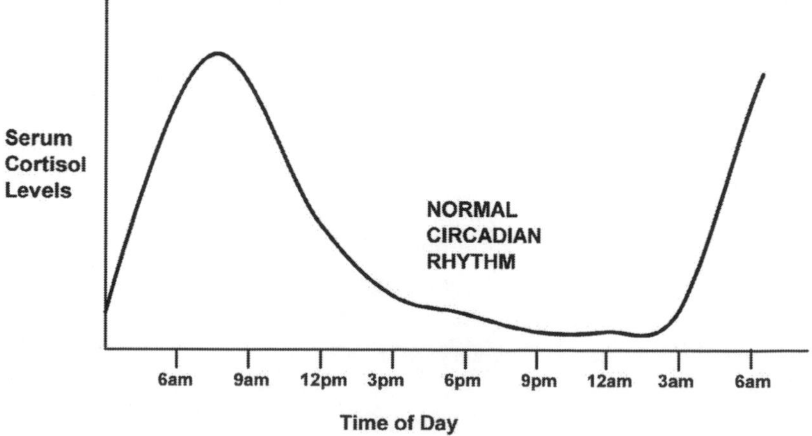

ACTH also rises in response to other stimuli such as eating, napping, standing, and stress. However, though these normal daily activities have a transient effect on ACTH secretion, they do not affect the underlying circadian pattern of ACTH production.

When you can produce cortisol naturally, cortisol levels will rise when there are high levels of ACTH. The increase in cortisol will stop ACTH from continuing to rise. If you have CAH, the suppression of ACTH is achieved by giving cortisol replacement medications. If cortisol medications are given when ACTH is high, androgen overproduction can be prevented.

**How Much Medication is Needed?**

Cortisol requirements can vary from person to person. As a result, doses of glucocorticoids must be carefully adjusted to the individual.

Normally, doses are initially based on "body surface area" (BSA). Body surface area is a measurement of your skin's surface. It is a function of height and weight, and is expressed in units called "meter-squared" ($m^2$).

BSA can be determined from tables or calculated using standard formulas. A number of Internet websites will also calculate BSA, when you input personal information. A partial listing of these websites is included in the appendix.

Normally, you produce cortisol at a rate of 6-10 $mg/m^2/day$ (six to ten milligrams per meter-squared per day). When you have CAH, you will need somewhat more than that—about 12-20 $mg/m^2/day$—in replacement cortisol medication. This is because a portion of oral medication is destroyed by stomach acids. Doses in excess of 20 $mg/m^2/day$ may be associated with a reduction in growth.

The rate at which cortisol is broken down and eliminated from the blood is also a factor in determining the size of the dose required. If you eliminate glucocorticoids rapidly from the blood, you may require higher-than-average doses to reduce ACTH production. If you eliminate cortisol slowly, you may require smaller-than-usual doses.

Although those with milder forms of CAH may be able to produce some cortisol, glucocorticoid requirements are generally similar whether salt-wasting is present or not. However, salt-wasters who are inadequately treated with mineralocorticoids may require higher-than-normal glucocorticoid doses, to remain in good control. In those cases, glucocorticoid doses can usually be lowered when mineralocorticoid treatment is improved.

## Tablets vs. Liquids

One of the most important factors in influencing the outcome of CAH treatment is the precise adjustment of glucocorticoid doses. In general, the more potent the medication, the less room for error.

Small increases or decreases in dose can be difficult to achieve, when using tablets. This is because tablets come in fixed strengths. When intermediate doses are desired, they can only be achieved by breaking a pill into smaller pieces. This can result in imprecise dosing, especially if the medication used is very potent, like prednisone or dexamethasone.

Because tablets will sometimes break unevenly, some dose-to-dose variability can also result. To minimize this possibility, a straight razor blade, very sharp knife, or pill cutter should be used to split pills. Pill cutters can be purchased at most pharmacies.

Glucocorticoids also come in liquid preparations, which can be easier to calibrate. However, doses of a very concentrated preparation can be difficult to adjust. Thus, you must also consider the concentration (strength) of the liquid.

Concentration is usually expressed in the units "mg/ml" ("milligrams per milliliter"). A preparation with a concentration of "5 mg/ml" will contain five milligrams of medication in one milliliter of fluid. A preparation with a concentration of "10 mg/ml" will contain ten milligrams of medication in the same one milliliter of fluid—in other words, it will be twice as strong.

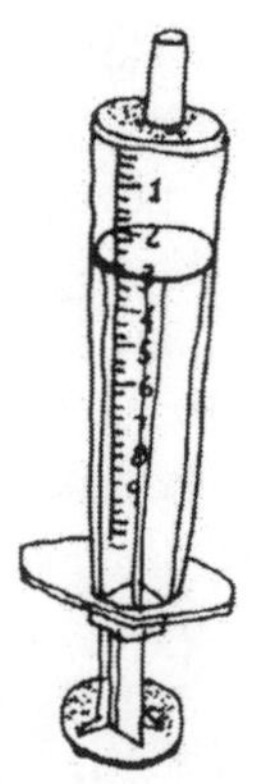

ORAL SYRINGE

When measuring liquid medications, a dosing syringe—similar to a hypodermic syringe, without the needle tip—should be used. Dosing syringes eliminate the problem of air bubbles and air pockets, which can result in inaccuracies in dosing. In addition, the plunger in the dosing syringe helps to insure that the medicine is not left on the surface of the dispensing device. ***Teaspoons and medicine droppers should be avoided because they are imprecise.***

Dosing syringes are usually calibrated in units called "cc" ("cubic centimeters"). A cc is the same as an ml. Both are equivalent to about one-fifth of a teaspoon. Thus, there are about five ccs (or five mls) in a teaspoon.

## THE DIFFERENT GLUCOCORTICOIDS USED TO TREAT CAH

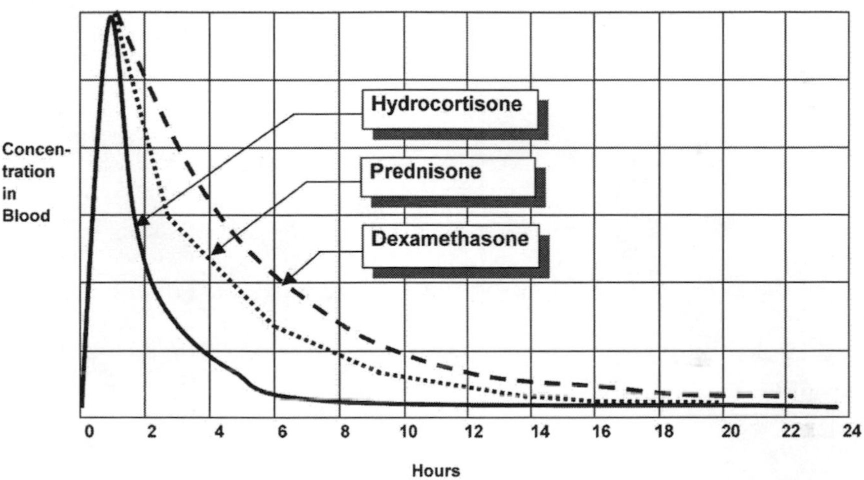


Cortisone, a synthetic form of cortisol, was the first glucocorticoid to become widely used in clinical medicine. In the early 1950s, Dr. Fuller Albright at the Massachusetts General Hospital in Boston and Dr. Lawson Wilkins at Johns Hopkins University in Baltimore showed that cortisone could be used to treat CAH. In the half century since this important discovery, cortisone has largely been replaced by hydrocortisone—which is preferred because of its greater bioavailability—and treatment for CAH has become increasingly refined.

Today, there are three glucocorticoids used to treat CAH—hydrocortisone, prednisone, and dexamethasone. Hydrocortisone is most commonly used, while prednisone and dexamethasone are used much less often. These medications differ from each other in strength (potency) and length (duration) of action. Their different biochemical properties help to determine how each is used in treatment.

**COMPARING GLUCOCORTICOIDS**

| Name of Glucocorticoid | Chemical Properties | | Dosing | | Available Preparations | | |
|---|---|---|---|---|---|---|---|
| | Relative Strength * | Duration of Action per Dose** | Typical No. of Doses/Day | Typical Dose/$m^2$ | Tablets | Liquids | Brand Names |
| **HYDROCORTISONE** | 1 | ~4-6 hrs | 2-3 | 12-18 mg/$m^2$/day | 5.0; 10.0 mg | Not Available | Cortef; Hydrocortone |
| **PREDNISONE** | 5-10* | ~6-10 hrs | 2 | 2-4 mg/$m^2$/day | 0.5; 1.0; 2.5 mg ;<br><br>5.0; 10.0 mg: not used*** | 1 mg/5 ml;<br>1 mg/1 ml;<br>5 mg/5 ml | Pediapred;<br>Prelone;<br>Orapred |
| **DEXAMETHASONE** | 80-100* | ~16 hrs. | 1 | 0.20-0.27 mg/$m^2$/day | 0.25; 0.50 mg not used*** | 0.1 mg/1 ml;<br>0.5 mg/5 ml;<br>1 mg/1 ml; not used*** | Decadron;<br>Alpharma;<br>Morton Grove; |

* *The relative strength, when compared to hydrocortisone, in controlling adrenal gland activity. These may differ from the numbers listed in standard drug equivalency tables.*

** *"Duration of Action" refers to how long the medication remains in the blood after a dose is given.*

*** *Not used by many physicians because these forms are too strong.*

## Hydrocortisone

Hydrocortisone is the least potent of the three glucocorticoids and has the shortest duration of action. Since its introduction to clinical medicine, hydrocortisone has continued to be the drug most often prescribed for CAH treatment.

Unlike prednisone and dexamethasone, hydrocortisone has some salt-retaining properties. However, at the relatively small doses used to treat CAH, its mineralocorticoid properties are minimal. Salt-wasters who are treated with hydrocortisone will still need fludrocortisone to replace deficient aldosterone, as well as sodium supplementation in infancy.

### *Figuring Typical Doses of Hydrocortisone*

Hydrocortisone is similar in potency to cortisol. For CAH treatment, average daily doses range between 12-20 mg/m$^2$/day. A typical dose for a child might be between 5 mg/day and 10 mg/day. A typical dose for an adolescent might be between 15 mg/day and 25 mg/day.

A typical dose of hydrocortisone stays in circulation for four to six hours. As a result, hydrocortisone is typically given three times a day, though some physicians prescribe it only twice a day. Twice a day therapy may be particularly useful in children prone to over-treatment.

Often, the total daily dose is simply equally divided, and given at roughly even intervals throughout the course of the day. E.g. a total daily dose of 7.5 mg might be split 2.5, 2.5, 2.5. Other times, a physician will prescribe a higher proportion of the total dose to be given in the morning, e.g., 12.5 mg total, split 5.0, 5.0, and 2.5. Sometimes, the higher amount will be prescribed at night.

### *Available Preparations of Hydrocortisone*

In the past, all three glucocorticoids used to treat CAH were available in both tablet and liquid form. However, since 2000, when a very commonly used form of liquid hydrocortisone (*Cortef* liquid) was recalled from the marketplace, no other commercial liquid hydrocortisone has been made available. As a result, hydrocortisone is now available only in tablet form.

*Cortef*, made by Pharmacia-Upjohn, is the brand most commonly prescribed. *Hydrocortone* is also hydrocortisone, but is made by Merck, a different manufacturer. Both *Cortef* and *Hydrocortone* are available in 5 or 10 mg tablets.

As a substitute for the liquid *Cortef*, some local pharmacies will make "custom" liquid preparations. However, because hydrocortisone does not dissolve easily in liquids and the effectiveness of these special formulations has not been tested, most doctors are not in favor of this practice. Thus, when using hydrocortisone, physicians generally recommend that only tablets be used.

## Prednisone

Prednisone and the closely related compound "prednisolone" are of greater potency and longer duration of action than hydrocortisone. Based on the relative potencies published in standard drug equivalency charts, prednisone is generally assumed to be about five times stronger than hydrocortisone. However, recent reports suggest that when used for the treatment of CAH, prednisone may be closer to ten times stronger than hydrocortisone. As a result, less prednisone may be needed than previously assumed.

Prednisolone is similar in potency to prednisone. However, prednisolone has a slightly shorter duration of action than prednisone and is eliminated from circulation at a slightly more rapid pace.

### *Figuring Typical Doses of Prednisone*

Prednisone is usually prescribed at a total dose of 2-4 $mg/m^2/day$. Thus, a typical dose for a young child might be 1.0 mg twice a day (a total of 2.0 mg), while the dose for an adolescent might be 2.5 mg twice a day (a total of 5.0 mg). However, because the use of prednisone in treating CAH has not been fully studied, these doses may be excessive. As a result, very close monitoring is needed to be sure a child on prednisone is not over-treated.

Prednisone generally stays in circulation for six to eight hours. As a result, it is typically given twice a day. The daily total can be split evenly, with half given in the morning and half given in the evening (for example, 2.5 mg twice a day). Sometimes, a larger proportion may be prescribed either in the morning or at night (for example, 2.5 mg in the morning and 1.25 mg at night).

### *Available Preparations of Prednisone*

Prednisone is currently available in both tablet and liquid forms. The 2.5 and 5.0 mg tablets are recommended to allow for more precise dosing. The 10.0, 20.0, and 50.0 mg pills are not used because they are too strong. Prednisolone also comes in tablet form, in a 5.0 mg strength.

Liquid preparations are usually made from prednisolone. *Pediapred* is the most dilute preparation, with a concentration of 5 mg/5 ml. *Prelone* is three times as strong as *Pediapred*, with a concentration of 15 mg/5 ml. *Orapred* is the strongest form of liquid prednisone, with a concentration of 20.2 mg/5 ml.

## Dexamethasone

Dexamethasone is the strongest and longest acting of the three glucocorticoids. Its high potency requires extreme precision with dosing. Because of this, few endocrinologists use dexamethasone to treat CAH.

It was previously believed that dexamethasone was "growth toxic." As a result, its use was avoided in children. However, endocrinologists prescribed it assuming that it was thirty to forty times stronger than hydrocortisone. In fact, it may be closer to eighty to one hundred times more potent, when used for treatment of CAH. As a result, much less dexamethasone is needed than previously believed. When utilized at the correct doses, dexamethasone can be successfully used to treat CAH and allow normal growth. *However, exquisite care is needed along with close monitoring.*

### *Figuring Typical Doses of Dexamethasone*

Typical dexamethasone doses are between 0.2 and 0.27 mg/m$^2$/day, though doses can range between 0.15-0.3 mg/m$^2$/day. Thus, a young child might take 0.1 mg/day; while the dose for an adolescent might be 0.3 mg/day.

A dose of dexamethasone stays in the circulation for sixteen to twenty hours. Because of its long duration of action, dexamethasone is typically given only once daily. Most physicians prescribe the full dose in the morning.

### *Available Preparations of Dexamethasone*

Because dexamethasone is so potent, it is especially important that doses are very carefully measured. Inaccurate dosing can quickly cause problems with both under- or over-medication.

Dexamethasone is available in both tablet and liquid form. Because of its strength and the need to closely control dosing, doctors recommend that only the liquid form of dexamethasone be used in children. Unlike hydrocortisone, dexamethasone readily dissolves in water solutions. Thus, liquid dexamethasone preparations may be used without fear of the medication "settling out" of the solution.

Currently available liquid dexamethasone preparations include a "dilute" elixir with a concentration of 0.1mg/1 ml (also written as 0.5 mg/5 ml). This preparation contains 0.1 milligrams of dexamethasone (one-tenth of 1 milligram) in 1 milliliter of solution. Another liquid preparation is ten times as strong, with a concentration of 1.0 mg/1 ml (1.0 milligrams of dexamethasone in 1 milliliter of solution). Both of these preparations are sold under the trade name *Decadron*. A third, less widely available preparation has a concentration of 2 mg/5 ml. This preparation is sold under the trade name *Dexsol*. The dilute elixir (0.1 mg/ml or 0.5 mg/5 ml) allows for the most accurate dosing.

A dosing syringe must be used, when administering liquid dexamethasone. If a syringe is used properly in conjunction with the dilute elixir, it is possible to measure dexamethasone to increments as small as 0.01 mg (equivalent to about 0.8 mg of hydrocortisone).

Dexamethasone tablets are available in 0.25 and 0.5 mg sizes. The relatively large amount of medication contained in each tablet makes tablet use suitable for some adolescents and adults, but difficult for young children.

## LONG-TERM SIDE EFFECTS OF GLUCOCORTICOIDS

Glucocorticoids have a wide range of applications in clinical medicine. In addition to their use in treatment of adrenal insufficiency, their anti-inflammatory properties are effective in treating conditions such as arthritis, asthma, skin rashes, and inflammatory bowel disease. Their immuno-suppressive properties play a critical role in successful organ transplantation.

When used to treat inflammatory diseases, the doses of glucocorticoids given can easily be more than ten times the amount of cortisol that the body normally makes. When high doses are given for many months, a number of complications can occur. These problems include the loss of bone (osteoporosis), cataracts, stomach ulcers, skin thinning, poor wound healing, and an increased chance of infections. In some patients, use of glucocorticoids at high doses can cause anxiety, depression, mood swings, and even psychosis.

In contrast, the doses of glucocorticoids needed to treat CAH are considered "physiologic." This means that they are closer to what the body normally makes. As a result, there should be fewer long-term side effects; however, because treatment for adrenal insufficiency is a lifelong proposition, and the balance between under-medication and over-medication can be difficult to strike, care must still be taken to avoid glucocorticoid excess, when treating CAH.

♦♦♦

## WHAT YOU MAY BE CONCERNED ABOUT: FREQUENTLY ASKED QUESTIONS

♦ ***Are there any homeopathic alternatives to glucocorticoid medications?***

No. There are no homeopathic alternatives to glucocorticoids.

♦ ***Glucocorticoids are "steroids." Aren't steroids supposed to be harmful to your health?***

When most people say "steroids," they are thinking of the drugs taken by athletes to increase muscle mass and strength. These are synthetic forms of androgens, known as *anabolic* steroids. However, *all* hormones made from cholesterol are classified as steroids, including the synthetic forms of mineralocorticoids and glucocorticoids. These are the steroid medications referred to when talking about treatment of CAH. These drugs are needed to maintain normal body function and do not have the same effects as anabolic steroids.

♦ ***Do you have to be treated if you have a mild form of CAH?***

While the risk of adrenal crisis is not as great if you have a mild form of CAH, lack of treatment can still result in the problems associated with excess androgen production. These include cosmetic problems such as acne, balding, and hirsutism; and reproductive problems such as lack of menstrual periods in women and infertility in both sexes.

Once they set in, these problems may be difficult to get rid of. Early treatment with glucocorticoids can make the problems less severe, or prevent them from happening altogether.

♦ ***Is it possible to discontinue treatment after adult height is reached?***

While you do not have to worry about growth issues once adult height is reached, lack of treatment can still result in the problems outlined above. You may also have trouble getting over routine illnesses because of marginally working adrenal glands, and be vulnerable to life-threatening adrenal crisis during illness.

♦ ***Are there any medications that can cause an adverse reaction to glucocorticoids?***

It is safe to take glucocorticoids with most prescription or over-the-counter drugs, though you should always let your doctor know if you are taking other medicines. Sometimes, another drug can affect the rate at which you metabolize glucocorticoids. If cortisol elimination is speeded up, your glucocorticoid dose may need to be increased. If cortisol elimination is slowed down, your dose may need to be reduced.

In addition, glucocorticoids are often prescribed for common childhood conditions, such as allergies or asthma. Thus, if you are also given glucocorticoids for treatment of a different condition, the amount that you need to treat the CAH will be less. If you continue to take the full amount that you are given for CAH, along with the steroids that are prescribed for these other conditions, you may become over-treated.

♦ ***Can my child safely undergo routine vaccinations?***

A child with CAH can safely get all routine childhood vaccinations. However, if fever develops after a vaccination, you should give oral stress doses, until the fever is gone. See chapter 9 for details.

♦ ***Since the liquid Cortef was recalled, I am nervous about liquid medications. Aren't tablets always safer?***

Some drugs, such as hydrocortisone, do not easily dissolve in water. Liquid preparations of these medications are usually prepared as "suspensions," in which small amounts of the drug float, or are "suspended," within the liquid. If suspensions are not shaken or mixed properly, the medication can settle at the bottom of the bottle, causing the drug to be unevenly distributed. Because of this problem, tablets are more dependable for giving hydrocortisone.

Other drugs, such as prednisone and dexamethasone, do dissolve easily in water. Thus, liquid forms of these medications can be used.

♦ ***My pharmacist makes a liquid form of hydrocortisone for me. Is this OK?***

Some local pharmacies will make "custom" or "compounded" liquid preparations of hydrocortisone. Many doctors say this practice should be avoided, as hydrocortisone does not easily dissolve in liquids. The stability, safety and usefulness of these preparations have not been thoroughly tested in children with CAH.

♦ ***Do you have suggestions for how to give pills to a baby? Can I just put the Cortef in the bottle of baby formula?***

It is not recommended that you put the medication in your baby's formula. Because it is not known how long *Cortef* will remain stable after it dissolved, it is best that pills be crushed or dissolved just before they are given. Also, because *Cortef* is not completely water-soluble, some of the medication can settle at the bottom of the bottle, or stick to the sides of the bottle, putting your child at risk for not getting the full dose.

Try softening the pill with a little water or juice and giving it to your baby with a soft baby spoon, oral medication syringe, or baby nipple. This way you can be sure that your baby is getting his full dose. Some parents like to nurse immediately thereafter, or follow with a formula "chaser." When your baby is older, you can crush the pill and put it in a spoonful of something he likes, such as applesauce or pudding.

♦ ***Is it important to give medication on a very strict schedule?***

Within reason, medication should be given at roughly the same times every day. Test results are more meaningful when they can be compared against an established pattern of dosing. At the same time, fluctuations in daily routines are a part of life, and you should not worry if times vary slightly from day to day.

♦ ***What is the best time to give medication? Some doctors prescribe the largest dose at night, while others prescribe the largest dose in the morning, and still others prescribe the same amount of medication each time. Why are there so many different approaches?***

A major goal of CAH treatment is to block adrenal androgen secretion. In many cases, giving glucocorticoid doses at evenly spaced intervals of the day is sufficient to do this. However, when using glucocorticoid medications that require more than once a day administration—such as hydrocortisone or prednisone—it can be difficult to make small increases in the total daily dose, while still giving the same dose each time. To avoid giving too much total daily medication, doctors will usually just increase one dose at a time, usually the early morning or the late evening dose.

♦ ***Giving a larger dose at night or in the morning sounds like two contradictory ideas. Which is better?***

Normally, there is a twenty-four-hour, or circadian, rhythm in the production of ACTH and cortisol, with levels starting to rise around 3 a.m. and peaking around 8 a.m. To block this early morning ramp-up in ACTH, and the corresponding rise in 17-OHP and androgens, some doctors will give a larger dose at night. Glucocorticoids given at night also appear to be more potent.

Other doctors give the larger dose in the morning, to "mimic" the a.m. cortisol peak. Giving the larger dose in the morning also gives a child more circulating cortisol during the waking hours.

While there have been a number of studies done on the time of administration of the different glucocorticoids, results are varied and often contradictory. As a result, it is difficult to say, with certainty, which way is best. The answer may differ depending on the specific glucocorticoid that is used, the total dose that is given, and the constitution of the particular individual.

♦ ***What is meant by dosing to mimic circadian rhythm? It sounds like a good idea to give the medication as nature intended. Is this something we should be doing?***

Because ACTH starts to rise around 3 a.m., it has been suggested that patients might benefit from an extra dose of glucocorticoid medication, given at 3 a.m. However, giving a dose in the middle of the night poses the obvious problems of interrupted sleep for both parent and child, as well as the risk of choking when giving medication to a child who is not fully awake. Regularly giving the medication may also be very difficult to do with such an inconvenient dosing schedule. If doses are missed, this will counteract possible benefits that 3 a.m. dosing is believed to have.

It is also important to note that very few studies have been done on the efficacy of this approach. While there are one or two studies that suggest that patients on this dosing regimen may have improved control on lower doses of glucocorticoids, it remains to be seen whether those benefits can be sustained. It is also difficult to know whether final outcome in these patients will be different enough to justify such an inconvenient approach.

♦ ***What should we do if we forget a dose?***

Missed doses should be given as soon as they are remembered. Occasional missed doses are not cause for panic or alarm.

♦ ***Should medication be taken with food?***

When given at high doses, glucocorticoids can sometimes cause stomach upset and should be taken with food. At the doses given to treat CAH, stomach irritation is not usually a problem.

♦ ***Are there differences between generics and name brands?***

In general, no. Though there will always be slight variations in products put out by different manufacturers, these differences should not be enough to affect the overall performance of a drug. However, if your child's behavior or well-being seems to change noticeably shortly after you have changed medication brand, you should point this out to your doctor.

♦ ***How do we adjust dose times when traveling to a different time zone?***

If there is not a great difference between the two time zones (say, two or three hours), just give all doses, on the day of travel, at the regular times in the old time zone (e.g., 7 a.m., 3 p.m., 9 p.m. Eastern Standard Time). The next day, give the medication at the same clock times, but in the new time zone (e.g., 7 a.m., 3 p.m., 9 p.m., Pacific Standard Time).

If the time difference is greater than a few hours, you will also want to be mindful of the amount of time elapsed between doses. In that case, you may have to shift dose times up or back for a couple of days, until you can adjust to the new time zone. Remember that, while it is important to give medication on a set schedule under normal circumstances, it may be necessary to vary from the routine when unusual circumstances occur. As long as proper precautions are taken and common sense is utilized, this should not be a cause for concern.

♦ ***Why does my child's dose seem to be fluctuating or even going down? Shouldn't it only go up, since his BSA can only increase?***

Doses according to BSA are very general and used only as a starting point. After an initial dose is determined, adjustments up or down are based on test results and physical signs of under-treatment or over-treatment. While doses generally increase as a child grows, many factors can cause control to change. Thus, some up-and-down dose adjustments are common.

♦ ***How can I convert from a dose of one glucocorticoid (e.g. hydrocortisone) to the equivalent dose of a different glucocorticoid (e.g. dexamethasone)?***

The relative potencies published in standard drug equivalency tables are usually based on a glucocorticoid's ability to treat inflammation, rather than its ability to suppress androgen production. If one uses the commonly published dose comparisons for prednisone or dexamethasone, over-treatment will occur. Rather, for treatment of CAH, prednisone should be considered to be about 10 times stronger than hydrocortisone and dexamethasone, 80 to 100 times stronger than hydrocortisone.

♦ ***Why would the potency of a glucocorticoid change depending on the condition that is being treated?***

Drug equivalencies are very general. Many factors can influence the effective potency of a drug including individual metabolism, severity of the condition being treated, and time of administration of the medication. When studies have been done utilizing glucocorticoids in different settings, it has been demonstrated that relative potencies can vary greatly depending on the conditions of the study.

♦ ***If prolonged use of glucocorticoids can cause osteoporosis, should I be giving my child calcium supplements?***

Studies done on children with CAH generally show that bone density is normal. Some studies on adults, however, report low bone density in individuals with CAH. Since many children and adolescents do not take their recommended daily requirements of calcium, some doctors recommend giving calcium supplementation.

♦ ***Can chewing Cortef tablets (versus swallowing them whole) ruin teeth?***

The answer to this question is not known. However, it is better to swallow tablets whole, rather than chewing them. Doing so helps to ensure that the entire dose is taken.

♦♦♦

# 6

# Monitoring Glucocorticoid Treatment in Congenital Adrenal Hyperplasia

*All children with CAH need close and regular medical follow-up. This includes the evaluation of physical growth and maturation, along with laboratory testing of adrenal hormone levels. In this chapter, we provide details about how hormone levels are followed in children with CAH; discuss the different methods of testing; and explain how bone ages are used to assess long-term control.*

**ESTIMATING GENETIC HEIGHT POTENTIAL**

| | (A) | (B) | (C) | (D) | (E) |
|---|---|---|---|---|---|
| | **Mom** | **Dad** | **Average of Parents' Heights**<br>**(A + B) / 2** | **Genetic Potential (Boy)**<br>**C + 3"** | **Genetic Potential (Girl)**<br>**C – 2"** |
| **Example 1** | 5' 4" | 5' 6" | (5' 4" + 5' 6") / 2 = 5'-5" | 5' 5" + 3" = 5' 8" | 5' 5" - 2" = 5' 3" |
| **Example 2** | 5' 2" | 6' 0" | (5' 2" + 6' 0") / 2 = 5' 7" | 5' 7" + 3" = 5' 10" | 5' 7" - 2" = 5' 5" |

MONitoring treatment in CAH is as important as the treatment itself. Yet monitoring methods vary from institution to institution and from doctor to doctor. Many articles and textbook chapters emphasize the importance of monitoring, yet few provide specific details. Not surprisingly, it can often be difficult to obtain clear information about appropriate testing regimens and acceptable hormone levels in CAH.

Although monitoring and testing in CAH may seem confusing, there are several approaches that you can use to gauge how you are doing. It is also important to emphasize that looking at changes in physical growth and maturation is as important as—if not more important than—the laboratory testing in CAH.

## MONITORING GROWTH AND MATURATION IN CAH

Rates of growth provide very important clues about the adequacy of CAH treatment in childhood. In general, if you are treated adequately from infancy, you should be able to maintain normal patterns of growth. You should also be able to grow at a pace that is consistent with your genetic potential.

Genetic potential is assessed by looking at the heights of the parents. Sometimes doctors will use standard formulas to make height projections. These can vary slightly, but are usually based on the average of the parents' heights, adjusted for gender.

For example, to estimate the adult height of a boy, you can take the average of the parents' heights and *add three* inches. To estimate height for a girl, it would be the average of the parents' heights, *minus two* inches.

### Normal Growth

Growth in childhood generally follows pretty set patterns. Patterns that deviate from the norm can often be a warning sign to the doctor that something is amiss.

#### *Early Growth*

The most rapid period of growth in life is during the first two years after birth. During the first year of life, you will grow an average of ten inches. During the second year of life, you will grow an average of about five inches. From two years of age, until the start of puberty, growth levels off to about two to two and a half inches per year.

### *Growth During Puberty*

Growth picks up again when you hit puberty. Puberty begins when the ovaries in girls, and the testes in boys, become active. This normally happens sometime between the ages of eight and eleven, if you're a girl, and between the ages of ten and thirteen, if you're a boy.

Puberty is a process of physical and sexual maturation that culminates in your ability to reproduce. From the beginning of puberty until sexual maturity is complete, the process takes about three to four years.

In girls, the earliest sign of puberty is the development of breast buds. In boys, it is the enlargement of the testicles. These events are normally followed by the development of other sexual characteristics—pubic hair, underarm hair, underarm odor, and acne—in both sexes.

In boys, the scrotum will also change in size and appearance. The penis will lengthen, muscle mass will increase, and the voice will deepen.

In girls, the breasts will increase in size and shape, and body proportion will change. Toward the end of puberty, menstrual cycles will start.

Puberty is marked by periods of rapid growth in both boys and girls. Girls usually have a growth spurt during the early part of puberty, while boys have their biggest spurt in the second half of puberty. During the peak of puberty, growth can increase to as much as five inches a year.

At the end of puberty, growth slows then finally stops altogether. Girls usually reach final adult height around fifteen years of age; boys, around seventeen years of age. Final height is reached when the growth plates in the skeleton become calcified. After the growth plates are eliminated, no more height is possible.

## Growth and CAH

If you are growing normally, you will usually grow along the same percentile for height, from infancy through adolescence. However, if you are over-treated or under-treated with glucocorticoids, you can grow more slowly or more quickly than normal.

To assess treatment, height and weight should be monitored and plotted on standard growth charts (see appendix). Following changes in height and weight, your physician can detect signs of over-treatment and under-treatment.

On the growth charts, the distribution of height and weight in the general population is depicted by a set of curves. Each curve corresponds to a different percentile line of growth. "Percentile" has to do with your

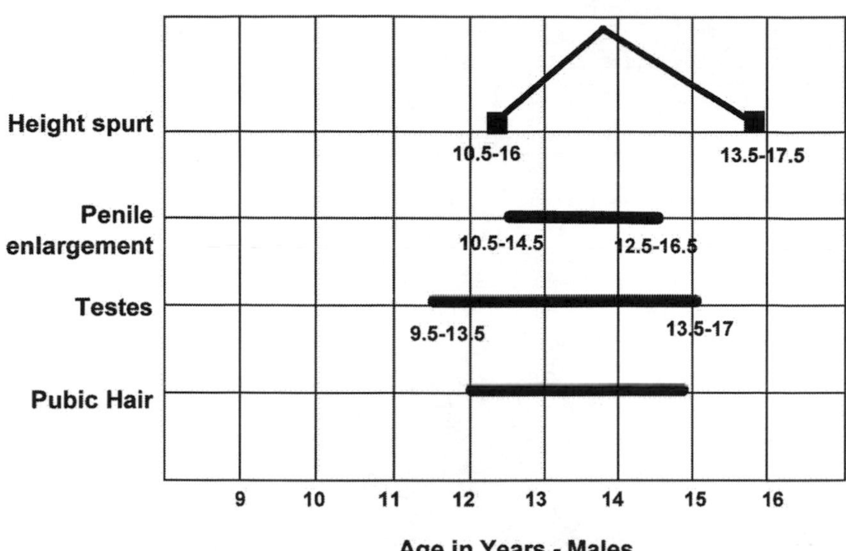


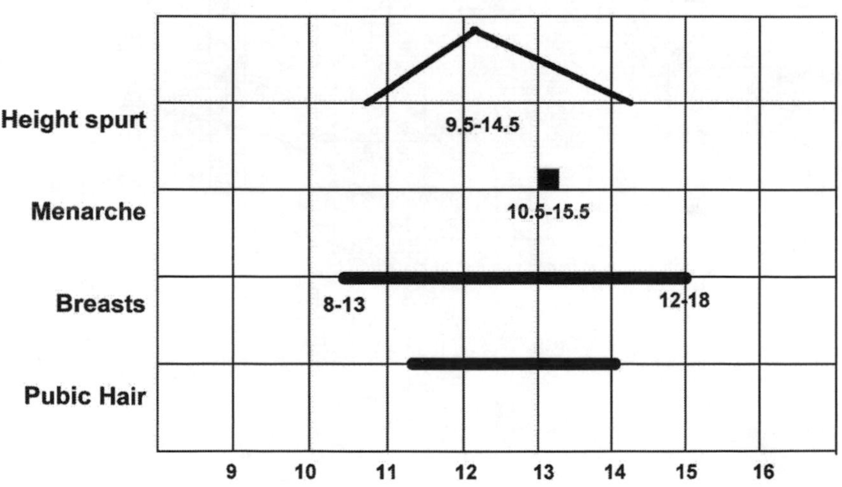


**PUBERTAL MILESTONES IN BOYS AND GIRLS.**
Adapted from J. M. Tanner, *Growth at Adolescence* (Springfield, Ill.: Blackwell Scientific Publications, 1962).

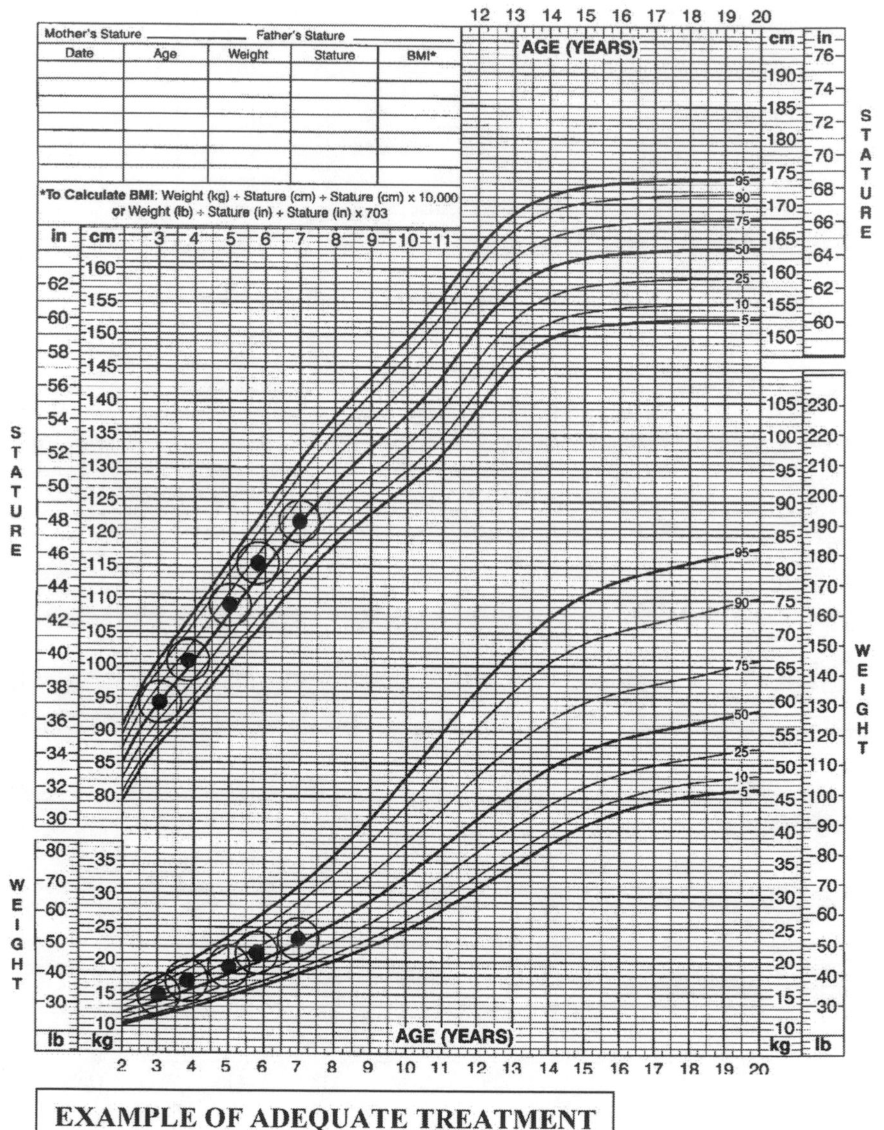


**EXAMPLE OF ADEQUATE TREATMENT**

ranking in comparison with others. The 50th percentile line represents the mean score for the population.

For example, if you are growing along the 50th percentile line for height, it means that you are taller than 50 percent of the population, and smaller than the other 50 percent of the population—in other words, you are exactly average. If you are growing along the 90th percentile line, you would be taller than 90 percent of other kids, i.e., taller than average. If you are growing along the 10th percentile line, you would be taller than only 10 percent of other kids, i.e., smaller than average.

## THE IMPORTANCE OF REGULAR FOLLOW-UP

To optimize treatment and ensure your child's normal development, frequent follow-up with a qualified professional is essential. Most practitioners will see a CAH child every three or four months. This gives sufficient time to see changes in height and weight, and responses to treatment. It is best to see the same doctor at each visit.

### Your Child's Doctor

A child with CAH is usually managed by a specialist called a pediatric endocrinologist. Pediatric endocrinologists are doctors who are specially trained to treat endocrine disorders in children.

The average pediatrician will care for 5,000-10,000 children during the course of a career spanning thirty to forty years. Because CAH is so unusual—about 1 in 20,000 births—most generalists will probably never see a case of CAH. As a result, they will not have the experience to treat this condition.

In contrast, pediatric endocrinologists see *only* patients with endocrine disorders. While there are many endocrine disorders—including more common ones such as diabetes—most pediatric endocrinologists have the experience to treat CAH. Because there are considerable differences in managing CAH in adults versus children, your endocrinologist should also be one who is specifically trained in pediatrics.

Continuity of care (being seen by the same person) is also important. A single care-provider has the advantage of being able to detect subtle signs of over-treatment or under-treatment. This is difficult if you are seen by a different practitioner each time, even if that doctor is within the same practice.

### What to Expect At Office Visits

Office visits will typically include careful measurements of height, weight, and blood pressure. The doctor will also look for physical signs of under-treatment and over-treatment, as well as signs of puberty.

During the visit, or around the time of visits, laboratory testing may be performed to assess hormonal control. Bone age x-rays may also be obtained every six to twelve months. Most physicians do not begin obtaining bone ages until after a child is two or three years old.

| HEIGHT AND WEIGHT: CONVERTING FROM ENGLISH TO METRIC UNITS | | | | |
|---|---|---|---|---|
| | **From Units of:** | **To Units of:** | **Multiply By:** | **Example:** |
| **WEIGHT** | Pounds | Kilograms | 0.4545 | 95 lbs x 0.4545= 43.18 kg |
| | Kilograms | Pounds | 2.2 | 43.18 kg x 2.2 = 95 lbs. |
| **HEIGHT** | Inches | Centimeters | 2.54 | 60 inches x 2.54 = 152.4 cms. |
| | Centimeters | Inches | 0.394 | 152.4 cms x 0.394 = 60 inches |

## Signs of Over-Treatment With Glucocorticoids

If you are getting too much glucocorticoid medication, then you are "over-treated." When glucocorticoid doses are too high, growth will slow and weight will increase. This means that you will fall to a lower percentile on the height chart, while climbing to a higher percentile on the weight chart.

Sometimes it can take three to six months to see changes in height. Changes in weight can be seen much sooner, often in as little as two or three weeks. As a result, it can be very useful to monitor weight at home, in between visits to the doctor.

Normally, a child gains two to three pounds for every inch of height. For the average child, this means a weight gain of five to seven pounds per year. If weight increases more quickly than that—especially right after a dose change—it can be a sign that the dose is too high. Sometimes, weight gain can occur even without a proportionate increase in appetite or food intake.

Over-treatment can also cause the weight on your body to be redistributed. A round or "moon-shaped" face is a sign of glucocorticoid excess. Another is the development of a fat pad, resembling a "buffalo hump," at the back of the neck.

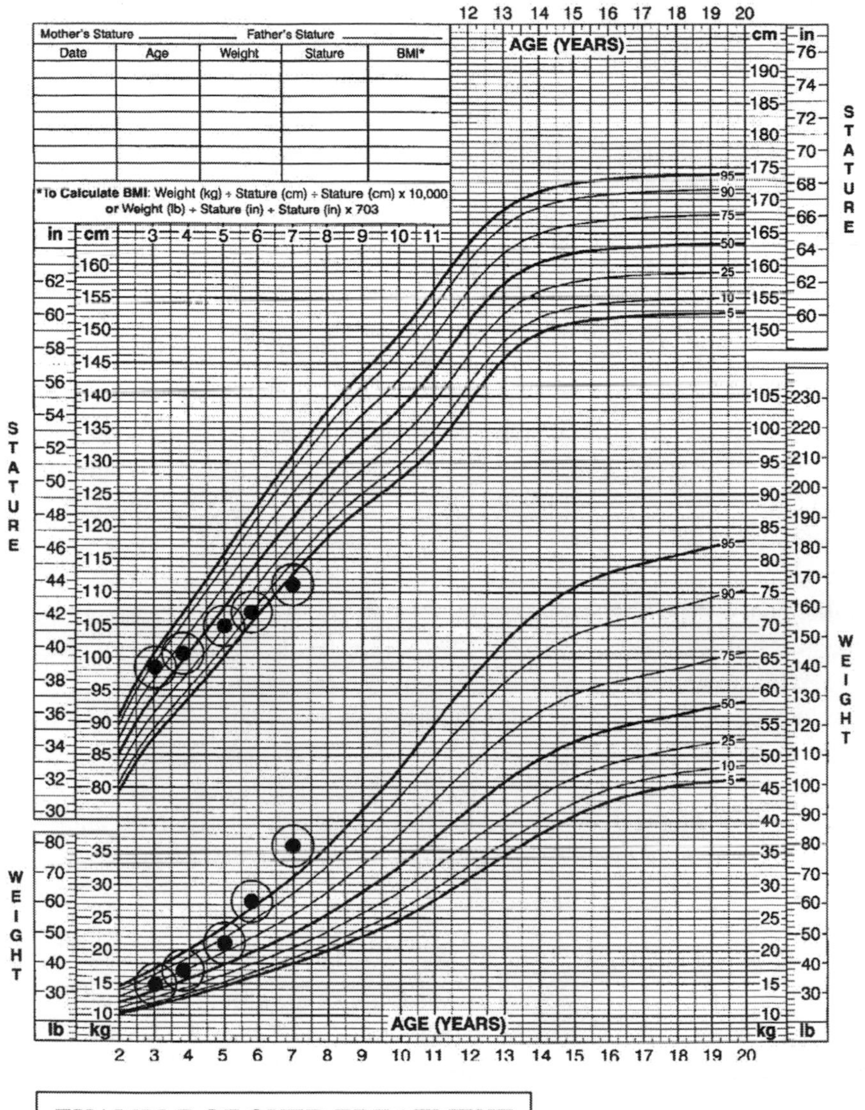


**EXAMPLE OF OVER-TREATMENT**

If over-treatment is significant, reddish stretch marks (called "striae") may develop along the abdomen and other parts of your body. Stretch marks occur when a lot of weight is gained in a relatively short period of time. (This can happen even if you don't have CAH.)

Over-treatment can also cause an increase in body hair. Whereas *under*-treatment will result in increased sexual hair (i.e., pubic and underarm hair), *over*-treatment can result in hair growth on the back.

## Signs of Under-Treatment With Glucocorticoids

If you are not getting enough glucocorticoid medication, then you are *under*-treated. Under-treatment will lead to increased ACTH and androgen production, and low levels of cortisol.

When you are under-treated, the pituitary gland will increase its production of ACTH. ACTH causes your skin to darken. Thus, a very tan appearance can be a sign that you have high levels of ACTH. The knuckles on your fingers can appear to be dark or "dirty-looking."

When you are under-treated, your adrenal glands will produce excess androgens. Androgens help to speed up growth. Your pattern of growth will then be the opposite of what it is when you are over-treated. That is, you will climb to a higher percentile on the height charts, while falling on the weight charts.

Excess androgens can also cause signs of sexual development to appear or increase. These include symptoms such as adult-type body odor, pubic hair, armpit hair, and acne. In girls, the clitoris may enlarge. In boys, the penis may increase in size and there may be more frequent erections.

With under-treatment, there may also be changes in behavior. Some parents report that children seem to be moodier and more aggressive when they are under-treated.

Under-treatment can also result in excessive tiredness, fatigue, headache, or stomach pain. Rather than as a result of excess androgen production, these symptoms may be due to low levels of cortisol.

## Signs of Puberty

Children who are under-treated will often exhibit signs of sexual maturity (pubic hair, armpit hair, body odor, acne, etc.). These physical traits are caused by an excess of androgens and do not necessarily mean that a child is undergoing true puberty.

"True puberty" starts when the pituitary gland in the brain becomes active, causing the ovaries in girls, and the testicles in boys, to also become active. When these glands mature, they will start to produce their own hormones. The ovaries will start to make estrogen and the testicles will start to produce testosterone.

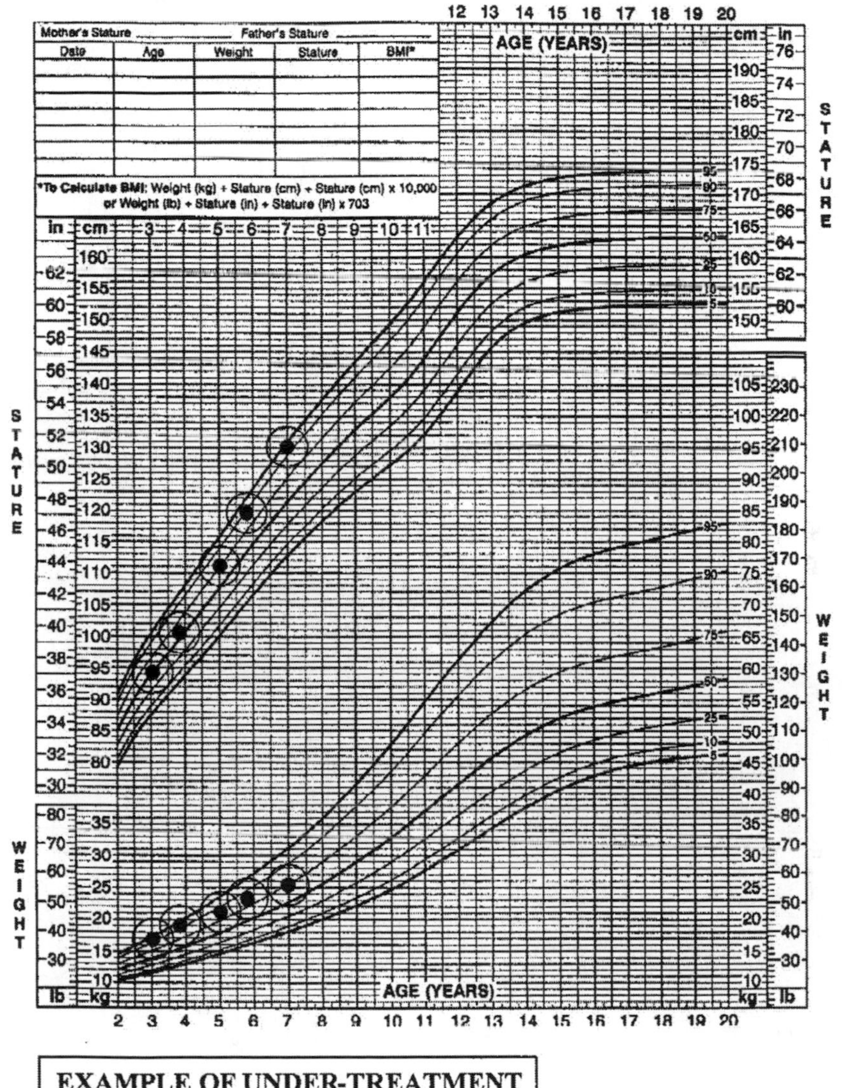


**EXAMPLE OF UNDER-TREATMENT**

Estrogen will cause the formation of breasts in girls, while testosterone will cause the testicles to enlarge, in boys. Thus, to check for puberty, your doctor will look for physical signs of breast development or testicular enlargement. To assess the development of the testicles, the doctor may use sizing beads called an "orchidometer."

If there is no breast development or testicular enlargement, then the child is not undergoing "true puberty." Rather, the symptoms of sexual maturity will be due to excess androgens caused by under-treatment, not maturation of the ovaries or testicles.

However, because pituitary activity can be affected by adrenal androgen levels, true puberty can also develop at a very young age, when you have CAH. This occurs because of a negative feedback relationship between the pituitary gland and adrenal glands. When there are persistently high levels of androgens, pituitary gland activity is suppressed. When androgen levels suddenly fall, pituitary activity will increase. Thus, in those who are diagnosed late or who have been chronically under-treated, puberty can be triggered when treatment is started or medication increased.

If true puberty begins before the age of seven in girls, or before the age of nine in boys, it is said to be early or "precocious." Because precocious puberty can complicate the treatment of CAH, additional medications may be recommended to help delay the progression of puberty in those affected children (see chapter 8.)

| GLUCOCORTICOID TREATMENT | |
|---|---|
| **Signs of Under-treatment** | **Signs of Over-treatment** |
| • Tiredness or fatigue<br>• Headache<br>• Loss of appetite<br>• Loss of weight<br>• Moodiness<br>• Acne<br>• Excessive tan appearance<br>• Premature development of:<br>- pubic hair<br>- underarm hair<br>- underarm odor<br>• Progressive genital enlargement<br>• Rapid growth | • Rapid weight gain<br>• Large appetite<br>• Round or "moon" face<br>• Excessive hair on back<br>• Sleeplessness<br>• Slow growth in height<br>• "Buffalo hump" at back of neck<br>• Striae ("stretch marks") along abdomen<br>• Headache |

## Monitoring Blood Pressure

Blood pressure generally provides clues about the adequacy of mineralocorticoid treatment. However, blood pressure can also be affected by glucocorticoid treatment. Thus, it is regularly monitored in all children with CAH.

If you have 21-hydroxylase deficiency, high blood pressure can be an indication that glucocorticoid doses are too high. When you have 11-

hydroxylase deficiency, it can be an indication that glucocorticoid doses are too *low*. If you have 11-hydroxylase deficiency, you will overproduce the hormones deoxycorticosterone and 11-deoxycortisol. Both those hormones have salt-retaining properties. Thus, if they are insufficiently suppressed with glucocorticoids, hypertension can result.

## THE USEFULNESS OF BONE AGES

One of the best tools for monitoring changes in physical maturation is the "bone age." By measuring your relative degree of skeletal development, the bone age provides a wonderful marker of long-term growth and androgen secretion.

### What is the "Bone Age"?

The growth centers ("epiphyses") in your skeleton can be easily visualized by taking an x-ray of your hand. At each stage of life, the growth centers have a characteristic shape and size. By comparing the appearance of the growth centers with those found in a book of standards, a "bone age" can be determined.

In childhood, growth and developmental milestones are often more closely correlated to the bone age, rather than to actual (chronological) age. When you are growing normally, the bone age approximates the actual age, though there may be differences of one to two years. If there is an abnormal growth pattern, the bone age may be significantly older (called "advanced") or younger (called "delayed.")

### Bone Age and CAH

If glucocorticoid treatment and growth is on target, the bone age will approximate chronological age. However, if there have been extended periods of under-treatment or over-treatment, the bone age may be significantly advanced or delayed.

An advanced bone age is an indication of under-treatment. A six-year-old who has been under-treated for a period of time may have a bone age of nine years. One who is late-diagnosed, and has been exposed to excess androgens for an extended period of time, may have a bone age of ten to twelve years. In contrast, a delayed bone age can be an indication of over-treatment. A six-year-old who has been chronically over-treated may have a bone age of three to four years.

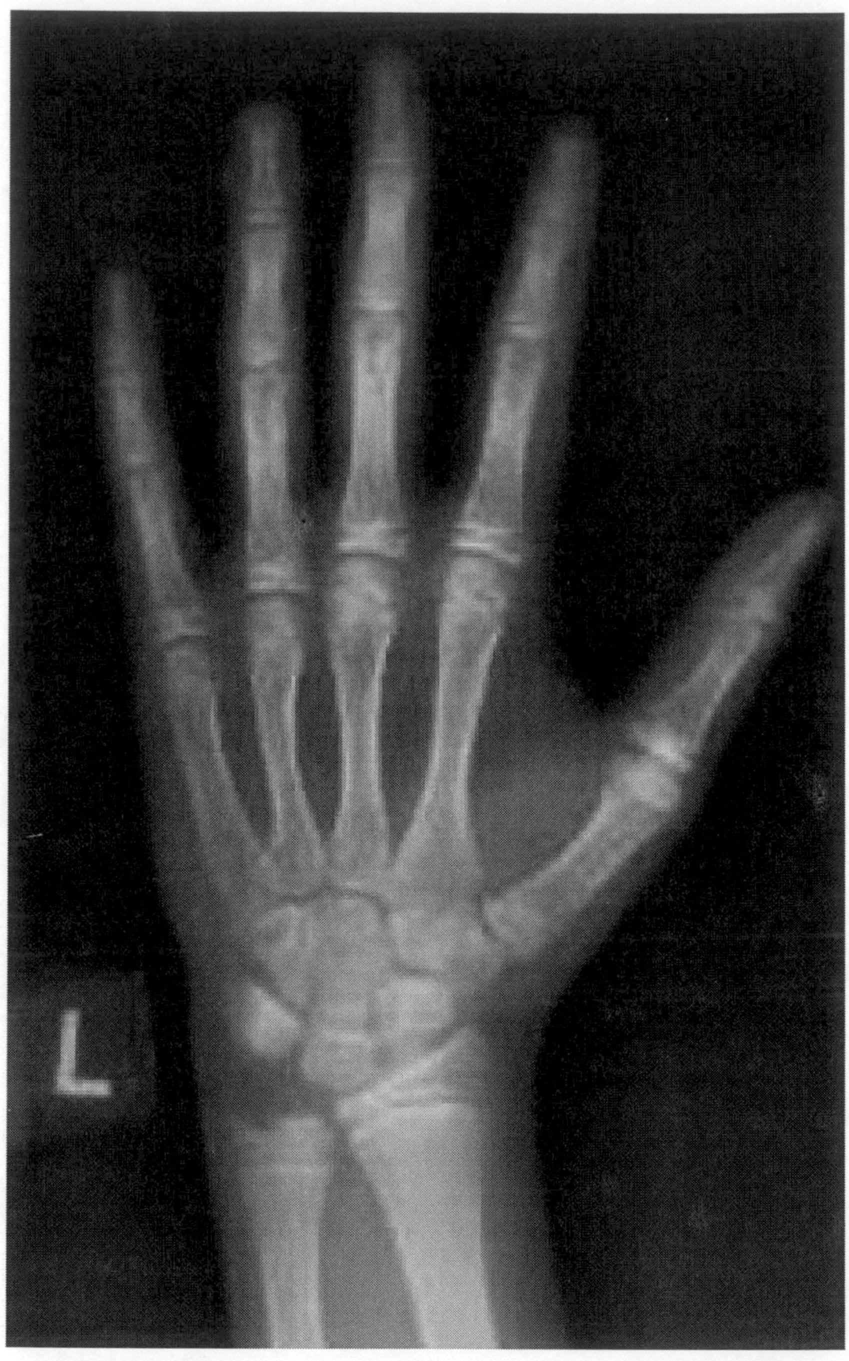
L

Advanced bone age can compromise adult height by shortening the length of time left to grow. Delayed bone age can also impact final height, as deferred growth may not be completely recouped.

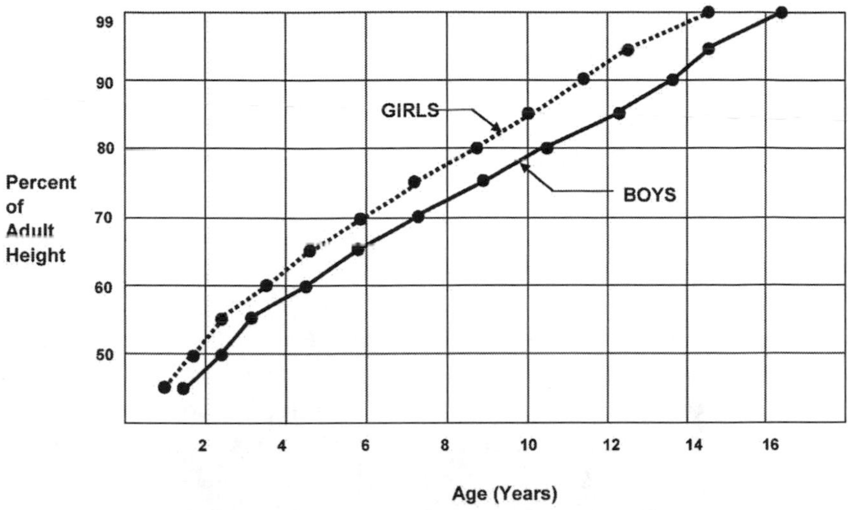


**PERCENT OF GROWTH COMPLETED RELATIVE TO BONE AGE.** Based on W. W. Greulich and S. I. Pyle, *Radiographic Atlas of Skeletal Development of the Hand and Wrist*, Stanford University Press, 1959.

## Bone Age and Height Predictions

Bone age is often used to help make height predictions. Research has shown that there is a correlation between bone age and the percentage of final height completed. Thus, by knowing bone age and current height, projections can be made about final adult height.

Because changes in bone age often lag behind periods of excess androgen secretion, it can take some time for advancement in bone age to be detectable on x-rays. Thus, it is also important to note that height predictions based on bone age can be imprecise, with an error margin of approximately two inches. In general, predictions based on bone ages tend to over-predict final height.

## Who Should Read the Bone Age X-Ray?

Bone age x-rays are read by your pediatric endocrinologist, or a radiologist skilled in bone age interpretation. In some cases, the pediatric endocrinologist may be more experienced at interpreting bone ages than a general radiologist. General practitioners, including pediatricians and internists, are usually not trained to read bone ages.

Because reading bone age involves interpreting a visual image, there can be some variability in interpretation from person to person. As a result, it is useful to have each bone age read by the same doctor. It is also useful for the doctor to review successive bone ages at the same time in order to get an accurate picture of the pace of skeletal maturation.

## MONITORING OF HORMONE LEVELS

The monitoring of hormone production in CAH usually involves the laboratory testing of either blood or urine. Several different approaches can be used.

Blood testing is the most common method of assessing control. It is preferred by many doctors because of its convenience. However, because adrenal hormone levels naturally fluctuate during the course of the day, a single blood test may not accurately reflect the extent of adrenal gland activity.

In comparison, urine testing can be used to measure hormone production over the course of an entire twenty-four-hour day. As a result, urine testing may give a better picture of adrenal control. However, because urine testing is viewed as inconvenient, it is not commonly used. Testing blood hormone levels several times a day using filter paper specimens has also been shown to be an effective monitoring tool. However, this method of testing is not widely available in the United States.

### Blood Testing

When testing blood, several hormones are usually measured to assess adrenal gland activity. These include ACTH, 17-OHP, androstenedione, and testosterone. If you are a salt-waster, tests to monitor mineralocorticoid treatment are also needed (see chapter 7.)

| BLOOD ADRENAL HORMONES LEVELS IN CHILDREN WITHOUT CAH | | | |
|---|---|---|---|
| **Hormone** | **Normal Pre-pubertal Levels*** | **Normal Mid-pubertal Levels*** | **Normal Pubertal & Adult Levels*** |
| **17-OHP** (ng/dl) | **50** (3-100) | **80** (10-150) | **100** (25-250) |
| **Androstenedione** (ng/dl) | **25** (8-50) | **70** (50-100) | **115** (70-200) |
| **Testosterone** (ng/dl) | **5** (3-10) | **Males: 150** (100-300)<br>**Females: 25** (15-35) | **Males: 600** (300-1000)<br>**Females: 30** (10-55) |
| **ACTH** (pg/dl) | **30** (10-60) | **30** (10-60) | **30** (10-60) |
| **Average number is given in bold. Normal range of levels is in parentheses.* | | | |

### *Blood Hormones Tested*

ACTH is a pituitary hormone. Adrenal gland activity is directly regulated by the release of ACTH. In approximately 75 percent of cases where adrenal hormone levels are elevated, ACTH is also found to be elevated. Thus—while not a direct measure of adrenal hormone production—ACTH can still be a good indicator of adrenal control.

The hormone 17-hydroxyprogesterone (17-OHP) is the direct precursor to cortisol in the glucocorticoid pathway of the adrenal cortex. When you have CAH due to 21-hydroxylase deficiency, you tend to build up 17-OHP. Thus, control of CAH is often assessed based on levels of 17-OHP. 17-OHP can be a sensitive barometer of adrenal gland activity. However, levels of 17-OHP can fluctuate widely and be elevated, even when other adrenal hormones are in good control.

The hormones androstenedione and testosterone reflect adrenal androgen production. Because androgens are responsible for most of the damaging effects of untreated, or under-treated, CAH, it is especially useful to look at androstenedione and testosterone levels in pre-pubertal children and females. Because testosterone also comes from the testicles in pubertal males, it is not as useful to look at testosterone levels in adolescent or adult males.

### *Time of Day of Testing*

Adrenal hormone levels vary naturally over the course of a twenty-four-hour day. Levels will also drop after a dose is given, but sometimes rise excessively after medication wears off. Thus care must be taken to consider the time of day and the timing of doses, when interpreting blood-test results.

Many endocrinologists advocate getting blood samples in the morning, before medication is given. Tests taken under these conditions reflect adrenal gland activity at its highest, when control is at its worst.

Others obtain blood tests after the dose is given. Tests taken after medication reflect adrenal activity at its lowest, when control is at its peak.

### *Evaluating Results*

In pre-pubertal children who do not have CAH, average 17-OHP levels are 50 ng/dl; average androstenedione levels are 25 ng/dl; and average testosterone levels are less than 5 ng/dl. However, if children with CAH are treated to achieve "normal" adrenal hormone levels, they will have problems with growth suppression and weight gain.

| **BLOOD ADRENAL HORMONE LEVELS IN CHILDREN WITH CAH** | |
|---|---|
| **Hormone** | **Acceptable levels** |
| **17-OHP** | 500-1000 ng/dl |
| **Androstenedione** | Up to 25 percent above those of children without CAH |
| **Testosterone** | Up to 25 percent above those of children without CAH |

To allow for normal growth, physicians will allow a CAH child's levels to go higher than normal. Thus, androstenedione and testosterone numbers that are modestly elevated (about 25 percent above normal) are considered acceptable, while 17-OHP levels can be allowed to go up to 500-1000 ng/dl (about ten times normal production). During puberty, levels of these hormones rise. Thus, "acceptable" numbers will also depend on a child's stage of pubertal development.

A recent study reports that when there is good control of adrenal gland activity, as evidenced by normal levels of ACTH, 17-OHP levels are generally less than 600 ng/dl in the morning, before medication is given, and less than 200 ng/dl during later parts of the day. When there is poor control of adrenal gland activity, 17-OHP can rise to an average of 10,000 ng/dl in the morning and 5000 ng/dl later in the day.

| ADRENAL HORMONES: COMMON UNIT CONVERSIONS | | | |
|---|---|---|---|
| **To Convert From Units of:** | **To Units of:** | **Multiply By:** | **Example:** |
| **ng/dl** (nanograms/deciliter) | **ng/ml** (nanograms/milliliter) | **0.01** | 600 ng/dl x 0.01 = 6 ng/ml |
| **ng/dl** (nanograms/deciliter) | **pg/ml** (picograms/milliliter) | **10.0** | 45 ng/dl x 10 = 450 pg/ml |
| **ng/ml** (nanograms/milliliter) | **ng/dl** (nanograms/deciliter) | **100** | 6 ng/ml x 100 = 600 ng/dl |
| **ng/ml** (nanograms/milliliter) | **µg/L** (micrograms/liter) | **1.0** | 150 ng/ml x 1.0 = 150 ug/L |
| **ng/L** (nanograms/liter) | **pg/ml** (picograms/milliliter) | **1.0** | 86 ng/L x 1.0 = 86 pg/ml |
| **pg/ml** (picograms/milliliter) | **ng/dl** (nanograms/deciliter) | **0.10** | 450 pg/ml x 0.1 = 45 ng/ml |
| **pg/ml** (picograms/milliliter) | **ng/L** (nanograms/liter) | **1.0** | 86 pg/ml x 1.0 = 86 ng/L |
| **µg/L** (micrograms/liter) | **ng/ml** (nanograms/milliliter) | **1.0** | 150 µg/L x 1.0 = 150 ng/ml |
| **µg/dl** (micrograms/deciliter) | **ng/dl** (nanograms/deciliter) | **.001** | 150 µg/dl x .001 = 0.15 ng/dl |

### *Units of Measure*

Adrenal hormone levels can somtimes be reported using different units of measure. Thus, when comparing lab results, it is important to check that direct comparisons are being made.

| ADRENAL HORMONES: CONVERTING FROM ENGLISH TO INTERNATIONAL UNITS | | | | |
|---|---|---|---|---|
| **Hormone** | **To Convert From Units of:** | **To Units of:** | **Mult. By:** | **Example:** |
| **17-OHP** | **ng/dl** (nanograms/deciliter) | **nmol/L** (nanomols/liter) | 0.03 | 1000 ng/dl x 0.03 = 30 nmol/L |
| | **nmol/L** (nanomols/liter) | **ng/dl** (nanograms/deciliter) | 33.05 | 45 nmol/L x 33.05 = 1487 ng/dl |
| **17-OHP** | **ng/ml** (nanograms/milliliter) | **nmol/L** (nanomols/liter) | 3.03 | 10.0 ng/ml x 3.03 = 30.3 nmol/L |
| | **nmol/L** (nanomols/liter) | **ng/ml** (nanograms/milliliter) | 0.33 | 45 nmol/L x 0.33 = 14.85 ng/ml |
| **Androstene-dione** | **ng/dl** (nanograms/deciliter) | **nmol/L** (nanomols/liter) | 0.03 | 50 ng/dl x 0.03 = 1.5 nmol/L |
| | **nmol/L** (nanomols/liter) | **ng/dl** (nanograms/deciliter) | 28.64 | 2.5 nmol/L x 28.64 = 72 ng/dl |
| **Androstene-dione** | **ng/ml** (nanograms/milliliter) | **nmol/L** (nanomols/liter) | 3.49 | 2.0 ng/ml x 3.49 = 6.98 nmol/L |
| | **nmol/L** (nanomols/liter) | **ng/ml** (nanograms/milliliter) | 0.29 | 2.0 nmol/L x 0.29 = 0.48 ng/ml |
| **Testosterone** | **ng/dl** (nanograms/deciliter) | **nmol/L** (nanomols/liter) | 0.04 | 30 ng/dl x 0.04 = 1.04 nmol/L |
| | **nmol/L** (nanomols/liter) | **ng/dl** (nanograms/deciliter) | 28.84 | 1.04 nmol/L x 28.84 = 30.0 ng/dl |
| **Testosterone** | **ng/dl** (nanograms/deciliter) | **pmol/L** (picomols/liter) | 34.67 | 30 ng/dl x 34.67 = 1040 pmol/L |
| | **pmol/L** (picomols/liter) | **ng/dl** (nanograms/deciliter) | 0.03 | 1040 pmol/L x 0.03 = 30 ng/dl |

Most laboratories in the United States use the units "ng/dl" ("nanograms per ***deci***liter") to measure the more common adrenal hormones—17 OHP, androstenedione, and testosterone. However, these hormones can also be measured in units "ng/ml" ("nanograms per ***milli***liter"). Because ng/dl differs from ng/ml by a factor of 100, it is important to know that you are comparing "apples to apples" when you are looking at numbers.

| COMMON NUMERICAL PREFIXES | | |
|---|---|---|
| **Symbol** | **Prefix** | **Power of 10** |
| d | deci | $10^{-1}$ |
| c | centi | $10^{-2}$ |
| m | milli | $10^{-3}$ |
| µ | micro | $10^{-6}$ |
| n | nano | $10^{-9}$ |
| p | pico | $10^{-12}$ |
| k | kilo | $10^{3}$ |

Laboratories outside the United States usually use different units altogether. To measure mass, units called "mols" are normally used instead of "grams." For example, 17-OHP is commonly expressed in units "nmol/L" ("nanomols per liter"), rather than "ng/dl" or "ng/ml." Converting from mols to grams is not straightforward. A mol is based on the molecular weight of an element. Thus, the number of grams in a mol is different for every hormone, and the conversion factor for each hormone has to be individually calculated.

Sometimes, a laboratory may use more uncommon units to report results. With a basic understanding of math and numerical prefixes, it should be possible to translate "unfamiliar" lab values to something that is more recognizable.

## Urine Testing

Whereas a single blood test measures hormone levels at a particular time of the day, a twenty-four-hour urine collection reflects levels over the course of an entire day. As a result, a twenty-four-hour collection is often considered the "gold standard' in assessing adrenal hormone production.

Urine collections also offer other advantages. Because you can do them at home, many parents and children find this method of testing to be very convenient. Urine tests can also avoid, or reduce, the need for needle-sticks, which can be traumatic for some children. However, because it is difficult to collect urine from very young children, urine testing is usually done only after a child has passed the toddler stage.

### *Urine Hormones Tested*

As with blood, different hormones are tested in the urine to gauge activity in both the glucocorticoid and androgen pathways of the adrenal cortex. The hormones measured in urine are the breakdown products (called "metabolites") of the equivalent hormones in the blood. Androgen production, in the urine, is assessed via the measurement of hormones called 17-ketosteroids (17-KS). The 17-KS are the metabolites of androstenedione and testosterone. Thus, measuring 17-KS in urine is comparable to testing androstenedione and testosterone, in blood.

To assess hormone production in the glucocorticoid pathway, "pregnanetriol" is measured. Pregnanetriol is the urinary metabolite of 17-OHP. Thus, measuring pregnanetriol in urine is comparable to measuring 17-OHP in blood.

"Creatinine" is another substance that is usually measured in the urine. It is a breakdown product of muscle. Creatinine is continuously released into the urine, at a rate of about 10-15 mg/kg (4-6 mg/lb) per day. While not a measure of adrenal gland activity, creatinine helps to assess whether a twenty-four-hour collection is complete or incomplete. A less-than-expected amount of creatinine in the sample suggests that urine has not been collected for a full twenty-four hours.

Urine testing is not normally used to assess the adequacy of mineralocorticoid treatment. Thus, if you are a salt-waster, you will still need to measure renin in your blood, twice yearly, to see if *Florinef* and salt amounts are adequate.

### *Evaluating Results*

Both 17-KS and pregnanetriol are normally measured in units "mg/24 hours." The values obtained in a twenty-four-hour collection can be compared to normal rates of excretion. Similar to the levels of adrenal hormones in the blood, the elimination of 17-KS and pregnanetriol increases with age.

Even in situations in which the 17-KS are normal—showing adequate treatment—pregnanetriol levels can be elevated. Thus, when 17-KS and pregnanetriol levels do not agree, many doctors place more emphasis on the 17-KS value.

| URINE HORMONE LEVELS IN HEALTHY POPULATION<br>*(Average number is given in bold. Normal range of levels is in parentheses.)* | | | |
|---|---|---|---|
| **Hormone:** | **Pre-pubertal*:** | **Mid-pubertal*:** | **Pubertal and Adult*:** |
| **17-Ketosteroids**<br>(mg/24 hrs) | **1.5** (0.2-3) | **Males: 5** (3-10.0)<br>**Females: 3.5** (2.5-8.0) | **Males: 15** (10-25)<br>**Females: 10** (6-14) |
| **Pregnanetriol**<br>(mg/24 hrs) | **0.5** | **1.0** | **2.0** |
| **Note: In CAH, levels of 17-ketosteroids that are normal, or modestly (about 25 percent) above normal, are acceptable. As with blood testing for 17-OHP, higher urinary levels of pregnanetriol can be accepted if the 17-KS are within target range.* | | | |

### *Performing a Twenty-Four-Hour Urine Collection*

In essence, a twenty-four-hour urine collection is a collection of all the urine that you void during a twenty-four-hour period. Collection periods usually span from one morning to the next.

On the day that you are ready to start collecting, you will urinate into the toilet upon waking. Thus, the first void of the *first* morning is *not* collected. From that point on, you will collect—and save—all the urine that is voided for the rest of the day and night—up to, and including, the first void of the next morning. Thus, the final sample collected is the first void of the *second* morning.

Urine should be saved in a special container provided by the lab or hospital. Some laboratories may require the addition of a preservative, before the collection is taken. Specimens should be kept refrigerated, or in a cool place, until they can be brought to the laboratory for analysis, within two or three days of doing the collection.

## Filter Paper (Blood-Spot) Testing

A single blood test can provide important insights into the adequacy of CAH treatment. But, because numbers can vary depending on the circumstances surrounding the test, results can be difficult to evaluate. A way to overcome the potential pitfalls of once-daily sampling is through the use of blood-spot testing.

Blood-spot testing is accomplished by taking *several* blood samples over the course of the day, via finger sticks. This is similar in idea to measuring blood sugar levels three or four times a day if you're a diabetic. By measuring 17-OHP levels at several different times of the day, you can identify times when levels are too high or too low, and adjust medication doses accordingly.

Blood specimens obtained by finger sticks are collected on specially treated pieces of filter paper, which are then sent to a laboratory for analysis. In the United States, samples may need to be sent to a state-run lab that performs newborn screening for CAH, as most hospital labs do not have the proper equipment to test filter paper samples. While this is not routinely done, it may be possible to arrange this through your endocrinologist.

Pediatrix Screening, a commercial laboratory in Pennsylvania, has recently instituted blood-spot testing for CAH patients. Contact information for this lab can be found in the appendix.

♦♦♦

## WHAT YOU MAY BE CONCERNED ABOUT: FREQUENTLY ASKED QUESTIONS

### ♦ *How can I find a pediatric endocrinologist in my area?*

Your pediatrician is probably your best first bet. Some patient support groups, such as CARES, may also be able to help you find a doctor, as well as connect you with other families who are affected by CAH. (See appendix.)

There are also a number of reference manuals that list physicians by geographic location and specialty. These manuals include information such as where your doctor went to medical school; how long he has been practicing; where he trained; and what institutions he is affiliated with. You should be able to find these books in the reference section of your public library.

### ♦ *Our pediatric endocrinologist always seems to have an "army" of other doctors trailing him or her. Is this really necessary?*

Many pediatric endocrinologists work in teaching hospitals and are responsible for helping to train the next generation of physicians. One of the best ways for new doctors to understand and respond to patient needs is by listening to and observing patients like you.

At the same time, if aspects of your doctor's visit make you uncomfortable, don't be afraid to speak up. Doctors wish to be sensitive to the needs of their patients. Your doctor may not realize how you feel, and would probably be happy to adjust the exam routine to make you and your child more comfortable.

♦ ***Our pediatric endocrinologist seems to have very limited hours and I can't get an appointment for months. Is this normal?***

Currently, there is a large nationwide shortage of pediatric endocrinologists. Thus, many pediatric endocrinologists have full clinics, and there may be a lengthy wait before you can be seen.

If your doctor books up months in advance, try making your next appointment on your way into, or out of, your current appointment. This way, you won't have to remember to make an extra phone call when it is time to schedule your next visit. You will probably also have a wider choice of available appointment dates.

♦ ***Is it absolutely necessary for the doctor to perform genital exams at each appointment?***

In some situations, a routine genital exam may not be necessary at every visit. However, in other cases, a genital exam—though uncomfortable—may be a critical part of proper monitoring. For example, the progression of puberty in boys is often assessed by examining the size of the testicles.

Talk to your doctor about this. Your doctor may agree that it is okay to have less frequent exams at this stage of your child's development. And if regular exams are still necessary, you may feel better once you know exactly what the doctor is looking for and why.

♦ ***Will treatment cause signs of puberty to regress, i.e., will pubic/ axillary hairs fall out, genitalia shrink in size, etc.?***

Once grown in, pubic and axillary hair will generally not fall out. However, enlarged genitalia will sometimes regress in size after commencement of treatment. Changes in size, however, are usually modest.

♦ ***How often should lab tests be done?***

On a routine basis, tests to monitor control are generally obtained every three to four months. If a dose change is necessary, many endocrinologists will retest after four to six weeks.

♦ ***Why can't doctors agree on what acceptable hormone levels should be? Why does "good control" vary so much from doctor to doctor?***

When using long-term measures of successful treatment—such as final height and/or fertility— studies have yet to conclusively link positive outcome with a specific level of hormonal control. As a result—though this is an issue that, understandably, frustrates many parents—"good control" is sometimes subjective and can vary, depending on a physician's experience with his or her patients.

Final data in CAH is also difficult to come by. Not only can it take fifteen to twenty years to follow a child to maturity, it is also difficult to keep a child on exactly the same protocol throughout the duration of treatment. This makes it even more difficult to make conclusions about the specific factors that determine final outcome.

♦ ***Our last tests were contradictory. They showed a high 17-OHP but low androgen numbers. Does this mean that there was a lab error?***

Probably not. Levels of 17-OHP can fluctuate widely, while levels of androstenedione and testosterone tend to be more stable. As a result, it is not unusual for these numbers to sometimes conflict with each other. When this happens, many physicians will give more weight to the androgen numbers, since high levels of androgens are responsible for most of the problems caused by under-treated CAH.

♦ ***If androgen levels carry more weight, why test for 17-OHP?***

In cases where the 17-OHP is low, a physician may decide to decrease dose, even if androgen levels are normal. Thus, it is good to test for both 17-OHP and androgens.

♦ ***Are there any negative effects of having elevated 17-OHP levels?***

An elevated 17-OHP indicates that control may be escaping and medication doses may be too low. However, in and of themselves, elevated levels of 17-OHP are not thought to be harmful.

♦ ***Why isn't cortisol usually measured as part of monitoring CAH treatment?***

In someone with CAH, cortisol levels will generally reflect the amount of glucocorticoid medication that has been given. It is more helpful to know the *effects* of glucocorticoids on the production of the other adrenal hormones. Thus, measuring 17-OHP and androgen levels is much more useful.

♦ ***Can illness affect blood test results?***

Yes. With illness, the need for cortisol increases. This will result in increased ACTH, which—in someone with CAH—will cause increased production of 17-OHP and androgens. As a result, it is best to avoid testing during illness, as results can be skewed. Wait for a week or more after the illness has resolved and stress dosing has stopped, then test.

♦ ***My child wasn't sick, but was upset and crying during the blood test. Can this affect the results?***

With emotional stress, 17-OHP levels can increase. However, androstenedione and testosterone levels should not change. If an emotionally distressed child returns very high 17-OHP numbers, but has low androgen numbers and otherwise looks to be in good control, your doctor may choose not to increase medication doses. In other situations, a retest may be suggested.

♦ ***My child is afraid of needle sticks. Is there anything that can help make blood-draws easier?***

Numbing creams can lessen the pain of needle sticks. These are usually applied twenty to thirty minutes before blood is taken. *Emla* is a prescription ointment that is now available as a generic. *Elamax* is one that is available over-the-counter.

♦ ***How do you account for changes in reference ranges between different laboratories?***

Different laboratories have different testing methods. Thus, there may be different ranges for "normal," depending on the method used. For the most part, however, these differences will not be appreciable.

♦ ***Does excess tanning from ACTH go away?***

Skin should lighten, once ACTH levels are brought down. However, this can take three to six months after proper treatment is rendered, sometimes longer.

♦ ***Can bone age go backwards?***

It is impossible for the bone age to go backwards. A younger bone age reading, or a reading that appears to go backwards, is most likely due to different interpretations by different physicians.

♦ ***Since interpretation of the bone age can be difficult, is it important to get a second opinion?***

Bone age interpretations can vary slightly even when two very experienced doctors are looking at the same film. However, discrepancies should not be significant. If interpretations of the same x-ray vary widely, you should discuss your concerns with your child's endocrinologist.

♦ ***Should CAH children get regular bone-density scans?***

Because decreased bone density has not been shown to be a problem for CAH children, bone-density tests are not routinely recommended. Yet, if your child has a persistent problem with bone fractures and there is a long-standing history of over-treatment (>2 years), a bone mineral density study may be considered.

### ♦ *How do I know what is due to CAH and what is part of normal growing up?*

Unfortunately, many times you probably won't know for sure. Questions often come up about potential links between CAH and other problems, both physical and mental. These run the gamut from moodiness, anxiety, ADD (Attention Deficit Disorder), hyperactivity, depression, insomnia, eating disorders, excessive sweating, and a host of other problems. While there may very well be a correlation between some of these issues and CAH, your doctor may find it difficult to make a definite connection, because of a lack of data and prior research. This can be frustrating for many parents.

Although it can be difficult to prove a problem's cause, you can still take steps to try to improve the situation. If behavior is new or cyclical, try keeping a diary. If patterns seem to develop around medication or testing, share what you have found with your doctor. In some cases, it may be possible to fix, or greatly improve, a situation just by making small adjustments to your routine. For example, if taking medication right before bed produces insomnia, but taking meds an hour before doesn't, your doctor may simply tell you to move the time of medication administration. Doing this allows you to fix the problem, even if it does not exactly answer the question "Why?"

In other cases, you may still have to treat a problem symptomatically, regardless of whether or not there is a link to CAH. In those situations, it may also be more useful to concentrate on how to improve the situation, rather than trying to find out exactly what is causing it. Ask your doctor for suggestions and recommendations.

# 7

# Mineralocorticoid Treatment & Monitoring in Congenital Adrenal Hyperplasia

*In addition to treatment with glucocorticoids, some children with CAH will need treatment with mineralocorticoids. In this chapter, we explain how mineralocorticoids act on the body. We also discuss how mineralocorticoid treatment is monitored in CAH.*

| MAJOR ELECTROLYTES IN BODY | | | |
|---|---|---|---|
| **Electrolyte** | **Charge** | **Needed To:** | **Normal Values** |
| ***Sodium (Na)*** | + | Maintain proper levels of water in body | 135-145 mmol/L |
| ***Potassium (K)*** | + | Maintain normal heart function | 3.5-5.3 mmol/L |
| ***Chloride (Cl)*** | - | Maintain proper salt balance | 95-105 mmol/L |
| ***Bicarbonate ($HCO_3$)*** | - | Neutralize acid | 18-24 mmol/L |

**IF** you are a salt-waster, you will need to replace missing aldosterone in addition to replacing deficient cortisol. This involves administering a medication known as"fludrocortisone" (trade name *Florinef*). *Florinef* is a synthetic aldosterone that helps your body maintain a proper balance of salts and fluids. When salts and fluids are not in balance, you can become dehydrated and go into shock.

## WATER AND ELECTROLYTE BALANCE IN YOUR BODY

Salts are simple chemical compounds that, when dissolved in water, separate into atoms which carry an electrical charge. These atoms are called "electrolytes."

Some electrolytes carry a positive electrical charge, while others carry a negative electrical charge. For your cells to function normally, there must be a balance between positive and negative charges.

A number of different electrolytes can be found in your body. These include positively charged electrolytes such as sodium, potassium, calcium, and magnesium, as well as negatively charged electrolytes such as chloride, phosphates, and bicarbonate. Like water, electrolytes are obtained from the foods that you eat and drink.

In addition to maintaining the electrical balance within your cells, electrolytes are needed to keep water in your bloodstream to maintain proper circulation. They are also essential components of the skeleton.

One important electrolyte is sodium. The amount of sodium in your body determines the amount of fluid that bathes your cells. Sodium is a component of "sodium chloride" (common table salt). When sodium chloride is dissolved in water, it splits into positive sodium atoms and negative chloride atoms.

### The Importance of Sodium

About two-thirds of your body weight is made up of water. Most of this water is contained within your cells. A smaller amount is in the space surrounding the cells. The rest is contained in your bloodstream.

The water in between the cells is called "extracellular" water. Most of the sodium in your body is contained in your blood vessels and in the extracellular water.

When the total amount of sodium in your body becomes too low, your body will tend to lose water. A deficiency in total body water means that the amount of fluid that bathes the cells (extracellular fluid), and the amount of blood (blood volume), will be low.

Too little water in the blood can lead to poor blood circulation and shock. It can also cause electrolyte levels in your blood to become abnormal.

### Normal Aldosterone Production

Your kidneys can sense the level of salts and fluid in your body. When the kidneys sense that blood volume or total body sodium is low, it releases a hormone called "renin." Release of renin will trigger the kidneys to release another hormone called "angiotensin." Angiotensin will cause the adrenal glands to produce aldosterone. Aldosterone will cause the kidneys to reabsorb sodium.

When more sodium is retained, more water will be retained. The increase in water will restore blood volume back to size, thus restoring proper blood circulation. It will also help you to maintain normal levels of electrolytes in your blood.

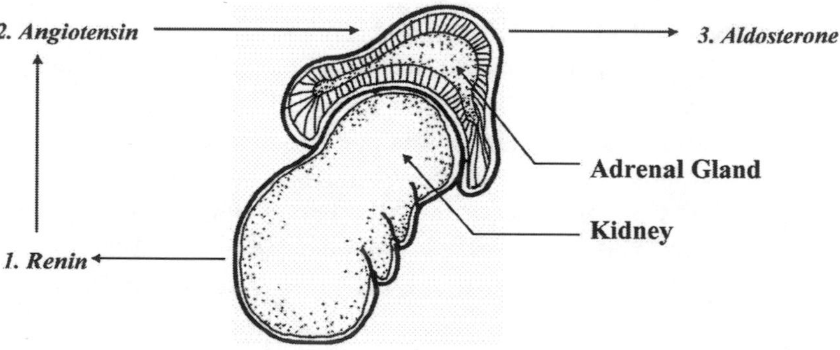


## WHAT HAPPENS IN CAH

If you have CAH and are a salt-waster, you cannot properly produce aldosterone. Thus, your body will not reabsorb sodium. Aldosterone is also important in helping your body get rid of excess potassium. Thus, without aldosterone, you will build up high levels of potassium.

### Poor Blood Circulation

When you have CAH, the series of events that leads to adrenal crisis are usually first related to the loss of sodium. When you lose sodium, you lose the fluid that bathes your cells, as well as the fluid in your bloodstream. As these fluid compartments become smaller and smaller, your blood pressure will fall and less blood will reach your cells. Lack of blood supply will cause your cells to become ill, leading to shock.

## Electrolyte Imbalance

Loss of body water can also produce abnormal concentrations of electrolytes in your blood. This is referred to as an "electrolyte imbalance."

In order for your body to function normally, the concentration of each electrolyte in your bloodstream must be kept within fairly narrow limits. "Concentration" refers to the amount of an electrolyte that is contained in a specific volume of blood, usually one liter.

When there are large quantities of electrolytes in that liter of blood, the blood will be more concentrated. When there are small amounts of electrolytes in the same liter of blood, the blood will be more dilute. Thus, electrolyte levels in the blood reflect not only the quantity of electrolytes in the body, but also the relative amount of water.

Electrolyte imbalance can be due to either a deficiency or excess of the total amount of an electrolyte in the bloodstream. It can also be due to either a deficiency or excess of the total amount of water in the bloodstream.

### *Hyponatremia (Low Sodium Levels in Your Blood)*

Normal sodium levels are between 135-145 mmol/L (135-145 millimoles per liter of blood). When levels go below 130 mmol/L, you face a dangerous situation called "hyponatremia." When you have CAH, hyponatremia is usually due to too little sodium in your body.

Your brain is very sensitive to the concentration of sodium in your blood. When sodium levels drop below 130 mmol/L, you can become sleepy, lethargic, and confused. As hyponatremia becomes worse, seizures can occur. This can be followed by brain injury, coma, and death.

| **HYPONATREMIA (Sodium Levels <130 mmol/L)** | | |
|---|---|---|
| **Causes of Hyponatremia In CAH** | **Symptoms** | **Consequences** |
| • Vomiting<br>• Diarrhea<br>• Not taking medication<br>• Not taking salt | • Lethargy<br>• Confusion | • Brain injury<br>• Seizures<br>• Coma<br>• Death |

### *Hyperkalemia (High Potassium Levels in Your Blood)*

Aldosterone not only prevents sodium loss, but also stimulates your kidneys to get rid of excess potassium. Without aldosterone, you can build up levels of potassium in your blood. Normal potassium levels are between 3.5-5.0 mmol/L. An excess of potassium in the blood is called "hyperkalemia." Hyperkalemia occurs when the concentration of potassium goes higher than 6.0 mmol/L.

| **HYPERKALEMIA (Potassium Levels >6.0 mmol/L)** | | |
|---|---|---|
| **Causes of Hyperkalemia In CAH** | **Symptoms** | **Consequences** |
| • Severe vomiting<br>• Severe diarrhea | • Irregular heartbeats (arrhythmia) | • Collapse of circulation<br>• Death |

Potassium is found in greatest amounts within the cells. In some situations, potassium can travel from inside the cell, to the bloodstream. If this happens, the concentration of potassium in the blood will rise. If you have CAH and cannot properly secrete aldosterone, the potassium that your cells normally release, and that you take in with food, can also build up in your bloodstream.

In general, there is more danger in having too much, rather than too little, potassium in the blood. When there is too much potassium in your bloodstream, your heart can beat irregularly. Irregular beating of the heart is called a heart "arrhythmia." Heart arrhythmias can cause your heart to stop beating altogether, resulting in death.

## TREATING MINERALOCORTICOID DEFICIENCY IN CAH

Mineralocorticoid treatment for CAH is accomplished by replacing deficient aldosterone with a medication called *Florinef*. *Florinef* is a synthetic aldosterone that helps you to retain sodium and get rid of potassium.

### *Florinef* Doses

*Florinef* comes in 0.1 mg scored tablets. Typical doses range between 0.05 mg (half a tablet) to 0.2 mg (two whole tablets) per day. Because *Florinef* is a long-acting medication, the dose is usually given only once a day, in the morning. If more than one tablet a day is needed, the total daily amount may be split into two, with half given in the morning and the other half given in the evening.

In contrast to glucocorticoid treatment, fine-tuning of *Florinef* doses is not needed. Your doctor will usually prescribe a "typical" dose, and then adjust up or down, guided by test results and blood pressure readings. Once a proper dose is found, it is usually not necessary to do much adjusting.

Generally, it is better to give slightly too much, rather than too little, *Florinef*. Unlike an excess of glucocorticoids, *Florinef* does not have bad effects on growth. If the dose is a little too high, blood pressure will rise and excess salt will be excreted in the urine to balance things out.

### Sodium Supplementation

*Florinef* works to retain sodium in your body. For *Florinef* to work properly, you must eat an adequate amount of salt. If *Florinef* is given without enough salt, electrolyte abnormalities and shock can still occur.

In children and adults, sodium needs can be met by the amount of salt in the diet. However, because baby formula and breast milk are low in sodium, extra salt must be given in infancy.

Usually, extra salt is given in the form of concentrated sodium chloride (NaCl) solutions, which are available by prescription only. These are available in different strengths, though the preferred preparation is one with a concentration of 23.5 percent (23.5 grams of sodium chloride per 100 ml of water). If a baby is bottle-fed, the salt solution can be added to a baby's formula. For breast-fed babies, the salt solution can be squirted into the back of the mouth, or placed in a feeding nipple and given to the baby, before nursing.

Salt needs can vary from child to child. The typical CAH baby needs 1.0-2.0 grams of sodium chloride supplementation per day. This is equal to a total of about one-quarter of a teaspoon of table salt per day. When using the 23.5 percent solution, this means giving a baby 1.0-1.5 ml of the concentrated salt solution four to six times a day (or a total of 4.0-6.0 ml of the 23.5 percent solution a day).

Less concentrated solutions are also available, e.g. 0.9 percent (0.9 grams of sodium chloride per 100 ml of water). Because the 0.9 percent solution is more dilute, a large amount of solution must be given in order to meet a baby's daily sodium needs. You can also use salt packets, like those found in fast-food restaurants, divided up over the course of the day. Each packet contains about a half gram, or approximately one-fifth of a teaspoon, of sodium chloride. As a child reaches one year of age and begins to eat table food, which typically contains a generous amount of sodium, salt supplementation can be reduced or omitted.

**COMPARISON OF SALT DOSES USING DIFFERENT PREPARATIONS**

****Because different kinds of salt supplements are used for CAH treatment, be sure to discuss your salt replacement dose with your endocrinologist. You should be sure you are giving the correct amount of salt, and not too much or too little.****

| Preparation | Typical size of dose | Amount of NaCl/ dose | Typical # doses/day | Total NaCl/day |
|---|---|---|---|---|
| **23.5% NaCl solution** (23.5 gm NaCl/100 ml; 0.235 gm NaCl/ml) | 1.0-1.5 ml | 0.23-0.35 gm | 4-6 | 1.0-2.0 gm |
| **0.9% NaCl solution** (0.9 gm NaCl/100 ml; 0.009 gm NaCl/ml) | 25-40 ml | 0.23-0.36 gm | 4-6 | 1.0-2.0 gm |
| **Table Salt** (6 gm NaCl/teaspoon) | 1/16-1/8 teaspoon | 0.3-0.6 gm | 4-6 | 1.0-2.5 gm (1/4-1/2 teaspoon per day) |

*NaCl: Sodium Chloride; gm: gram; ml: milliliter*

## MONITORING MINERALOCORTICOID TREATMENT

Mineralocorticoid treatment is monitored by looking at blood pressure, and renin and electrolyte levels in the blood. Aside from these measurements, there are few clues to either under-treatment, or over-treatment, with mineralocorticoids.

### Blood Pressure

Blood pressure gives clues about blood volume and the stretch of your blood vessels. Blood volume refers to the amount of fluid that is in your bloodstream.

If you have too much fluid in your bloodstream, you may have high blood pressure. Because excess salt and *Florinef* will cause you to retain water, a high blood pressure reading means that *Florinef* and/or salt doses are too high and need to be lowered. In contrast, a low blood pressure reading means that blood volume is too low and that *Florinef* and/or salt doses need to be raised. Low blood pressure is also a warning sign that mineralocorticoid deficiency may be severe.

If there is only a modest deficiency in mineralocorticoids, blood pressure is usually normal. Thus, while you should have normal blood pressure if you are adequately treated with *Florinef* and salt, a normal blood pressure reading is not always an indication that mineralocorticoid treatment is adequate.

When blood pressure is tested, it is important that the correct size blood pressure cuff be used. The width of the blood pressure cuff should be half the length of the upper arm. There are four standard sizes that are used, ranging from infant sizes to those suitable for adults.

Abnormal blood pressure readings are commonly related to the use of the wrong size blood pressure cuff. If the cuff is too small, the blood pressure reading will be falsely high. If the cuff is too big, the blood pressure will be falsely low.

Tables of normal blood pressure can be accessed at the following website <http://www.nhlbi.nih.gov/health/prof/heart/hbp/hbp_ped.pdf >. These values are correlated to a child's age, sex, and height. (Also see appendix.)

### Renin

Renin is a hormone that is released by the kidneys to control fluid levels in the bloodstream. Thus, renin levels in the blood—also referred to as PRA ("Plasma Renin Activity")—are a sensitive indicator of the adequacy of mineralocorticoid treatment.

When mineralocorticoid treatment is inadequate, your body will have low amounts of total sodium and fluids. This will stimulate the kidneys to produce renin. A high renin reading is therefore an indication that *Florinef* and/or salt doses need to be increased. When you are over-treated with mineralocorticoids, the opposite will happen. That is, blood volume will be high and renin levels will be low. This means that *Florinef* and/or salt doses need to be lowered.

Renin levels vary depending on your body position. They are generally lower when you are sitting or lying down, and increase when you stand. However, if you are over-treated with mineralocorticoids, your renin levels will be low, even when you are standing. Likewise, if you are under-treated with mineralocorticoids, your renin levels will be high, even when you are sitting.

Renin levels are normally high in infants and gradually fall over the first six months of life. Normal renin values can vary widely depending on the testing method used by a particular lab. Therefore, when interpreting renin values, you should refer to the ranges of normal values for that lab.

**Electrolytes**

When you have CAH, a major imbalance of electrolytes suggests that adrenal crisis may be occurring. However, it is also important to note that adrenal crisis can occur, even with normal electrolyte levels. In this event, the renin will be elevated.

Most commonly, electrolyte imbalances in CAH involve low sodium levels or high potassium levels. Thus, if the sodium is low, or the potassium is elevated, additional *Florinef* and/or salt is needed.

Along with sodium and potassium, the electrolytes normally measured include chloride and bicarbonate. Bicarbonate is the substance in the blood that neutralizes acid. Low bicarbonate levels in your blood suggest that there are high amounts of acid in your body. This occurs when low blood flow or shock sets in.

**Effect of Mineralocorticoid Deficiency on Glucocorticoid Treatment**

Difficulty controlling CAH can be a sign that mineralocorticoid replacement is insufficient. When too little *Florinef* and/or salt is given, treatment with glucocorticoids can be more difficult. This may be because the blood volume is slightly reduced triggering a small "stress response."

Under-treatment with mineralocorticoids can also result in slow weight gain and slow growth in children. However, when there is only a modest deficiency in mineralocorticoids, growth will continue normally.

♦♦♦

## WHAT YOU MAY BE CONCERNED ABOUT: FREQUENTLY ASKED QUESTIONS

♦ ***Why doesn't everyone with 21-hydroxylase deficiency take Florinef, since they all can't make aldosterone to some degree?***

In people who don't waste salt, *Florinef* treatment has not proven to be beneficial. It doesn't take much aldosterone to maintain fluid and electrolyte balance. Thus, a slight impairment in aldosterone production does not appear to affect cell function. If you take *Florinef* when you don't really need it, you run a greater risk of developing hypertension (high blood pressure).

♦ ***Why does a salt-wasting infant still need sodium supplementation, if he is taking Florinef? Once sodium balance is normalized, shouldn't Florinef alone be enough to keep him from losing salt?***

Although *Florinef* will promote salt reabsorption in someone with CAH, a salt-waster on *Florinef* will still tend to lose greater amounts of salt than someone who does not have CAH. Unless sodium is given to make up for these losses, electrolyte imbalance and shock can still occur.

♦ ***My salt-wasting child is taking Florinef, but still seems to crave excessive amounts of salt. Will this harm him or her?***

Usually, excess salt will be eliminated in the urine and not cause problems. However, when taking excess salt, it is important to be sure that the blood pressure is not elevated.

♦ ***My child is a salt-waster, but has never seemed to crave salt. Is this normal?***

Salt "cravings" vary according to the individual. As long as there are no signs of under- or over-treatment with mineralocorticoids, a taste for salt— or lack thereof—is not a cause for concern.

♦ ***Do Florinef doses often change depending on the season?***

No. *Florinef* doses generally remain pretty steady. However, in hot weather, extra salt may be needed to compensate for salt lost in sweat.

♦ ***When you are a salt-waster, can you have low sodium levels, without high potassium levels, and vice versa?***

Yes. An electrolyte imbalance occurs when levels of any of the circulating electrolytes become abnormal. Levels of specific electrolytes can become abnormal, independent of the levels of other electrolytes. For example, when you have CAH, potassium can often be normal, even when sodium is low. This occurs about 60 percent of the time, when there is adrenal crisis.

♦ ***If a salt-waster has to take in more sodium because he can't retain enough sodium, should he also try to take in less potassium because he cannot excrete enough potassium?***

Under normal circumstances, a salt-waster on *Florinef* will be able to get rid of extra potassium. Thus, she or he does not need to avoid foods that contain potassium. However, in situations where there is danger of adrenal crisis, you should avoid taking in extra potassium.

♦ ***Why are potassium levels sometimes too low in someone with CAH? Aren't you supposed to build up levels of potassium when you have CAH?***

If you have consistently low potassium levels while taking *Florinef*, your *Florinef* dose is probably too high. You can gain clues to over-treatment by looking at levels of renin. If the *Florinef* is too high, renin levels will be low.

♦ ***If renin levels are elevated, how do you know when to increase sodium and when to increase Florinef?***

To figure out if more salt or *Florinef* is needed, you can measure urinary sodium (Na) concentrations. If there are generous amounts of sodium in the urine (>50 mmol/L), more *Florinef* is needed. If the sodium level is low (<50 mmol/L), then more salt is needed.

♦ ***My child is suddenly very thirsty all the time even though it is not particularly hot out and he has not been particularly physical. Is this normal?***

Thirst in children can vary considerably, so your child's increased thirst may have nothing to do with CAH. At the same time, some parents report that their CAH children seem to have a greater thirst when they are under-suppressed or when the glucocorticoid dose has just been reduced. Thus, you may also want to be sure that there aren't other signs of under-suppression with glucocorticoids.

If your child also has increased urination in addition to excessive thirst, you should see your pediatrician. Excessive thirst, in conjunction with excessive urination, is seen in children with diabetes. Diabetes can affect CAH children, just as it can affect children who do not have CAH.

♦ ***Under-suppression with glucocorticoids causes rapid height gain, while over-suppression with glucocorticoids causes rapid weight gain. But my child is having trouble gaining both height and weight. Could anything else be going on?***

It has been suggested that inadequate mineralocorticoid treatment can result in slow growth and poor weight gain. Therefore, it is important to make sure that your child is receiving enough *Florinef* and/or salt.

At the same time, many children continue to grow normally, even in the face of inadequate mineralocorticoid treatment. If growth is slow, even after salt and *Florinef* doses have been adjusted, you should also look for non-adrenal causes of poor growth.

♦ ***My child's pulse rate is extraordinarily high. What could this signify?***

If your child has a very high pulse, you should see your doctor immediately. This can be the sign of an arrhythmia (irregular heart beat). Even with under-treatment, the heart rate should not be very rapid, unless there is dehydration or adrenal crisis.

♦ ***My child has problems with bedwetting. Could this be related to the salt or Florinef dose?***

If your child is taking the appropriate amounts of salt or *Florinef*, urine output should be normal. However, if he or she is getting too much salt or too little *Florinef*, there may be increased urination, which can contribute to a problem with bedwetting. To test for this possibility, your pediatrician or endocrinologist can check morning urine sodium levels. If the urine sodium level is high, there could be excessive salt intake or a too low *Florinef* dose, both of which can contribute to excessive urination.

Children can have problems with bedwetting, whether they have CAH or not. Thus, you should also be sure to investigate other possible causes with your pediatrician.

♦♦♦

# Other Medications Used in Treatment of Congenital Adrenal Hyperplasia

*Some children will need to be treated for problems separate from, but often associated with CAH, such as Central Precocious Puberty. In this chapter, we describe situations in which additional medications might be prescribed. We also touch upon experimental approaches and new drugs that are being developed for the treatment of CAH.*

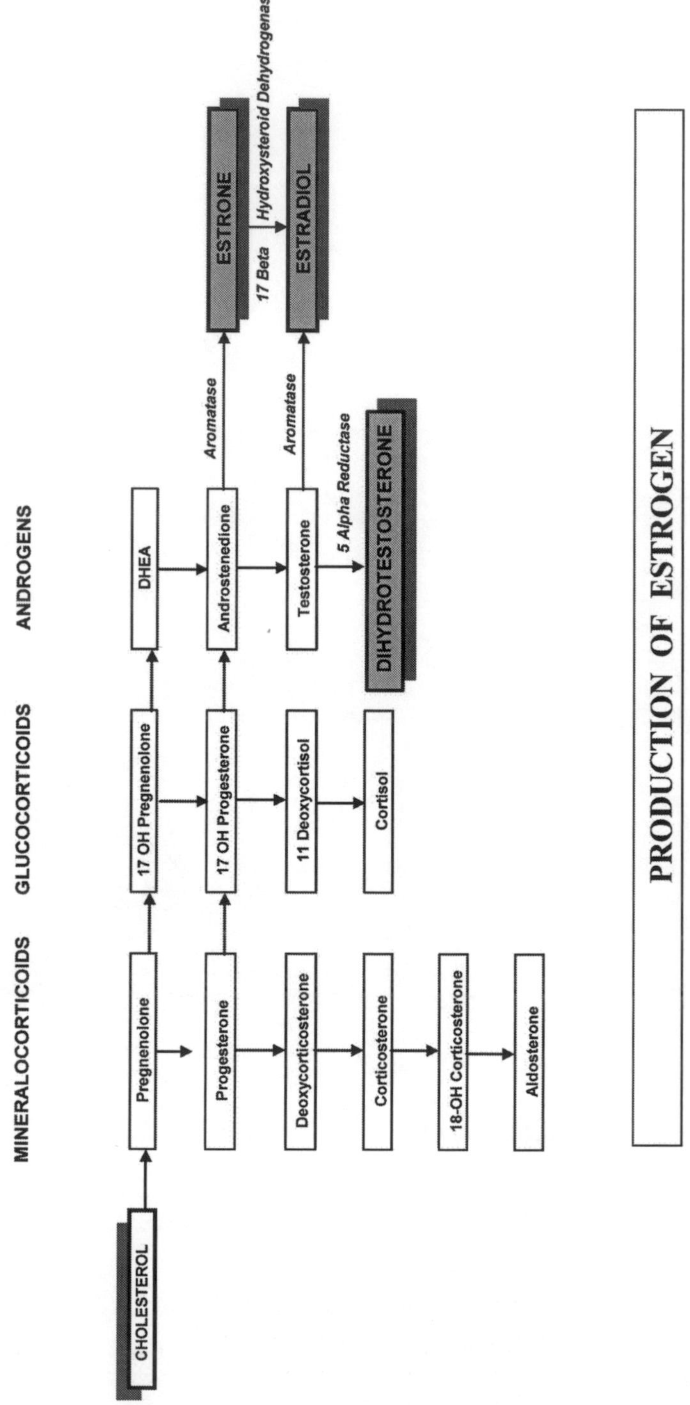


PRODUCTION OF ESTROGEN

**TREAT**ment for CAH is accomplished by replacing deficient cortisol with glucocorticoids, and deficient aldosterone with *Florinef*. In some cases, other medications may be prescribed. One that is commonly used is a drug called *Lupron ("depot leuprolide.") Lupron* is used to stop the progression of puberty in children with CAH.

## DRUGS USED TO TREAT PRECOCIOUS PUBERTY

Treatment for CAH can be complicated by the early onset of puberty. If puberty starts too early, growth will stop prematurely. To stop puberty, your doctor may prescribe monthly injections of *Lupron*.

*Lupron* is a type of medication known as a "GnRH (Gonadotropin Releasing Hormone) agonist." While glucocorticoids suppress the production of sex hormones in the adrenal glands, GnRH agonists stop the production of sex hormones in the gonads (ovaries or testicles).

### "True" Puberty

When you have CAH, you tend to overproduce androgens in your adrenal glands. An excess of androgens can cause you to develop physical symptoms of puberty such as pubic hair, underarm hair, underarm odor, or acne. However, the presence of these symptoms does not necessarily mean that you are undergoing "true" (or "central") puberty.

Puberty doesn't start until the pituitary gland in your brain begins to release hormones called LH ("Luteinizing Hormone") and FSH ("Follicle-Stimulating Hormone"). If you're a girl, LH and FSH will stimulate your ovaries to produce estrogen. If you're a boy, they will stimulate your testicles to produce testosterone. Testosterone is then converted to estrogen through the action of enzymes called "aromatase." Estrogen is responsible for advancing bone age and fusing the growth plates in your long bones. Because boys and girls will both have high levels of estrogen during puberty, early puberty then becomes a special concern for the child with CAH who already produces excess androgens from the adrenal glands.

### Precocious Puberty and CAH

The first detectable sign of true puberty is the development of breasts in girls and the enlargement of the testicles in boys. If these events occur before the age of seven in a girl, and before the age of nine in a boy, puberty is termed early or "precocious." Many CAH children will undergo puberty at a normal age. However, puberty can be triggered in some CAH children who are late-diagnosed, after glucocorticoid treatment is started. Before treatment, the pituitary gland is exposed to high levels of androgens. When androgen levels suddenly fall after treatment is started, the parts of the brain that control puberty (the hypothalamus and pituitary gland) may become active. This causes increased release of LH and FSH, causing puberty to start. Puberty can also be triggered when treatment is improved in children who have been chronically under-treated.

*Lupron* stops the pituitary gland from producing LH and FSH, which stops the gonads from making hormones. This will slow down bone maturation and growth, and may help to improve final height.

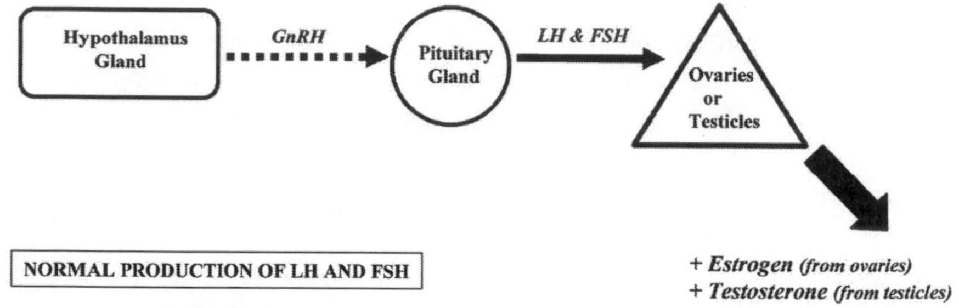


## How *Lupron* Works to Stop Puberty

The production of estrogen and testosterone is stimulated by high levels of LH and FSH. In turn, the production of LH and FSH is stimulated by the action of Gonadotropin Releasing Hormone (GnRH). GnRH is produced by the hypothalamus gland in the brain.

GnRH is normally released from the hypothalamus in short bursts. This pulsing pattern causes the pituitary gland to release LH and FSH. If GnRH is released continuously, LH and FSH production will stop. *Lupron* is a synthetic form of GnRH. When given at the appropriate doses, it causes the pituitary gland to stop making LH and FSH. Without LH and FSH, the testicles stop making testosterone and the ovaries stop making estrogen.

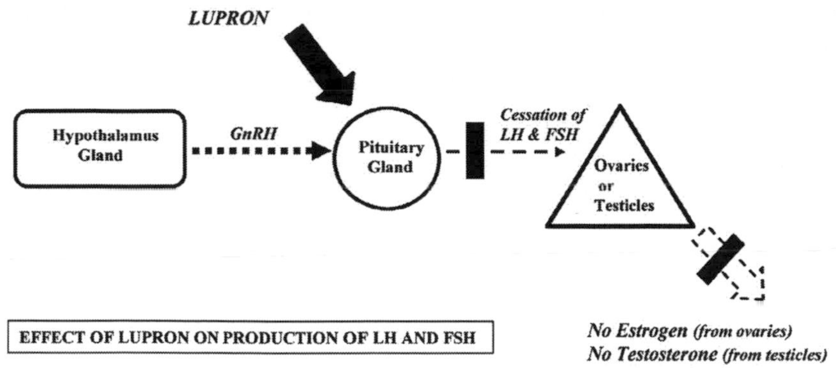


## How Puberty is Diagnosed

Puberty is most often diagnosed using a test called an LHRH stimulation test (or GnRH Stimulation test). This is a challenge test, similar in idea to an ACTH stimulation test.

To perform an LHRH stimulation test, blood is first drawn to measure levels of LH and FSH. A medication called *Factrel* is then injected into the arm. Blood is then taken every fifteen or twenty minutes, for one hour, after the *Factrel* has been given. *Factrel* will stimulate the release of LH and FSH. By looking at the pattern of LH and FSH production, it is possible to tell if puberty has started.

*Factrel* is the drug that has been traditionally used to test for puberty. However, because it is occasionally in short supply, *Lupron* is sometimes used instead. When *Lupron* is used, the protocol for testing and evaluating results may be slightly different than when *Factrel* is used.

## Common GnRH Agonists Used to Treat CPP

While different GnRH agonists can be used to treat early puberty, *Lupron* is the one that is most commonly prescribed. It is typically given by intramuscular injection every three or four weeks.

*Lupron* comes in fixed doses. The smallest pediatric dose is 3.75 mg, and the largest 15.0 mg. Intermediate doses are 7.5 and 11.25 mg. If a dose larger than 15.0 mg is needed, injections are given at shorter intervals of time.

Doses are based on the child's size at the start of treatment. Once pituitary suppression is achieved, it is generally not necessary to increase the *Lupron* dose, though this may not always be the case.

*Synarel* is a GnRH agonist that comes in the form of a nasal spray. However, because nasal sprays need to be administered several times a day, compliance can be difficult. Daily injectable forms of GnRH agonists, including *Lupron*, are also available.

### Side Effects of Treatment

The use of *Lupron* in children is considered to be safe and effective. Usually, there are few side effects. Most children get *Lupron* injected in the upper part of the thigh or in the buttocks. Sometimes, there may be soreness after an injection. If this happens, an over-the-counter pain reliever, such as *Tylenol* or *Advil*, can be given until the pain goes away. A numbing cream can also be applied prior to getting the shot.

Rarely, a sterile abscess may develop at the site of injection. This appears as an area of redness and tenderness, with a bump at the site of the injection. If this happens, you should let your physician know immediately.

## EXPERIMENTAL DRUGS AND APPROACHES

The mainstay of CAH treatment for the last fifty years has been the use of glucocorticoids and mineralocorticoids. However, because treatment of CAH is still not perfect, several experimental approaches have been suggested.

### Adrenalectomy

One proposed approach for treating CAH is the removal of the adrenal glands. When the adrenal glands are removed, you do not have to worry about excessive androgen production. Thus, lower doses of glucocorticoids can be used, making treatment easier.

Arguments against adrenalectomy include the fact that after adrenalectomy, the adrenal medulla will be lost, in addition to the adrenal cortex. The inability to produce enough adrenaline (epinephrine) can make you vulnerable in stressful situations. However, when you have CAH, you may already have impaired adrenal medullary function. Adrenaline is also made in other places in your body.

Surgical removal of the adrenal glands has not been widely employed in patients with CAH. Thus, there is currently little information on the long-term prospects of adrenalectomized individuals although preliminary reports sound promising.

## Anti-Androgens

Anti-androgens are drugs that block the sites, or "receptors," where androgen hormones bind. When androgen receptors are blocked, signs of masculinization—such as body odor, masculinization of the genitalia, pubic and axillary hair development, and acne—will regress.

Anti-androgens are sometimes prescribed to treat symptoms of androgen excess in adult women with CAH. They are rarely prescribed for children, except in the context of a clinical study. A potential complication of anti-androgens is liver damage, so careful monitoring is needed. Anti-androgen drugs include flutamide, spironolactone (*Aldactone*), and finasteride.

## Aromatase Inhibitors

Estrogen is made when androgens are converted into estrogen by enzymes known as "aromatase." Since estrogen is responsible for advancing bone age and closing of the growth centers, reducing estrogen production through the use of aromatase inhibitors is a strategy that is being tested in treatment of CAH. When coupled with anti-androgens, decreased skeletal maturation has been reported. Aromatase inhibitors include the drugs letrozole, anastrozole (*Arimidex*), and testolactone.

## Growth-Hormone Therapy

Growth hormone is normally produced in the pituitary gland. As its name implies, this hormone stimulates growth. People who are growth-hormone deficient tend to be small in childhood and end up as short adults.

Though children with CAH are not growth hormone deficient, recent studies have raised the possibility that growth hormone may help improve height in children with CAH. With growth hormone treatment, improvement in growth velocity has been seen in children with CAH, though it is still unknown if this strategy will lead to permanent increases in height.

Growth-hormone treatment involves daily injections of the medication until final height has been reached. Growth hormone is not currently FDA approved for treatment of CAH. It is also an extremely costly medicine. Thus, insurance approval may be difficult and, unless you are part of a clinical study where the medication can be obtained free or at a greatly reduced cost, the expense may be prohibitive.

Some physicians have also observed that growth hormone treatment leads to the more rapid elimination of glucocorticoids from the blood. Thus there may be a worsening of CAH control with growth hormone treatment.

♦♦♦

## WHAT YOU MAY BE CONCERNED ABOUT: FREQUENTLY ASKED QUESTIONS

♦ ***Will all children with CAH end up with precocious puberty and need treatment with Lupron?***

No. Early puberty is a problem for some children with CAH, but not most. Children who are more likely to be affected are those who are diagnosed in later childhood, rather than early infancy, or those who have been under-treated for long periods.

♦ ***My child has always been well controlled since infancy, but I noticed signs of pubic hair today. Does this mean she is undergoing puberty and will need treatment with Lupron?***

Not necessarily. The symptoms that usually accompany puberty—such as pubic hair, axillary hair, body odor, and acne—are due to excess androgen production, not maturation of the ovaries or testicles. The first sign of "true" puberty is the development of breast buds in girls, and the enlargement of the testicles in boys. If you see signs of excess androgens, but no sexual development, it may just mean that your child is under-suppressed. You should let your doctor know, but there is probably no reason to panic. He or she may suggest running some blood tests to better assess the situation.

♦ ***Is it always necessary to treat early puberty with Lupron?***

The use of *Lupron* can be a judgment call. Much depends on how old you are when puberty hits. Normally, puberty starts between the ages of eight and eleven in girls, and ten to thirteen in boys. Generally, the younger you are, the greater the benefits you will get from treatment.

♦ ***How long will my child need to be on Lupron?***

As long as treatment is progressing smoothly, most children being treated for precocious puberty will stay on *Lupron* until they reach an age where puberty would more normally occur, usually around age eleven or twelve if you are a girl, and twelve or thirteen if you are a boy. Alternatively, treatment may be continued until the bone age and the actual age are the same.

♦ ***How is pituitary suppression monitored, after Lupron is started?***

Monitoring is accomplished by a combination of laboratory testing and physical examination. In general, monitoring treatment with *Lupron* is much simpler than monitoring treatment with glucocorticoids. Usually, very few dose adjustments are needed.

During regular office visits, your doctor will check for signs of breast development in girls, and testicular enlargement in boys. Testicle size is sometimes measured using sizing beads called an "orchidometer." When *Lupron* is started breast tissue will either get smaller or stay the same. In boys, the testicles will not increase in size.

Blood testing involves checking levels of LH to see if they are very low. In boys, doctors can also look at testosterone, androstenedione, and 17-OHP levels. If the testosterone level is high, but the 17-OHP and androstenedione levels are not elevated, pituitary suppression may be insufficient.

♦ ***My child's growth has slowed down a lot since Lupron was started. Is this normal?***

Yes. *Lupron* will stop the gonads from producing estrogen and testosterone. With the decrease in sex steroid production, it is normal to see a decrease in growth rate. *Lupron* can also be associated with modest gains in weight.

♦ ***I was put on Lupron for endometriosis. Is this the same drug?***

Yes. Many medications are used for multiple purposes. The same is true of *Lupron*. In addition to endometriosis, *Lupron* is also used for treatment of prostate cancer.

♦ ***Our doctor is suggesting an experimental drug for my child. I don't know what to do.***

The nature of experimental therapy is that there is usually some element of risk. Thus, you should have a clear understanding of the risks versus benefits of treatment, prior to the start of any experimental treatment.

Some questions you might want to ask your doctor: *How many other children have been treated with this drug, and what have been the results? What are the side effects of the medication, both short-term and long-term? Are side effects reversible? How long will it take to see results, if the treatment is working? How much does the medication cost, and who will bear the cost if funding should dry up? What are our other options for treatment?*

If your child has been responding well to conventional therapy on glucocorticoids, the risks of treatment may not outweigh the benefits. But, if your child's response to conventional treatment has been poor, or if there are extenuating circumstances, you might decide that the risks are worth taking.

♦♦♦

# 9

# Stress Coverage During Illness

*One of the biggest concerns of parents is knowing what to do when their CAH child gets sick. In this chapter, we discuss "stress dosing" during illness. We give information about oral stress doses, emergency injections of Solu-Cortef, and situations when hospitalization, or a trip to the emergency room, may be necessary.*

*Though children with CAH can have a lower ability to cope with illness, it is also important to emphasize that, when proper precautions are taken, they can do well with illness.*

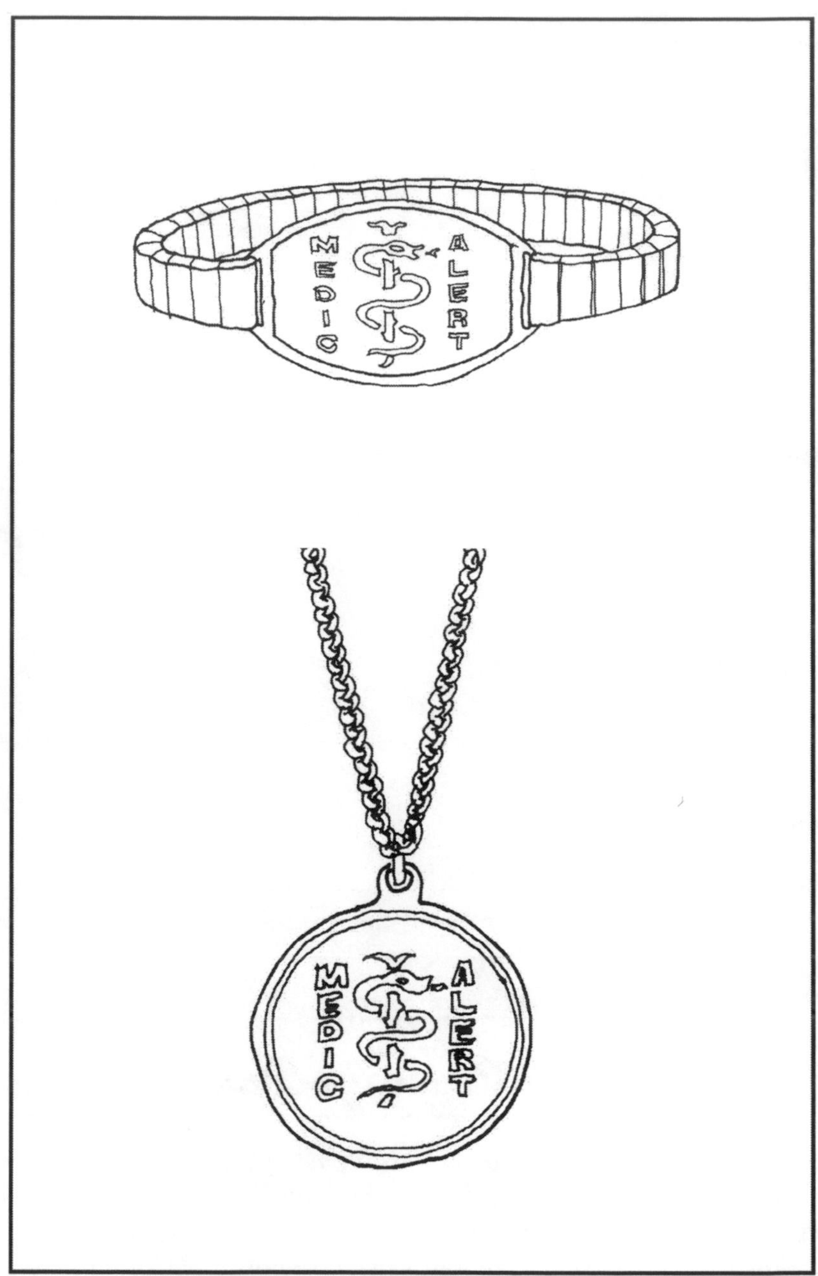
MEDIC
ALERT
MEDIC
ALERT

**WHEN** you are healthy, you normally produce cortisol at a rate of 6-10 mg/m$^2$/day. When you are physically stressed—such as with infection, trauma, or surgery—cortisol production increases to 50-100 mg/m$^2$/day. This is more than five to ten times the normal rate.

If you have CAH, you cannot adequately produce cortisol. As a result, you may be unable to generate a sufficient response to illness or trauma. Your normal daily doses of glucocorticoid medications may also be insufficient to handle your increased need. To minimize the risk of adrenal crisis, glucocorticoid doses need to be increased during illness. This is known as "stress dosing."

## THE DANGERS OF ADRENAL INSUFFICIENCY IN CAH

Without cortisol, you can go into "shock," a situation that occurs when not enough blood flows through your body. When there is inadequate blood flow, organ damage and brain injury can occur.

### What Is an Adrenal Crisis?

In CAH, the lack of adrenal steroids can result in inadequate circulation, electrolyte abnormalities, or low blood glucose levels. This is called "adrenal crisis." The consequences of adrenal crisis are severe. They include coma, internal organ damage, irregular heartbeats, and death.

Sometimes, adrenal crisis can develop gradually over time, such as when medication has not been taken for days or weeks. Other times, adrenal crisis can occur suddenly with illness.

Because cortisol requirements increase with illness, special precautions need to be taken if you have CAH and become sick. These precautions involve:

- Understanding when and how to give stress doses.
- Knowing what to do when you are vomiting, or have severe diarrhea, and cannot retain oral medication.
- Being prepared to give emergency injections of hydrocortisone called "*Solu-Cortef*."
- Knowing when to go to a hospital emergency room for intravenous fluids and hydrocortisone.

***Thus, you should be sure that you discuss a "stress dosing" plan with your doctor.***

In some situations, you may be able to "weather the storm" and get by without stress dosing, but under other circumstances, the "bottom falls out." Your body will not be able to cope with the extra stress and you will collapse.

Adrenal insufficiency can lead to adrenal crisis in both salt-wasters and non-salt-wasters. Thus, the same precautions apply to different forms of CAH.

**The Need for Stress Doses**

Stress doses of glucocorticoids are needed in situations that would normally trigger your adrenal glands to release more-than-normal amounts of cortisol. These include infection resulting in fever, surgery requiring general anesthesia, and major physical trauma resulting in fracture or severe bleeding.

Stress doses are not needed for minor illnesses such as common colds, or for minor cuts and abrasions. Stress doses are also not needed for physical activity or exercise, or emotional distress.

In some situations, you may need stress doses under certain circumstances, but not under others. For example, if you are undergoing routine dental work (such as a cleaning or filling), stress dosing is not needed, even if a local anesthetic (Novocaine or "laughing gas") is given. However, if you are getting dental surgery performed under general anesthesia, then stress dosing would be required. Likewise, you do not need to stress dose, when getting routine childhood vaccinations. But, if the vaccination results in a fever, then stress doses should be given.

In situations involving accidental injury, discretion needs to be used. For example, if you fall and suffer a bump or bruise, but immediately recover and carry on with what you were doing, you will probably not need a stress dose. However, if you suffer a blow to the head—and become unconscious, dazed, or disoriented—then a stress dose is needed. If the injury is serious—and results in severe bleeding or internal injuries—an intramuscular shot of hydrocortisone, and follow-up treatment in a hospital emergency room, may also be necessary.

It will take time to distinguish between the situations when oral stress doses are enough, or when a hydrocortisone injection or trip to the hospital emergency room may also be necessary. Not every person will respond the same way to illness, and not every person will respond the same way in every situation.

***If you are uncertain what to do during an illness, don't try to "ride out the storm." Rather, call your doctor for instructions. While it is best not to panic, remember that—in the event of an illness with CAH—it is always better to be cautious.***

| WHEN TO STRESS DOSE | | | |
|---|---|---|---|
| **Situation** | **Yes** | **No** | **Comments** |
| Fever | • | | Double dose for fever >101° F; Triple dose for fever >102 ° F |
| Surgery requiring general anesthesia | • | | Follow guidelines for stress dosing during surgery |
| Serious accidental injury | • | | Give IM injection and transport to hospital, as situation warrants |
| Minor scrapes and bruises | | • | - |
| Bone break | • | | Give IM injection and transport to hospital, if break is severe |
| Common colds (no fever) | | • | If fever occurs, stress dose as above |
| Routine dental work (cleaning, filling, etc.) | | • | No stress dose needed for local anesthesia |
| Oral surgery involving general anesthesia | • | | Follow guidelines for stress dosing during surgery |
| Vaccinations (no fever) | | • | If fever occurs, stress dose as above |

## GIVING ORAL STRESS DOSES

The first line of defense in treating illness in CAH is giving oral stress doses. Many routine illnesses can be successfully treated at home if medications and fluids can be taken by mouth.

### Fevers and CAH

The most common situation in which stress doses are needed is when there is a fever. A fever is an indication that your body is fighting an infection, usually caused by a virus or bacteria. A fever is defined as a body temperature higher than 100.4° F.

When body temperature climbs to between 101° and 102° F, many doctors recommend that you double your daily dose of glucocorticoids. When temperatures climb above 102° F, many doctors suggest tripling the daily dose. These increased doses should be given for each day that the fever is present, and continued for one day after the temperature has returned to normal (less than 100.4° F).

Sometimes you may also be prescribed an antibiotic if the fever is due to a bacterial infection, such as with an ear infection or Strep-throat. If that is the case, stress dosing is not necessary for the full course of the antibiotic. Like with other situations when fever is present, stress dosing is needed for each day that the fever is present, until one day after the fever has gone away.

| **BODY TEMPERATURES*** | | |
|---|---|---|
| **Threshold** | **Fahrenheit °** | **Centigrade°** |
| Normal body temperature | 98.6° | 37° |
| Fever | 100.4° | 38° |
| Threshold for double dosing | >101° | >38.3° |
| Threshold for triple dosing | >102° | >38.9° |
| **Note: These numbers indicate body temperatures taken orally or rectally. Temperatures taken under the arm may be up to 1° F lower.* | | |

## Stress Dosing With Hydrocortisone

When giving stress doses of hydrocortisone, ***each*** dose of the day should be doubled or tripled. For example, if you are taking 5 mg of hydrocortisone three times a day (a total of 15 mg/day), double dosing means taking 10 mg, three times a day (a total of 30 mg/day). Triple dosing means taking 15 mg, three times a day (a total of 45 mg/day). If your doses are unevenly split, each dose should be doubled or tripled.

**Stress Dosing with Prednisone**

Stress dosing using prednisone is accomplished by doubling or tripling each dose of the day. Most people take prednisone twice daily. If you are taking 1 mg of prednisone in the morning and 1 mg in the evening (a total of 2 mg/day), double dosing would mean taking 2 mg in morning and 2 mg in the evening (a total of 4 mg/day). Triple dosing would mean taking 3 mg in morning and 3mg in the evening (a total of 6 mg/day). If your total daily dose is unevenly split, each dose should be doubled or tripled.

**Stress Dosing with Dexamethasone**

Stress dosing with dexamethasone is accomplished slightly differently than stress dosing with hydrocortisone or prednisone. Because dexamethasone is usually given only once a day, stress dosing involves giving the medication more frequently, as well as giving a larger total daily amount.

For example, if you normally take 0.25 mg of dexamethasone in the morning, you would take an extra 0.25 mg in the evening to double dose (a total of 0.50 mg/day). To triple dose, you would triple the normal daily dose, then give half that amount in the morning, and half in the evening. For example, if your normal dose is 0.25 mg/day, 0.375 mg would be taken in the morning and another 0.375 mg would be taken in the evening (a total of 0.75 mg/day).

| EXAMPLES OF HOW TO DOUBLE OR TRIPLE DOSE | | | |
|---|---|---|---|
| **Glucocorticoid:** | **If Usual dose is: (mg)** | **To double dose: (mg)** | **To triple dose: (mg)** |
| **Hydrocortisone** | 5 / 5 / 5 *** | 10 / 10 /10 *** | 15 / 15 / 15 *** |
| **Prednisone** | 2.5 / 2.5 ** | 5.0 / 5.0 ** | 7.5 / 7.5 ** |
| **Dexamethasone** | 0.25.* | 0.25 / 0.25 ** | 0.375 / 0.375** |
| *** *morning / afternoon / evening dose;* ** *morning / evening dose;* * *morning dose* | | | |

**Over-the-Counter Fever Medications and the Need for Extra Fluids, Sugar, and Salt**

When you are ill with fever, you are at greater danger of becoming dehydrated. Dehydration means that your body fluid levels are low. When your body fluids are low, the risk of poor circulation and shock increases.

To prevent dehydration, it is very important to take in extra fluids. "Sports" drinks, such as *Gatorade* or *Powerade*, are good choices, if you have CAH. In addition to replenishing fluids, they provide sugar—a source of energy—and sodium.

Juice, soda, and freezer pops are also good sources of sugar and fluids. However, since they do not contain much sodium, pretzels or salted crackers (Saltines) can be given to provide extra salt.

When fever is present, doctors recommend over-the-counter fever-reducing medications. These include *Tylenol* (which is acetaminophen) or *Advil* and *Motrin* (which are preparations of ibuprofen). Some fever-reducing medications are available in suppository form, if you are vomiting and unable to take anything by mouth. However, if you are vomiting and have CAH, you need to be especially cautious.

### When Oral Medications are Vomited

When you have CAH, vomiting can be a big problem, even when there is no fever. Not only will you have the stress of the illness, but you will be unable to take, or keep down, needed glucocorticoids.

Vomiting also puts you in greater danger of becoming dehydrated. Because salt-wasters are more prone to dehydration than non salt-wasters, special attention is needed when vomiting or diarrhea occurs in a salt-waster. However, dehydration can also result in adrenal crisis in those who are non-salt-wasters, though this is less common.

It takes about an hour for a dose of glucocorticoid medication to be fully absorbed into the bloodstream. Thus, if vomiting occurs within one hour of taking medication, the dose should be given again. If vomiting occurs only once, and it has been more than an hour after the medication has been given, the dose does not have to be repeated. However, you should be on the lookout for signs of further illness.

If vomiting stops and liquids can be taken by mouth, triple doses should be given for the duration of the illness, and for one day after the illness subsides. However, if vomiting persists for longer than two hours, your doctor should be contacted and you should be prepared to go to the doctor's office or an emergency room. Prior to going to the hospital, your doctor may recommend that you give an injection of *Solu-Cortef.*

## GIVING A *SOLU-CORTEF* INJECTION

When oral glucocorticoid medications cannot be taken or kept down, an injectable form of hydrocortisone called *Solu-Cortef* may be needed. If nothing can be taken by mouth, getting the medication via injection may be the only way to insure that you are getting adequate cortisol.

### Warning Signs of Adrenal Crisis

If you become increasingly ill, in spite of being stress dosed, then you may not be getting enough glucocorticoid medication, or not absorbing the medication quickly enough. In that case, doctors recommend getting an injection of *Solu-Cortef.*

Signs of impending adrenal crisis include being excessively tired, sleepy, dizzy, or confused. You may also be pale and sweaty, and have signs of dehydration, such as dry lips and infrequent urination.

Typically, a single dose of *Solu-Cortef* contains between 50 and 100 mg of hydrocortisone, which is a lot of medication. Thus, a shot gives you a large, sudden boost of cortisol.

## What to Look For After Giving an Injection

Sometimes you can "bounce back" after getting an injection of *Solu-Cortef.* If that is the case, you may be able to be closely monitored at home by your physician by phone, while continuing with normal oral stress dosing.

In other instances, a *Solu-Cortef* injection may still not be enough, and your doctor may want you to go a hospital. If you become unresponsive, unconscious, or fall into a coma, an injection of *Solu-Cortef* should be given *immediately*. 911 (Emergency Services) should be called and you should be taken to the hospital by ambulance.

## What is *Solu-Cortef*?

*Solu-Cortef* (hydrocortisone succinate) is hydrocortisone that has been mixed with a compound called "succinate." Because hydrocortisone has both glucocorticoid and mineralocorticoid properties at high doses, it is preferred over prednisone or dexamethasone in emergencies.

Normally, hydrocortisone is not readily water-soluble. However, when coupled with succinate, it is very water-soluble and is readily absorbed into the bloodstream when given by injection. The combination of its salt-retaining properties and its water-solubility makes *Solu-Cortef* ideal in a crisis.

*Solu-Cortef* comes in a convenient *Acto-vial* preparation. This is a glass vial that consists of two chambers, separated by a rubber barrier. One chamber contains hydrocortisone powder, while the other contains a solution (diluent) to dissolve the medication. To mix the two, you push down on the top of the vial, forcing the diluent into the powder. The mixed solution is then drawn into a hypodermic syringe and given via injection.

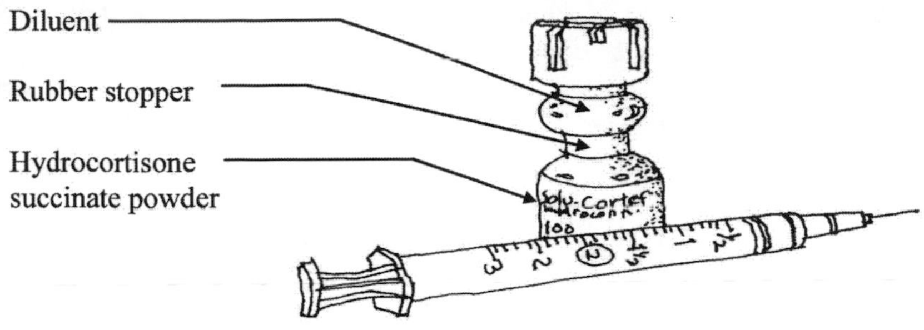


**SOLU-CORTEF ACTO-VIAL**

You should have at least two *Solu-Cortef Acto-vials*, along with sterile syringes at home, to be prepared for illnesses. When traveling out of the country, or to remote areas where medical care may be difficult to find, several vials of *Solu-Cortef* and syringes should be taken. The medication and syringes are available by prescription only.

*Solu-Cortef* also comes in vials that contain *only* the powdered medication. This preparation must be mixed with a separate sterile diluent, before it can be used for injection. So as not to be caught unprepared in an emergency, you should make sure that you are always prescribed and given the *Acto-vial* preparation by your pharmacist.

## How Much *Solu-Cortef*?

Most commonly, a vial of *Solu-Cortef* contains 100 mg hydrocortisone powder, and 2.0 ml (2.0 cc) solution. When mixed, the entire 2.0 ml of solution (containing 100 mg of medication) can be administered to children over five years of age (above ~thirty-five pounds). For children less than five years of age, half of the mixed vial (1.0 cc containing 50 mg of medication) can be given.

*Solu-Cortef* also comes in a vial that contains 250 mg of hydrocortisone, and 2 ml (2 ccs) of solution. Note that, when mixed, this solution will be more than twice as strong as the 100 mg vial. (A full 2.0 cc dose would deliver 250 mg of hydrocortisone, while a 1.0 cc dose would contain 125 mg of hydrocortisone.) In order to get the same amount of medication, only about half the reconstituted solution would need to be given.

There is little harm that will result from giving too much *Solu-Cortef*. In an emergency, it is better to give too much, rather than too little, medication.

Whereas precise dosing of glucocorticoids is needed for the day-to-day treatment of CAH, precise dosing is not needed in emergencies.

### Where to give *Solu-Cortef*

*Solu-Cortef* should be injected intramuscularly (into a muscle). Injections can be given in the front of the mid-thigh or in the upper arm.

### Other Injectable Steroids

Besides *Solu-Cortef*, there are several different glucocorticoid preparations that can be used in emergency situations. The common feature of these medications is that they are easily dissolved in water and can be given via intramuscular injection or intravenous infusion.

Another injectable cortisol preparation is *Cortone Acetate* (cortisone acetate). Though it also has mineralocorticoid properties, the base compound cortisone must first be converted to cortisol (hydrocortisone) before it is chemically active. As a result, cortisone acetate is not as well suited for emergency situations as *Solu-Cortef*.

Prednisone preparations can be given in emergencies. Prednisone injectables include *Hydeltrasol*, which is the sodium phosphate ester of the prednisone derivative, prednisolone; and *Solu-Medrol*, which is methylprednisolone sodium succinate. Methylprednisolone is widely used in clinical medicine for treating allergic conditions and asthma.

Dexamethasone comes in preparations that can be given intravenously or intramuscularly. *Decadron* phosphate is a highly water-soluble sodium phosphate preparation of dexamethasone. *Decadron* phosphate is widely used in hospitals for treating inflammation and brain and spinal swelling.

Both prednisone and dexamethasone medications stay in the blood much longer than preparations derived from cortisol. However, because they lack mineralocorticoid properties and there is less experience using these drugs for adrenal crisis, many physicians prefer *Solu-Cortef* in emergencies.

| HOW TO GIVE A *SOLU-CORTEF* INJECTION | |
|---|---|
| **Step 1**.<br><br>Wash hands, assemble equipment:<br>• *Solu-Cortef Acto-vial*<br>• Hypodermic needle and syringe<br>• Alcohol wipe | 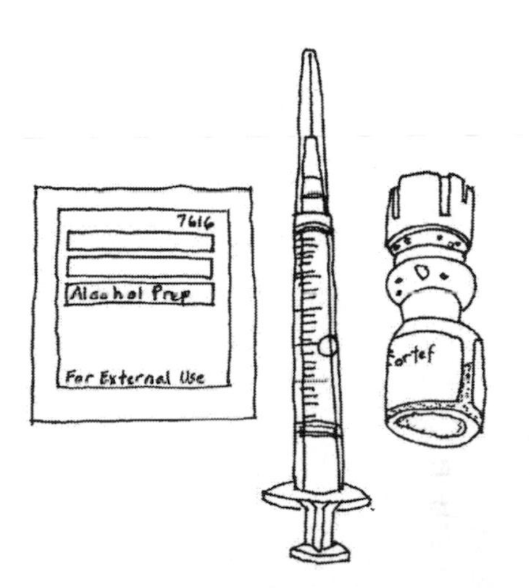  |
| **Step 2**.<br><br>Mix medication by pushing down firmly on top of the vial of *Solu-Cortef*. This will release the stopper and allow the diluent (liquid), which is in the top chamber of the *Acto-vial*, to mix with the dry powder, which is in the bottom chamber of the *Acto-vial*. |  |

| HOW TO GIVE A *SOLU-CORTEF* INJECTION | |
|---|---|
| 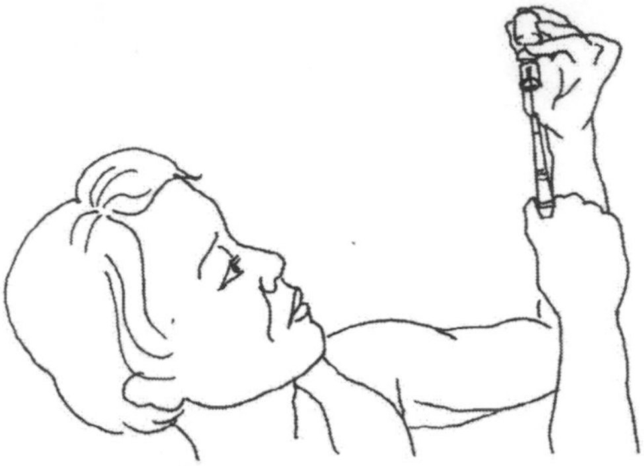 | **Step 3.**<br><br>Remove protective cover on top of *Acto-vial.* Clean rubber top with alcohol wipe. Insert needle into vial and draw up medication. |
|  | **Step 4.**<br><br>Pinch large area of skin together, at site of injection (the top of the thigh is a good spot). With other hand, push needle gently, but firmly, into the muscle. Inject medication by pushing down on plunger until it can go no further. |

## GOING TO THE EMERGENCY ROOM

In some situations, an emergency room visit may be necessary, even if a *Solu-Cortef* injection has been given. These include situations when there is continued vomiting, or if you feel very sick. At the hospital, medication and liquids can be given intravenously instead of orally. This assures that you will be able to get the cortisol and fluids that you need.

***If you are not sure what to do, call your doctor. If you cannot reach your doctor, go to the Emergency Room.***

## What to Expect at the Hospital

Because CAH is uncommon, the emergency room physician may not have experience in caring for someone with CAH. As a result, you should contact your pediatrician and/or endocrinologist prior to going to the hospital. To ensure proper attention, it is helpful to have instructions relayed to hospital personnel, by your physician, prior to your arrival.

Upon arrival at the hospital, it is important to emphasize that you need to be seen promptly, and that hydrocortisone should be given shortly after arrival. If you cannot be seen by a physician for an extended period of time, the intramuscular dose should be repeated every six hours.

For children less than fifty pounds, 50 mg of hydrocortisone is given. For children greater than fifty pounds, 100 mg of hydrocortisone is given. If you are greater than one hundred fifty pounds, 200 mg of hydrocortisone is given. Even if *Solu-Cortef* has been given at home, many physicians will give hydrocortisone in the emergency room, because it is possible that the shot was not given correctly or the medication may have been out of date. A double dose of the medication will not typically cause problems.

If there is dehydration, "normal saline" (0.9 percent NaCl) at a dose of 20-30 ml/kg, is given intravenously over thirty minutes to help restore the blood volume to normal. This may need to be repeated. Afterward, intravenous solutions consisting of 5 percent dextrose and half normal saline (D5W-1/2NS) can be given, at a rate of 1,500-3000 ml/m$^2$/day.

If you are severely ill (low blood pressure, dehydration, fever higher than 103° F), 100 mg/m$^2$ of hydrocortisone is given over the course of a twenty-four-hour day by many doctors, with doses administered every four to six hours. If you are moderately ill (normal blood pressure, fever less than 103° F), 50 mg/m$^2$/day may be sufficient, after you have received initial treatment.

In some cases, you will be hospitalized for a day or two. In other cases, you may be able to go home after six to twelve hours, if you are improved after receiving fluids and steroids. Before you are sent home from the hospital or emergency room, you should not appear dehydrated, should have urinated, and should be able to drink without vomiting.

| STRESS DOSING WHEN IN HOSPITAL | | |
|---|---|---|
| **Treatment** | **Initial Dose** | **Follow-up Dose** |
| **Hydrocortisone** | <50 lbs: 50 mg<br>>50 lbs: 100 mg<br>>150 lb:200 mg | 100 mg/m$^2$/day<br>Give doses every 6 hrs |
| **Intravenous Fluids** | 20-30 ml/kg of normal saline (0.9% NaCl); May need to be repeated | 5% dextrose and ½ normal saline (D5, ½ NS)<br>1500-3000 mg/m$^2$/day |
| *<: less than: >: more than. All treatments are given intravenously (IV).* | | |

## STRESS DOSING DURING SURGERY

Cortisol production increases more than five times when you are having surgery. Thus, stress doses of glucocorticoids are needed if you have CAH and are going to the operating room. Stress dosing is needed for all surgical procedures that require general anesthesia, which is anesthesia in which you are made asleep.

At the start of the case, shortly after the IV is placed, doctors recommend that intravenous hydrocortisone be given. Hydrocortisone is then given every two to four hours during the operation, and at the end of the operation. After surgery, intravenous hydrocortisone is given every four to six hours until you can take medication by mouth.

When medication can be taken orally, triple dosing is recommended for the first day or two after surgery. The dose can then be decreased to a double dose, and weaned to the normal dose by post-operative day three or four.

If you develop post-operative fevers, vomiting, or other complications, it is advisable to continue stress dosing, following the usual guidelines, until the complications have resolved.

| STRESS TREATMENT DURING INFANT SURGERY** | | | |
|---|---|---|---|
| *Adapted from J. Schnitzer and P.K. Donahoe. "Surgical Treatment of Congenital Adrenal Hyperplasia." Endocrinology and Metabolism Clinics of North America. 30(143), 2001.* | | | |
| **Time** | **Drug** | **Dose** | **Route of Administration** |
| Pre-operative (on-call surgery) | Cortisone acetate microcrystals | 25 mg | SQ |
| Surgery, initial stage (just after anesthesia and intravenous fluids are begun) | Hydrocortisone | 50 mg | IV bolus |
| Post operative— First 24 hours | Hydrocortisone | 50 mg | IV or IM every 6 hours |
| Post-operative— Beyond first 24 hours | Hydrocortisone; Florinef | Resume daily oral medication | PO |
| SQ = Subcutaneous; IV = Intravenous; IM = Intramuscular; PO = by mouth. **For older children, doses are increased based on size. | | | |

## SAFEGUARDING WELL-BEING

If you have CAH, there will be times when you will need to rely on others to help you get proper medical treatment. Children can get sick or suffer an injury while away from their parents. Adults can also get sick or hurt and be unable to speak for themselves, or their children. As a result, proper precautions need to be taken to ensure safety, especially in the event of an accident.

### Medical Alert Tags

If you have CAH, or any serious medical condition, you should wear a medical alert bracelet or necklace. This is a special piece of jewelry that is designed to alert emergency room physicians to the fact that you have a medical problem.

Parents should encourage their children to wear their medical alert tags at all times. However, because of the risk of choking, bracelets and necklaces are not recommended for children less than four years of age. These younger children may wear their medical alert tags around the ankle.

For someone with CAH, the *MedicAlert* tag should indicate—at a minimum—that you have an adrenal insufficiency and should be treated with hydrocortisone. A suggested inscription is ***"Adrenal Insufficiency—Treat with Cortisol."***

While there are a number of different companies that produce medical alert tags, *MedicAlert* is a non-profit organization that will also relay other important information to the emergency room physician. By calling a toll free phone number inscribed on the tag, the caring physician will be able to find out your name and home phone number; your doctors' names and phone numbers; and whether you have any allergies, or are taking drugs for other medical conditions.

To be maintained in their database, *MedicAlert* charges a small annual membership fee. Contact information for *MedicAlert*, as well as other similar organizations, is included in the appendix.

## Telling Others About CAH

Everyone who cares for a child with CAH should be given the information that they need to properly provide for their care. This includes schools, daycare centers, babysitters, and relatives who may care for a CAH child on a regular basis.

### *Your Child with CAH*

All children with CAH should know that they have a condition that makes it harder for them to tolerate illnesses. From an early age, they should be taught to inform their parents, teacher, school nurse, or other responsible adult, if they feel warm; develop vomiting or diarrhea; develop severe neck or headaches; or otherwise feel out-of-sorts.

As children grow older and acquire more verbal skills, they might also be taught some of the terms relevant to their condition, as well as the names of the medications that they take. Young adults and teens, who often spend nights away from home, might also be taught how to inject themselves with *Solu-Cortef.*

Since CAH is a life-long condition and responsibility for treatment will one day revert to the child, it is probably not a bad idea for you to discuss as much as you feel your child can comprehend, and handle, from an early age. An illustrated medical encyclopedia, showing the basic parts of the human body and the location of the adrenal glands, can be helpful when doing this.

Encourage your child to ask questions, but let him or her set the pace. The specifics of what to tell a child, and when, is a judgment call that each parent must make. In general, it is probably best to be matter-of-fact and straightforward with the answers.

### *The School and Other Regular Caregiver*

The child's teacher and school nurse should know that the child has CAH. The school nurse should be aware that children with CAH arc at risk of circulatory collapse with illness and severe trauma.

It is suggested that parents meet with school staff every year to go over the precautions that need to be taken, if the child becomes ill at school. The school should clearly understand when parents need to be contacted; what to do if the child is injured or develops a fever or vomiting; and when it may be necessary to call 911. Extra glucocorticoid medication, in the event that a child will need to be stress dosed, as well as a vial of *Solu-Cortef* and syringe, should be kept in the school nurse's office.

In addition to verbal instructions, parents are advised to supply the school with written instructions. A sample letter that can be submitted to schools is available in the appendix.

♦♦♦

## WHAT YOU MAY BE CONCERNED ABOUT: FREQUENTLY ASKED QUESTIONS

♦ ***My child is not a salt-waster. Do I still need to worry about adrenal crisis?***

Yes. The same stress dosing guidelines should be followed, regardless of the severity of CAH.

♦ ***How quickly can adrenal crisis occur?***

This is difficult to say. In some people, adrenal crisis can occur within several hours of getting sick, though this is rare. In others, it may take much longer. Because it is difficult to predict how you will fare in a given situation, it is best to begin oral stress dosing, as soon as illness and fever is recognized.

♦ ***How can I tell if my child is lethargic or just sleepy?***

It may sometimes be difficult to distinguish between lethargy and normal sleepiness, especially if you are talking about a young infant, who spends much of his or her time sleeping. It can be helpful to consider whether there are other physical signs of illness, e.g., parched lips, lack of urination, weak cry, difficulty waking up, etc. If your child is just sleepy, you should be able to wake or arouse your child. If you cannot do this, then emergency attention is needed, including giving *Solu-Cortef* and calling 911.

♦ ***If my child is ill, but has already taken his regular dose of medication, should I wait until the next regular dose is due before I double or triple the dose?***

Giving exact doses of medication on a regular schedule is important when you are talking about the day-to-day management of CAH. But when you are sick, it is much more important to make sure that there is adequate glucocorticoid medication to handle the stress of illness. Thus, stress doses should be given as soon as you detect fever and illness.

♦ ***Should I give the Solu-Cortef injection myself, or let the EMT or doctor at the hospital give it?***

If you call 911, give the injection before the ambulance arrives. Most ambulances do not normally carry *Solu-Cortef*, and EMTs and emergency room physicians are often prohibited from administering medication supplied by someone else. It can also take a while to get medication ordered at the hospital to your child. Thus, if your child is severely injured or ill, you should not delay giving a *Solu-Cortef* injection.

♦ ***What size hypodermic should be used to give an injection of Solu-Cortef? Where do I get the syringes?***

In general, a syringe used to deliver an emergency injection should have enough capacity to hold an entire vial of *Solu-Cortef*, after it has been mixed, as well as a needle tip long enough to reach into a muscle. While different size syringes and needles will work for different people, a syringe with a capacity of 3 ccs, fitted with a 22 gauge needle that is 1 and 1/2 inches long, should work in almost all cases.

Hypodermic needles can only be obtained via prescription. So as not to be caught unprepared in an emergency, make sure you have a prescription for the needles, in addition to the prescription for the *Solu-Cortef.*

♦ ***There are two different dates on my Solu-Cortef prescription, one on the bottle and one on the pharmacist's label. Which one do I go by?***

The date on the bottle reflects the actual shelf life of the medication, as determined by the drug manufacturer. The date on the pharmacist's label indicates the date on which the prescription expires at the pharmacy, usually a maximum of one year from when the drug is dispensed. Because a vial of *Solu-Cortef* has a shelf life of several years, the medication is good until the date stamped on the bottle, even if the pharmacist's label might indicate an earlier expiration date.

♦ ***If it is better to err on the side of caution, should I always give my child a Solu-Cortef shot when he or she is sick, just to be on the safe side?***

While illness should always be taken seriously in a CAH child, it is also important to note that injections are not needed every time a CAH child gets sick. In most cases, an injection will not be needed. Call your doctors if you are not sure what to do.

♦ ***After my child goes home from the hospital, can he immediately go back to normal doses of steroids? Or do the doses need to be weaned down slowly?***

In general it is best to continue stress dosing until one day AFTER your child has recovered from being ill. Thus even your child looks fine the next day after being ill, it is wise to give an extra day of stress doses.

♦ ***Does Florinef need to be increased during illness?***

No. Standard *Florinef* doses generally permit the body to retain normal levels of sodium during illness. Thus, you do not need to increase doses of *Florinef.* However, you should give plenty of fluids as well as some salty snacks (saltines, pretzels, etc.), in order to minimize the risk of dehydration.

♦ ***Should I get my child a flu shot each winter?***

Yes. Because it is much more difficult to tolerate illness when you have CAH, flu shots are recommended.

♦ ***What about the chicken pox vaccine?***

It is now recommended that all children receive the chicken pox vaccine. Though some vaccinated children will still get the chicken pox, these cases are usually mild.

♦ ***I have used up most of our regular supply of glucocorticoid medication because my child has been sick, and I have needed to stress dose. What should I do?***

Call your doctor and ask him or her to submit a new prescription to the pharmacist. You should be able to get additional medication before your refill date, if the original order is overwritten.

♦ ***My child doesn't want to call attention to himself by wearing his Medic Alert bracelet. What if we engrave the emergency instructions on another piece of jewelry, such as the back of a watch?***

The *MedicAlert* symbol is universally recognized by medical professionals. If instructions are "disguised" or "hidden," they may be overlooked or disregarded by EMTs or doctors at the hospital. This will defeat the purpose of engraving the emergency instructions on a piece of jewelry in the first place, so is not a good idea. If your child is self-conscious, perhaps he or she can wear a medical alert necklace, rather than a bracelet, since a necklace can be tucked underneath clothing.

♦ ***What is a 504 plan? Should I have one in place for my child?***

A "504 plan" refers to Section 504 of the Rehabilitation Act of 1973, a federal law enacted to protect the rights of disabled children in the public schools. The definition of "disabled" is a broad one. Some school administrators may interpret it to include any child with a medical condition, including CAH, while others may adopt a more narrow view.

If your child is designated as a "504," it means that the school needs to come up with a written plan to accommodate your child's special needs.

This is usually done as a joint effort between the parents and school administration. The plan is then updated and reviewed annually.

Whether your school administrator decides to designate your child as a 504 or not, you should still meet with school representatives annually to go over your child's needs. A standard letter for schools, which outlines the basics of CAH and gives emergency instructions, is included in the appendix of this book. A copy of the provisions of Section 504 is also included in the appendix.

♦ ***We are going on a long trip, far from home. What should I do to be prepared?***

Bring several vials of *Solu-Cortef*—along with needles, syringes, and alcohol wipes—as well as extra oral medication. Also pack over-the-counter items, such as *Advil* or *Tylenol*; medications for motion sickness, such as *Dramamine* or *Benadryl*; and *Pedialyte* or *Gatorade*.

Because most emergency room physicians, as well as the medical personnel on a cruise boat, will have limited experience in treating children with CAH, you should also bring treatment guidelines for emergency room physicians, a copy of which can be found in the appendix. You may also want to let your own physician know that you will be away and ask that they be available to provide advice to ER physicians, in case your child should become ill.

While you should always be prepared for emergencies, especially in situations where you may not have easy access to a doctor or hospital, there is no reason to cancel your vacation, just because your child has CAH. If you are properly prepared, chances are likely that your child will be just fine, even if he or she should get ill.

♦ ***Will we be able to get on an airplane with a hypodermic needle and syringes? What if we are stopped by security?***

Parents generally report that they have had no problem flying, while carrying an emergency injection kit. However, if you are traveling, you may want to bring a signed letter from your doctor, just in case. A copy of a standard letter is included in the appendix.

♦ ***What should I do if my child is in a lock-down situation at school? How will he be able to get his or her medication?***

Emergency medical personnel are usually present, even in lock-down situations. So it should be possible to get medication to your child. At the same time, it is important to remember that, unless your child becomes very ill during the middle of a lock-down, he or she will not be in immediate peril, even if he or she misses a few doses of medication.

♦ ***Can hydrocortisone suppositories be used instead of a Solu-Cortef injection when my child is ill?***

A suppository generally contains less hydrocortisone than a vial of *Solu-Cortef* (25 mg vs. 100 mg.) A suppository will also not take effect as quickly as an intramuscular injection. Thus, it should not be considered an equivalent substitute. In addition, suppositories cannot be used if your child has diarrhea.

Some doctors may prescribe hydrocortisone suppositories as an alternative to *Solu-Cortef*, in situations where the *Solu-Cortef* is difficult to find because of drug production shortages. Other doctors do not feel comfortable using hydrocortisone suppositories and prefer the injections. Talk to your endocrinologist about this.

♦ ***Do you have suggestions for what to put in an emergency shot kit?***

You should have a vial of *Solu-Cortef*, needles and syringes, and several alcohol wipes, along with instructions for how to give the injection. You should also have copies of emergency letters with your doctor's name and phone number. All of this can fit into a hard eyeglass case for easy transport.

Remember that *Solu-Cortef* must be stored at room temperature, so it should not be left in the glove compartment of your car. Exposure to extreme heat or cold can render the medication ineffective.

# 10

# Surgical Restoration for Girls with Congenital Adrenal Hyperplasia

*Contributed By Dix P. Poppas, M.D. and Rosalia Misseri, M.D.*

*Institute for Pediatric Urology*
*Children's Hospital of New York Presbyterian*
*Weill Medical College of Cornell University*

*Girls with CAH are often born with genitals that appear like those of a boy. Parents of female infants are then faced with deciding whether their child should have surgery to correct function and make the genitals look more typically female. Many physicians recommend early surgical intervention. Others believe surgery should wait until the patient is old enough to give consent.*

*In this chapter, we give an overview of surgery in girls with CAH. Our goal is not to examine the controversies that can be associated with genital restoration, but rather to discuss the risks and benefits of surgical therapy. By understanding what surgery entails, parents can better understand the options for their daughters.*

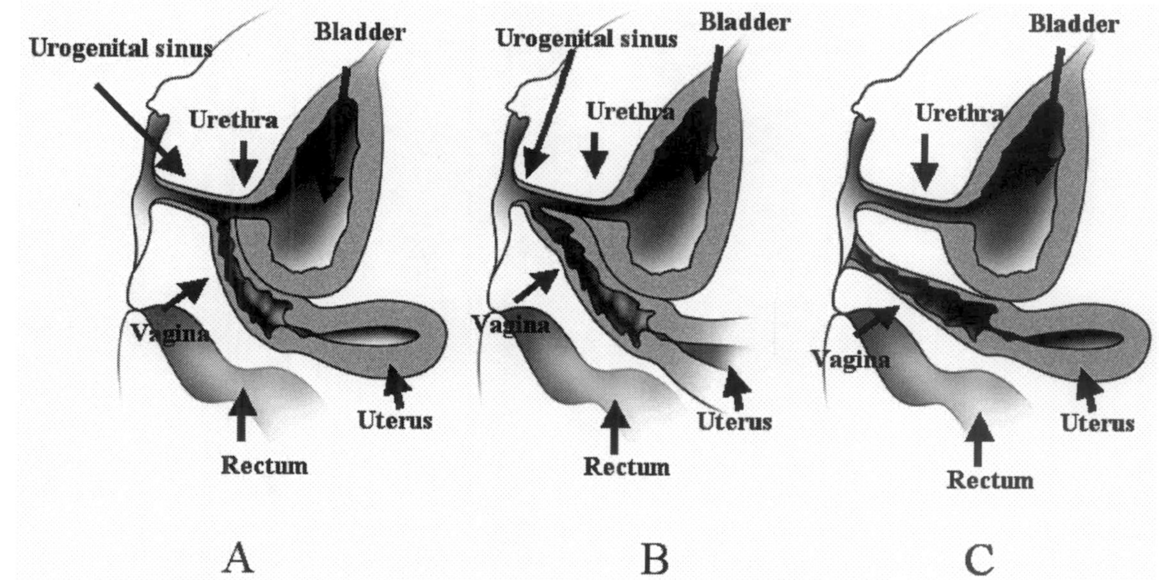


A. **High Vaginal Confluence**: The vagina is connected to the urethra close to the bladder.
B. **Low Vaginal Confluence**: The vagina is connected to the end of the urethra, far from the bladder.
C. **Normal Anatomy**: The vagina and the urethra open onto the perineum separately.

**PROBLEMS OF THE REPRODUCTIVE AND URINARY SYSTEMS IN GIRLS WITH CAH**

CAH is usually accompanied by varying degrees of masculinization of the female genitalia. When this happens, the result is the joining of the female urinary and reproductive systems. The more these two systems combine, the more difficult it becomes for girls to have normal urinary, reproductive, and sexual function.

However, masculinized girls with CAH have the ability to develop and function normally. In the past ten years, doctors have greatly expanded their understanding of the anatomy of the female genitalia. Considerable advances in surgical techniques have also emerged to help improve the functional, cosmetic, and psychological results of surgical restoration, including the preservation of genital sensitivity and orgasmic potential.

## FEMALE GENDER

Excess androgens can cause the clitoris, labia, and vagina in CAH girls to develop abnormally, but they do not affect the formation of the ovaries, fallopian tubes, cervix, or uterus. Although girls with CAH can be born with genitals that resemble those of a boy on the outside, they have two normal X chromosomes and female internal reproductive organs. Without surgery, masculinized girls may have problems with urination, menstruation, and sexual intercourse. With proper medical treatment and—in some girls—surgery to separate the urinary and vaginal tracts, these problems can be corrected or alleviated.

Though surgeons constantly strive to improve their technique, genital surgery may not be without complications. As such, doctors recommend that masculinized girls be evaluated early in life and that parents have a thorough understanding of the risks and benefits of surgical restoration so that they can know all the options available for their child.

## ANATOMICAL PROBLEMS IN GIRLS WITH CAH

Girls with CAH can have a wide range of problems with the urinary system and genitals. These include varying degrees of clitoral enlargement; fusion of the labia majora with the absence of labia minora; and the formation of a urogenital sinus (UGS). The term "urogenital sinus" refers to the tract (or tube) that is formed when the vagina joins with the urethra.

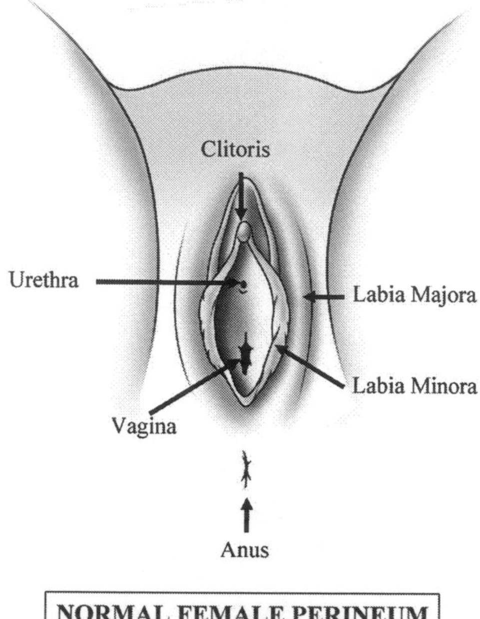


**NORMAL FEMALE PERINEUM**

Typically, the vagina and urethra are two distinct structures that open separately onto the perineum (the area between the anus and the external sex organs.) When a urogenital sinus exists, the vagina and urethra join together to form a single structure. Internally, the two may join at varying distances from the perineum.

When masculinization is very severe, the two join together close to the bladder and far from the perineum. This is known as "high vaginal and urethral confluence." When masculinization is less severe, the vagina and urethra join together far from the bladder and close to the perineum. This is known as "low (or 'distal') vaginal and urethral confluence." The anus is usually found in a normal location in girls with CAH.

Many attempts have been made by doctors to classify abnormalities of the urogenital system. The one most frequently used is the Prader scale (also see chapter 4.) Girls who are a Prader 3, 4, or 5 typically have a mid or high vaginal and urethral confluence, while girls who are a Prader 2 typically have a low vaginal and urethral confluence. Girls who are a Prader 1 have mild clitoral enlargement, but no urogenital sinus.

| COMPARISION OF PRADER LEVELS | | | |
|---|---|---|---|
| **Prader Level** | **Clitoris** | **Labia** | **Urogenital Sinus (UGS)** |
| **1** | Enlarged | Normal | No UGS; vagina and urethra open separately onto the perineum |
| **2** | More enlarged | Partially fused | UGS with low vaginal and urethral confluence |
| **3** | Increased clitoral enlargement | Completely fused | UGS with mid-level vaginal and urethral confluence; vagina and urethra open together onto the perineum |
| **4** | Very enlarged; looks like small male phallus | Completely fused; labia look like scrotum, but with less pigmentation and rugation | UGS with high vaginal and urethral confluence; vagina and urethra share same opening at *base* of phallus |
| **5** | Indistinguishable from male phallus | Indistinguishable from male scrotum | UGS with high vaginal and urethral confluence; vagina and urethra share same opening at *tip* of phallus |

## THE PEDIATRIC UROLOGIST

If your daughter is born with genital abnormalities, you will be referred to a doctor called a pediatric urologist. Pediatric urologists are doctors who specialize in the anatomy and physiology of the urinary and reproductive tracts in children.

### What to Expect at the First Visit

At your first visit, the pediatric urologist will perform a detailed evaluation of your daughter's prenatal and postnatal history. This will include discussion of her current medications, laboratory results, and the need for further x-ray studies. It will be helpful if the urologist speaks with your pediatrician and endocrinologist before your meeting. This way, he or she will be completely up to date with your daughter's diagnosis and medical history, by the time you meet.

Parents should state their reasons and expectations for visiting the urologist. This will ensure that the urologist understands your concerns. It will also provide a foundation for further discussion.

A physical exam will be performed. The doctor will evaluate your daughter's size, weight, and general physical appearance. It will be important to determine if she looks over-treated (or cushingoid), as evidenced by a round facial appearance. Because children on high doses of steroids heal more slowly and are more prone to infection, they may be poor surgical candidates. Thus, if your daughter is found to be cushingoid, surgery should be delayed until over-treatment is corrected.

A detailed assessment of the genitalia will be performed. The urologist will note the overall external appearance of the genitals, and then focus on the size, shape and consistency of the clitoris and labioscrotal folds. The labioscrotal folds will be examined for their relationship to the clitoris and for the degree of fusion, rugation (wrinkling), and pigmentation (color.) After that, the opening of the urogenital sinus—where urine exits the body—will be identified. The location and anatomical relationship of the UGS to the clitoris, labioscrotal folds and anus will also be assessed.

### Tests Needed

Often, x-rays will have been obtained prior to your visit. If not, they will be ordered at this time. The doctor may ask for an ultrasound of the abdomen and pelvis—which is useful to examine the kidneys, bladder, uterus, ovaries and the adrenals—and an x-ray of the vagina, urethra, bladder, and urogenital sinus called a "genitogram." To perform a genitogram, a catheter is placed into the opening of the urogenital sinus. A liquid dye (called "contrast") is then injected through the catheter.

When combined with the physical exam, the ultrasound and genitogram will be helpful for planning any surgical restoration. Because every child's anatomy will be different, due to differing levels of masculinization, any surgery done must be tailored to the needs of your child.

### Discussion of Treatment Options

Once the examination is complete, the findings should be discussed with the urologist to see if surgery should be considered. There should be a detailed review of the potential risks and complications of surgical restoration, as well as its expected benefits. There should also be discussion about the pros and cons of performing surgery in infancy, versus waiting until the child is older. Additionally, you should ask about the option of ***NOT*** performing any surgical restoration.

## SURGICAL PROCEDURES AND TECHNIQUES

The major features of surgical restoration are clitoroplasty, labioplasty, and vaginoplasty. Several techniques for vaginoplasty are used, depending on the anatomical findings in the child. Your surgeon should have considerable experience working with CAH girls in order to understand these variations and surgical approaches. In general, the more masculinized the genitalia, the more complex the surgery.

### Clitoroplasty

Clitoroplasty (also known as "clitoral reduction") refers to surgery performed on the clitoris, in order to reduce its size. Because some consider clitoroplasty to be cosmetic, rather than medically necessary surgery, it can be controversial.

In the past, complete removal of the clitoris (called "clitorectomy") was often recommended. This should ***NEVER*** be considered today. Another outdated technique called a "clitoral recession" involved moving the clitoris behind the pubic bone. This often resulted in pain, when the clitoris was sexually aroused. Clitoral recessions should also be avoided today.

Today, the nerve and blood supply to the clitoris are left intact to allow for maximum sexual function and sensation, while the erectile bodies (the parts of the clitoris that cause erection) are partially reduced to prevent the painful erections that can be caused by the erectile bodies. After a clitoroplasty, the clitoris has a normal appearance.

## Labioplasty

Labioplasty refers to the surgery that is performed on the labia. The goal of labioplasty is to separate the labia majora, which can be partially or completely fused in girls with CAH, and to form labia minora, which are often absent in girls with CAH. To form the labia minora, the foreskin that covers the clitoris is moved. The labia majora are then brought below (inferior to) the new vaginal and urethral openings that will be formed during the vaginoplasty.

## Vaginoplasty

Vaginoplasty refers to surgery on the vagina. The goal of vaginoplasty is to create a vagina that will allow sexual intercourse and normal menstrual and urinary function.

There are several different types of vaginoplasty. The type of vaginoplasty that is best suited for your child is dependent on the level at which the urethra and vagina join together.

### *Cut Back Vaginoplasty*

The cut-back vaginoplasty is typically used when there is labioscrotal fusion with no associated urogenital sinus. This is seen in girls who are only mildly masculinized.

### *Flap Vaginoplasty*

The flap vaginoplasty is used when there is a low vaginal and urethral confluence. A U-shaped flap of skin is developed in the perineum and brought up to the urogenital sinus, which is then opened posteriorly until a normal sized vaginal opening is formed. The U-shaped flap is then sewn to the urogenital sinus to form the posterior part of the vagina.

### *Total Urogenital Mobilization*

In this procedure, the entire urogenital sinus is moved (or "mobilized") toward the perineum. This procedure is most commonly used in girls with a mid level or high vaginal and urethral confluence.

This procedure has been reported to have better cosmetic results than older surgical techniques, and less risk of post-operative complications such as the formation of a "fistula" (an abnormal connection between the bladder or vagina and skin) and vaginal "stenosis" (narrowing of the vaginal entrance.) Using this technique, the vagina is not separated from the urethra. Rather, both openings are brought flush to the perineum.

### *Pull-through Vaginoplasty*

The pull-through vaginoplasty is used for very high vaginal confluence. This complex situation, where the confluence is very high, is found in only about 5% of patients with CAH.

In pull-through vaginoplasty, the vagina is separated from the urogenital sinus, and tissue from the sinus is used to lengthen the urethra. The mobilized vagina may reach the perineum, but in most cases, extra skin (called a "skin flap") is required to achieve this.

## PREPARATION FOR SURGERY

Before undergoing any form of genital surgery, all children should receive antibiotics. This will help to prevent infection after surgery. The urologist may also recommend that a laxative or enema be given prior to the operation, to empty the intestines of stool.

Children with CAH also require stress dose steroids before, during, and after surgery, in order to prevent adrenal crisis (see chapter 9.) Thus, your daughter may be admitted to the hospital one day prior to surgery, where stress dose steroids will be administered under the guidance of her endocrinologist.

Once your daughter has been brought to the operating room and has been anesthetized, a cystoscopy and vaginoscopy (examinations of the UGS, bladder, and vagina with an instrument called an "endoscope") will be performed. The length of the common sinus; the location of the vaginal entry into the sinus; the size and position of the vagina; and the presence of a cervix will be noted. Along with the results from the genitogram, the findings from these endoscopic exams will help to determine the best surgical approach for your child.

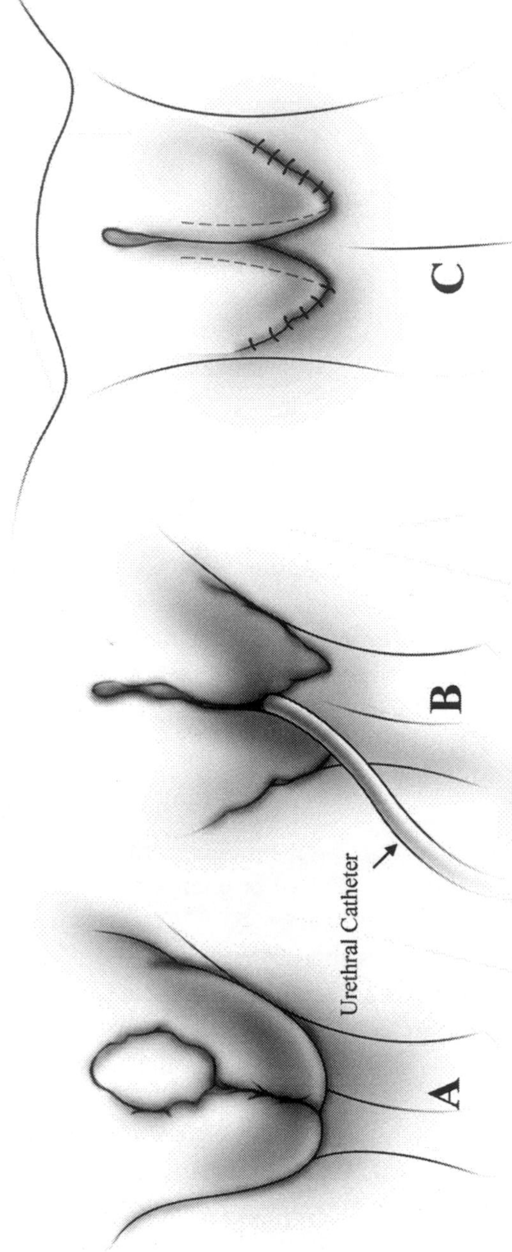


A. Before Operation (Pre-operative): Note the fused labia and enlarged clitoris.
B. Immediately after operation (immediate post-operative): Temporary urethral catheter used to drain urine.
C. Later after Operation (post-operative): Sutures will dissolve 2 to 4 weeks after surgery.

**GENITAL AREA BEFORE AND AFTER SURGERY**

## TIMING OF SURGERY

Opinions vary about the best time for a girl to undergo genital surgery. With safe neonatal anesthesia, most surgeons agree that clitoroplasty is best carried out in infancy, usually when the child is between 4 and 6 months old; however, opinions diverge over the optimal time for vaginoplasty and labioplasty.

Some surgeons feel that all three procedures—clitoroplasty, vaginoplasty and labioplasty—should be performed at the same time in infancy, *only* in girls with a low vaginal and urethral confluence; while in girls with a high vaginal and urethral confluence, the vaginoplasty and labioplasty should be delayed until after puberty. This is because early vaginoplasty may lead to vaginal stenosis and the need for vaginal dilation or additional vaginal surgery at a later time.

Other surgeons believe that, regardless of vaginal location, all three procedures should be performed at the same time, in infancy. There are several reasons for this second approach.

Girls with a urogenital sinus can have problems with dribbling after urination (also known as "vaginal voiding.") This occurs as a result of urine flowing from the urethra, into the vagina, during urination. When the child stands up after urinating, the urine drips out of the vagina and onto her underwear, resulting in chronic irritation, poor hygiene and increased risk for infection.

Vaginal voiding can often be misdiagnosed as "urinary incontinence," or lack of bladder control. If the problem is not detected and corrected early, a girl may end up having to undergo extensive and inappropriate x-rays and examinations in an effort to locate the source of the problem.

When clitoroplasty, labioplasty, and vaginoplasty are performed at the same time in infancy, the foreskin that covers the clitoris may be used in the vaginoplasty and labioplasty. This can help to increase local tissue sensitivity and improve the appearance of the genitalia. Furthermore, genital tissue is thicker and has a better blood supply in infancy, due to exposure to maternal estrogens in the womb, making vaginal mobilization easier at a young age. Tissue also heals better, and with less scarring, the younger the patient. Additionally, some doctors believe that girls are able to undergo a more natural psychological and sexual development when they grow up with genitals that look typical.

## COMPLICATIONS AND RISKS OF GENITAL SURGERY

An important first step in making the best decision for your daughter is finding the right surgeon. Having an experienced surgeon will help to reduce the potential complications that may occur as a result of the surgery. This point is emphasized in the *2002 CAH Consensus Statement* from the Lawson Wilkins Pediatric Endocrine Society and the European Society for Pediatric Endocrinology, which states that surgery "should only be performed in centers with significant experience," and further defines this as "a center with experience of at least 3-4 cases/year." However, because there are only a few places in the United States that meet these criteria, you may have difficulty finding an experienced surgeon in your area.

The surgeon should also be someone you can communicate with and trust. He or she should be willing to tell you exactly how many genital surgeries he or she performs each year, as well as freely discuss the outcome of those surgeries. The surgeon may also put you in contact with past patients and parents, so you can discuss their experience.

### General Complications

Any surgery performed on a patient with CAH requires appropriate stress steroid management. Because your daughter in unable to produce cortisol, she is at risk of adrenal crisis during, or immediately following, surgery. An experienced surgeon will coordinate the proper stress dosage of steroids with your endocrinologist to prevent adrenal crisis from occurring.

### Blood Loss

Blood loss will occur during any surgery. However, the amount of blood lost during genital surgery is well controlled. Following surgery, bandages may be blood stained, but this is usually minimal. In unusual instances, blood loss may be significant and a blood transfusion may be needed.

### Infection

Infection of the surgical area is a possible complication, though it is rare. The tissue in the genital area has an excellent blood supply, which helps to reduce the risk of local infection; however, because steroids reduce the body's ability to fight infection, children taking steroids might be at a higher risk for developing infection during surgery. Therefore, they are usually given a combination of oral and intravenous antibiotics, before and after surgery, to prevent infection from happening.

**Vaginal Stenosis**

Once the vagina is surgically placed in the desired location, the opening may narrow with time. This is called "vaginal stenosis." Stenosis is a common complication of any vaginoplasty.

Some surgeons recommend dilating the vagina as soon as narrowing begins. Others recommend doing nothing until the patient is older. Because access to the vagina is not considered necessary prior to puberty, many doctors will not attempt to correct vaginal stenosis until after a girl begins to menstruate (usually after 12 years of age). Also, because vaginal dilation can be traumatic and painful, psychological distress and distrust can result, if dilation is performed repeatedly in young children.

If the stenosis is severe or restricts menstrual drainage, dilation is usually successful in correcting the problem. However, the use of dilators requires a motivated and mature patient. It may take several months to achieve the desired result.

If the stenosis is mild to moderate in severity, and menstrual drainage is not restricted, correction of the stenosis can be further delayed until a girl desires correction for sexual intercourse. Should she desire surgical correction, the stenosis can also be corrected using a simple outpatient procedure.

**Loss of Clitoral Sensation**

Loss of clitoral sensation due to surgery is a major concern for patients, parents and surgeons. In the past, functional outcome of clitoral surgery was extremely poor. However, studies that attempt to evaluate clitoral sensitivity and orgasmic potential after surgery are often based on surgical approaches more than 20 years old, when clitorectomies or clitoral recessions were common recommendations. Modern approaches to clitoroplasty are based on maintaining clitoral nerve and blood supply. Thus, genital sensitivity and orgasmic potential should be better preserved.

The outcome of modern clitoroplasty is now being studied in a prospective way by following girls for many years after surgery. No definitive studies are available yet, though early post surgical reports are encouraging. Long-term results should be known in the next five to ten years.

## CONSIDERING OPTIONS

Because of the intricacies involved in surgical restoration and the potential for serious complications, the selection of an expert, experienced surgeon is of utmost importance. Parents should ask how many times, and how recently, a surgeon has performed genital restorations. Parents should also ask about the complications seen in patients who have had similar operations.

The decision to perform, or not to perform, surgical restoration resides with the family. This decision making process is best supported by a pediatric team that includes an endocrinologist, urologist, psychologist and geneticist.

♦♦♦

## WHAT YOU MAY BE CONCERNED ABOUT: FREQUENTLY ASKED QUESTIONS

♦ ***How long will my daughter need to stay in the hospital for the surgery?***

Typically, children are admitted to the hospital one day before surgery—for blood work, fluids, and antibiotics—and discharged three days after surgery.

♦ ***Will she be able to urinate normally after surgery?***

Most children are able to urinate without difficulty and can go home without catheters or drains.

♦ ***Will we need to do anything special regarding wound care or diapering, after her surgery?***

Normal diaper changes and genital care are usually all that is required. No bandages or bandage changes are necessary. However, children should avoid all straddle toys, bouncy chairs, and bikes, until they have been seen by the urologist for a follow up visit, after surgery.

♦ ***When, and how often, will she need to go back for a follow-up visit with the urologist?***

Most surgeons will want to see your daughter one week after the surgery, to see how well she is healing After that, visits are necessary once a year, for three years, in order to evaluate the surgical site. After three years, no further genital exams need to be performed, unless there are complications.

Many urologists encourage the continuation of yearly visits even after the three years are up. This is so your daughter will know that support exists to answer her questions as she goes through adolescence and young adulthood.

♦ ***Without surgery, is it possible for a girl to menstruate properly?***

This will depend on the degree to which a girl is masculinized. With increased masculinization and a higher vaginal and urethral confluence, menstrual flow usually becomes more difficult. However, if the opening of the vagina is narrow, regardless of its entry point into the urethra, menstrual flow may be restricted.

♦ ***How about to carry children and deliver a baby vaginally?***

Once successful correction of the genitalia has been performed, a woman should be able to conceive naturally and carry a pregnancy to term; however, vaginal delivery is not recommended if genital surgery has been performed. In those cases, a Caesarean section is advised.

♦ ***How many surgeries should a physician have performed, before he or she is considered an expert?***

It is difficult to pinpoint an exact number; however, some believe that a surgeon should have performed at least twenty genital restorations, and at least three per year, before being considered an expert. In general, the more experienced the surgeon, the greater the potential for a successful outcome of surgery. It is also important that surgeons follow-up with their past patients, in order to determine long-term results.

♦ ***How long have current methods of clitoroplasty been used?***

Like that of all surgery, the approach to clitoral surgery is constantly evolving. The major advance in this area occurred about 20 years ago when Drs. Hendren and Donahoe at Massachusetts General Hospital in Boston, Massachusetts, published their technique for clitoroplasty. Since then, doctors' knowledge and understanding of clitoral anatomy and nerve supply have improved greatly. As a result, current approaches to clitoroplasty offer a much greater opportunity for preserving clitoral sensation, orgasmic potential, and cosmetic appearance than surgical techniques used in the past.

♦ ***In what situations are dilators used?***

Dilation is used to correct vaginal stenosis, which can occur after vaginoplasty. However, even if the vaginal opening begins to narrow after surgery, dilation is not recommended until a child reaches adolescence. Then, it is done to enlarge the vaginal entrance in preparation for future sexual intercourse and, in some cases, may be needed in order to allow for normal menstruation.

Dilation should never be performed in a girl with a urogenital sinus, unless she has had surgery to separate the vagina from the urethra. Doing so can result in serious injury and infection.

♦ ***What is the likelihood of having to have repeat surgeries, even assuming that the surgeon is skilled?***

If the surgeon is highly skilled, additional clitoral surgery following clitoroplasty is rarely ever needed; however, additional vaginal surgery may be needed if dilation is unsuccessful in correcting vaginal stenosis. This should be done only when a patient is psychologically prepared and her surgeon has confirmed that surgery is an option.

♦ ***What do we know about long-term cosmetic results of surgery? In other words, if surgery looks good today, how do we know that it is still going to look good twenty years from now?***

If surgery is performed correctly by an experienced surgeon, the genitals should develop normally as the child grows. However, appearance is very subjective. Even without surgery, there can be wide variation in the appearance of the external genitalia.

♦♦♦

# 11

# Prenatal Treatment of Congenital Adrenal Hyperplasia

*After learning to co-exist with CAH, some parents decide that they are ready to "try again." While this decision can be viewed as a triumph of sorts, concerns can still remain about the affected status of the unborn child, especially if that child is a girl.*

*In this last chapter, we discuss the pros and cons of treating pregnant mothers with dexamethasone. While routinely offered by some doctors, this procedure—which has been found to reduce masculinization in girls with CAH—is still viewed as experimental by others.*

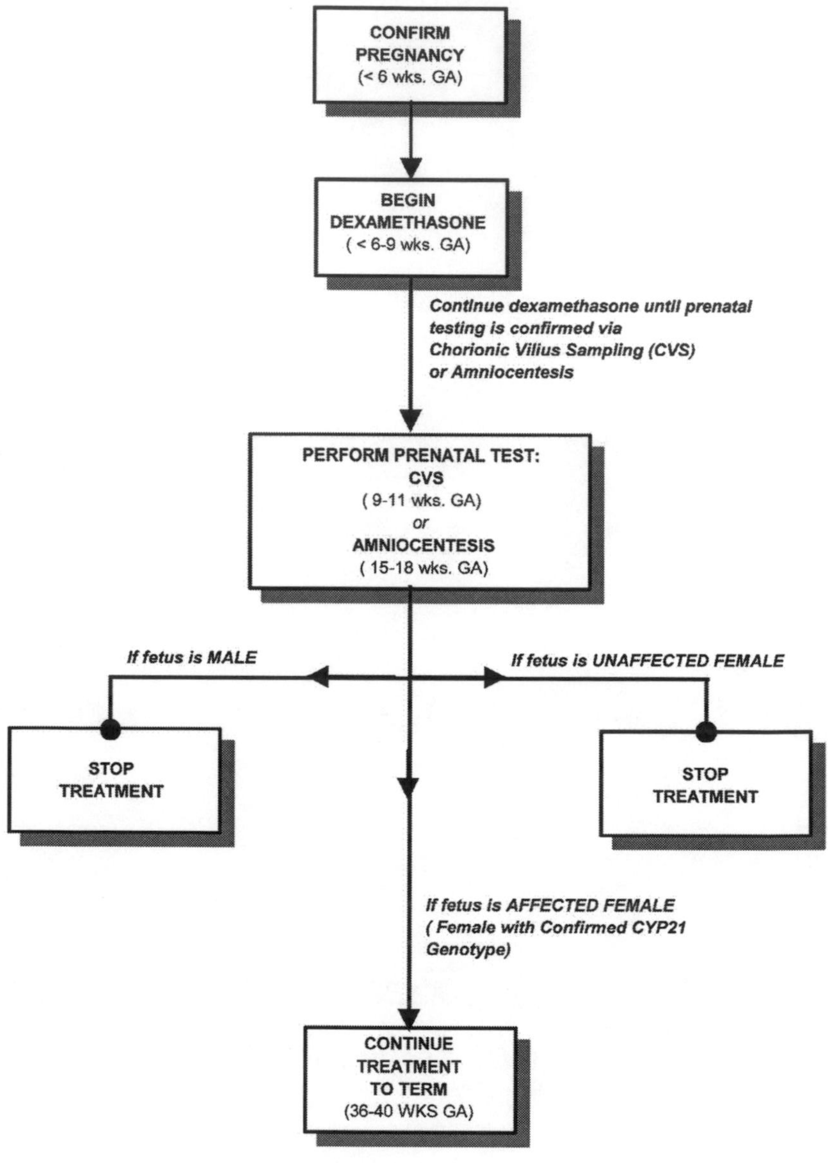


**GA: Gestational Age (measured from last menstrual period)**

**MILESTONES DURING PRENATAL TREATMENT**

**GIRLS** with CAH are often born with masculinized external genitalia. This can cause a number of complex problems, both social and medical. Recent studies have shown that prenatal masculinization can be prevented, or reduced, if mothers are treated with dexamethasone during pregnancy. This has generated considerable interest for many reasons.

When masculinization is prevented in the womb (*in utero*), many of the problems that face parents and patients can be avoided. The need for many affected girls to undergo complex reconstructive surgery is reduced, and the emotional toll that is often taken on families when a child is born with ambiguous genitalia, or given an incorrect sex assignment at birth, can be alleviated. Thus, the potential benefits of treatment are indisputable.

However, prenatal treatment of CAH has only become widely available in the last decade. Presently, there are few studies available on the long-term effects of fetal exposure to glucocorticoids, and concerns remain about the unknown risks of treatment. As a result, it is important to realize that, while some medical professionals consider prenatal treatment of mothers to be routine, others still view it as experimental and controversial.

## GENITAL FORMATION IN THE WOMB

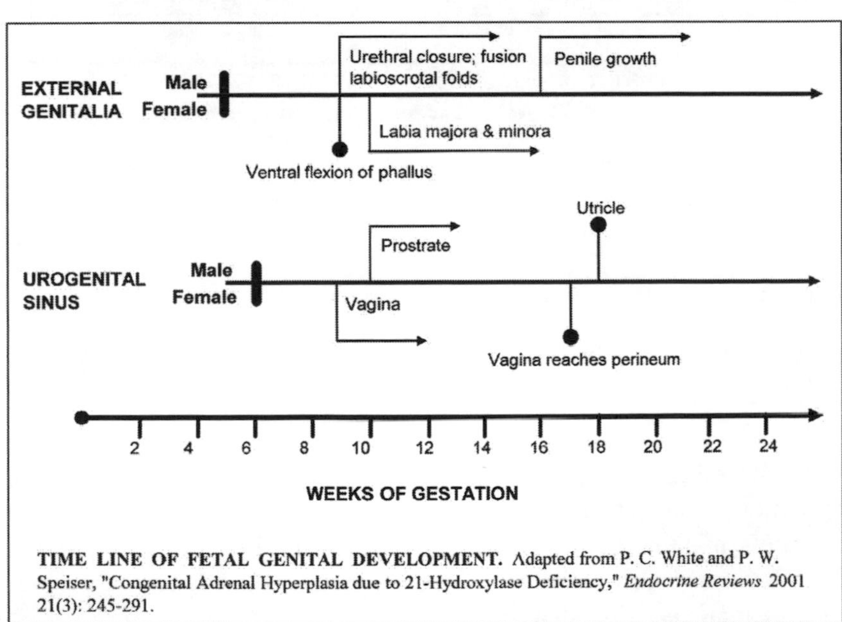


**TIME LINE OF FETAL GENITAL DEVELOPMENT.** Adapted from P. C. White and P. W. Speiser, "Congenital Adrenal Hyperplasia due to 21-Hydroxylase Deficiency," *Endocrine Reviews* 2001 21(3): 245-291.

The reproductive structures in a developing fetus form early in gestation. At about the seventh week of pregnancy, the external genitalia start to form as either male or female. If the baby produces male sex hormones (androgens), the genitals will develop into those of a boy. In the absence of male sex hormones, the genitals will develop into those of a girl.

By the sixth to seventh week of gestation, a baby's adrenal glands are already functioning and secreting steroid hormones. A baby with CAH will thus start producing excess androgens from this early stage. If the baby is male, these extra male hormones will not have an effect on genital development. But if the baby if female, these excess androgens will cause her genitals to develop like a boy's.

## DEXAMETHASONE TREATMENT

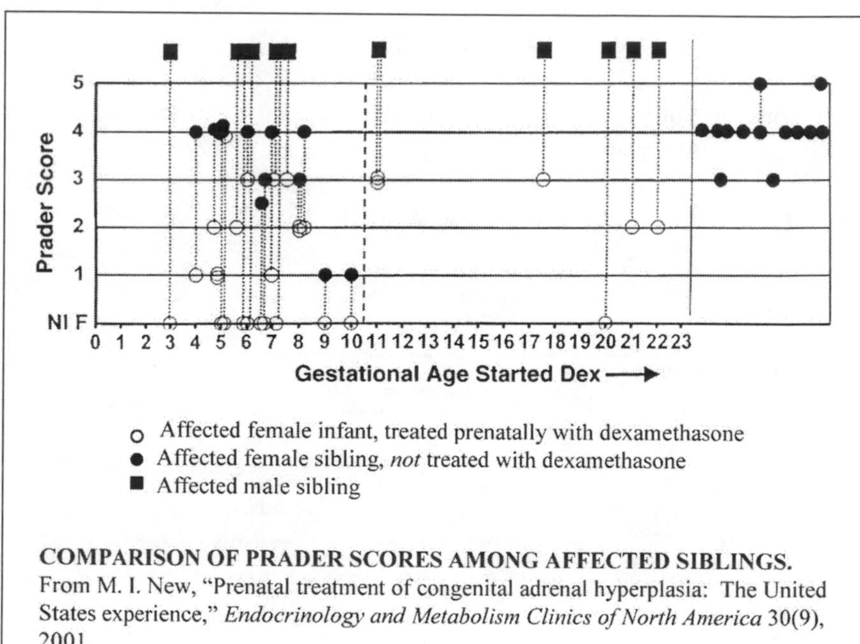


**COMPARISON OF PRADER SCORES AMONG AFFECTED SIBLINGS.** From M. I. New, "Prenatal treatment of congenital adrenal hyperplasia: The United States experience," *Endocrinology and Metabolism Clinics of North America* 30(9), 2001.

In the same way that dexamethasone suppresses adrenal androgen production in children and adults with CAH, dexamethasone suppresses the excess male hormones (androgens) produced by a fetus with CAH. When fetal androgen production in the baby is reduced, masculinization of the genitalia is reduced, as well.

Dexamethasone is effective for prenatal therapy because it has the ability to go from the mother's circulation, across the placenta, to reach the fetus. This ability to cross the placenta distinguishes dexamethasone from other glucocorticoids, like prednisone and hydrocortisone.

When affected sisters within the same family are compared, masculinization is less severe in the infant who has been treated prenatally with dexamethasone. However, it is also important to note that while prenatal treatment can prevent severe masculinization in many girls, some girls will still be somewhat masculinized, even with treatment.

## Timing of Treatment

The most important factor influencing the success of prenatal treatment is the timing of the start of treatment. Because a baby's genitals begin to form within the first two months of pregnancy, treatment should start as soon as possible after conception.

Most external genital development is completed by the time a fetus is ten weeks old. To achieve maximum benefit from prenatal treatment, a mother needs to start dexamethasone before the sixth to seventh week of pregnancy. To prevent labial fusion, treatment should begin before the eighth or ninth week.

Later initiation of treatment can minimize the amount of masculinization, but it may not prevent the formation of a scrotum and male-like phallus. Thus, once a woman is past ten weeks of pregnancy, the benefits of therapy do not outweigh the risks, and many physicians will not recommend treatment.

## How Much Dexamethasone Is Needed

Dexamethasone is given at a total daily dose of about 20 mcg/kg (20 micrograms per kilogram), based on a woman's pre-pregnancy weight. This is split into two or three equal doses.

For example, if you weigh 115 lbs (52 kg), your total daily dose would be about 1.0 mg/day (20 mcg/kg x 50 kg). Thus, you might take 0.5 mg of dexamethasone, two times a day. If you weigh 160 lbs (73 kg), your total daily dose would be about 1.5 mg/day (20 mcg/kg x 73 kg). In that case, you might take 0.5 mg of dexamethasone, three times a day.

## SIDE EFFECTS OF PRENATAL TREATMENT

Prenatal treatment for CAH has generally been found to be safe for both mother and child. However, because it has only become available in the past decade, the oldest treated patients are just now reaching adolescence. Thus, the long-term effects of treatment are still unknown.

Concerns about prenatal therapy center on the fact that, with each pregnancy, there is only a 1 in 8 chance that the baby will be a girl with CAH. Conversely, this means that 7 out of 8 infants will not benefit from treatment.

### Effects on the Baby

Available information has not revealed a higher rate of birth defects in infants exposed to dexamethasone in the womb. Nor has it revealed a higher incidence of spontaneous abortion. Thus, by objective short-term measures, prenatal treatment of CAH appears to be safe for the child.

However, in some CAH children who have been treated prenatally, abnormalities of the brain, including hydrocephalus (excess fluid in the brain) and agenesis (lack) of a part of the brain called the corpus callosum, have been reported. Other studies suggest that treated children may have an increased tendency towards shyness and being withdrawn. Until further studies are done, involving large numbers of children, it will be difficult to tell whether these associations are coincidental or can be attributed to prenatal exposure to glucocorticoids.

### Effects on the Mother

One of the most common side effects in pregnant women treated with dexamethasone is excessive weight gain. Whereas most women typically gain twenty-five to thirty pounds during pregnancy, women taking dexamethasone gain an average of forty pounds or more. Other reported side effects are moodiness, insomnia, extreme hunger, acne, and the development of severe stretch marks across the abdomen. Whereas stretch marks normally occur as a result of rapid weight gain in a short period of time, in pregnant women treated with dexamethasone, they can appear even if weight gain is normal.

Prenatal dexamethasone treatment is also associated with hypertension (elevated blood pressure), diabetes mellitus (high blood sugar), and preeclampsia (a condition in pregnant women that is characterized by high blood pressure, protein in the urine, and swelling.) While these problems are usually transient, they can still damage the health of the mother. ***Thus, close monitoring of pregnant women during prenatal treatment of CAH is essential, as the side effects of dexamethasone can be quite severe in some women.***

## TESTING THE FETUS FOR CAH

Dexamethasone treatment is needed through the course of the entire pregnancy *only* if it is determined that you are carrying a female infant with CAH. If the infant is male, or a female *without* CAH, treatment can be stopped. When dexamethasone is stopped, it is weaned over several weeks.

To determine if the fetus has CAH, fetal cells or tissue must be obtained for genetic testing. This is done using either "chorionic villus sampling" (CVS) or amniocentesis.

Both CVS and amniocentesis carry some risk. When considering these procedures, it is important that you discuss all the potential risks and benefits with your physician, in order to make an informed decision.

### Chorionic Villus Sampling (CVS)

CVS involves inserting a small catheter (tube) into the vagina, through the cervix, and into the uterus of the pregnant mother. A small amount of the placenta (the chorionic villi) is then extracted. Because part of the placenta comes from the fetus, placental tissue contains fetal genes that can be used for testing.

CVS is generally performed between the ninth and eleventh week of pregnancy. In comparison with amniocentesis, the advantage of CVS is that information about the fetus can be obtained sooner. Thus, dexamethasone treatment can be stopped sooner, if it is determined that the baby is ***not*** a girl with CAH.

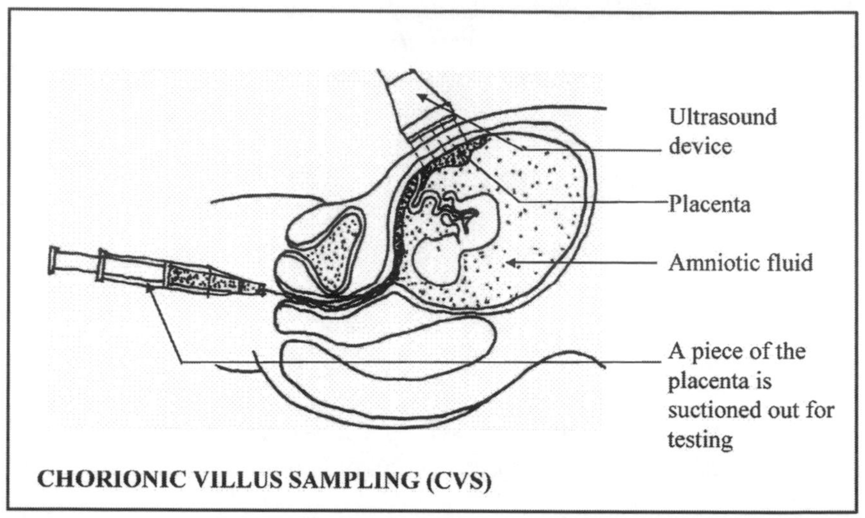


**CHORIONIC VILLUS SAMPLING (CVS)**

Similar to amniocentesis, the risks of CVS include miscarriage, bleeding, and infection. With CVS, however, the incidence of spontaneous abortion is higher. Limb defects, as a result of injury to the hands and feet of the fetus, have also been reported after CVS.

**Amniocentesis**

Amniocentesis is very commonly used to test for birth defects, even in routine pregnancies where CAH is not a concern. It involves taking a sample of amniotic fluid (the fluid which surrounds the fetus) from the womb. This fluid contains fetal cells, which are then used for testing.

Amniocentesis is performed by inserting a needle through the mother's abdomen into the fluid sac surrounding the baby. Ultrasound imaging is used as a guide. A sample of the amniotic fluid is extracted, then the needle withdrawn.

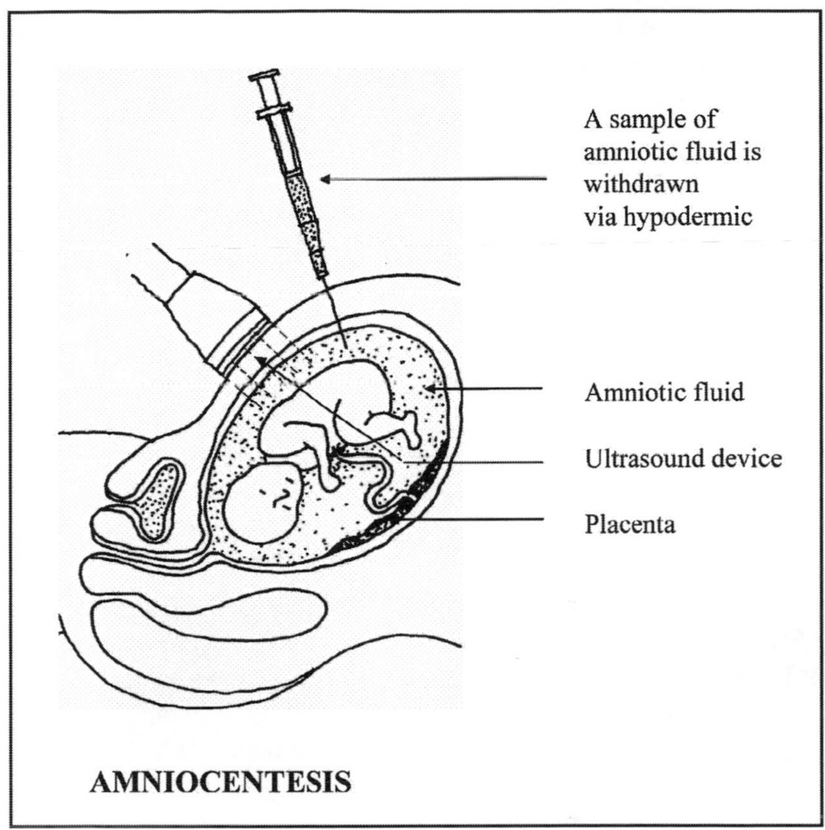


**AMNIOCENTESIS**

Amniocentesis is performed later in pregnancy than CVS, generally between the fifteenth and twentieth week of gestation. Because information about the baby cannot be obtained as quickly as with CVS, dexamethasone treatment will need to continue for a longer period of time, in the case of the baby who is found to be unaffected by CAH.

A larger sample of amniotic fluid can be obtained, than the amount of placental tissue gotten via CVS. Thus, one advantage of amniocentesis is that the fluid can also be tested for markers of other birth defects, such as alpha-fetoprotein. As with CVS, amniocentesis carries with it a risk of miscarriage, bleeding, and infection.

## PLANNING AHEAD FOR THE NEXT PREGNANCY

In order to fully understand the risks and benefits of prenatal treatment, prospective parents should consider genetic testing and counseling before the next pregnancy. In the event that a mother chooses to undergo prenatal therapy, dexamethasone treatment can then begin as early as possible. It is also recommended that a woman choosing prenatal treatment be followed by an obstetrician with experience in high-risk pregnancies.

♦♦♦

## WHAT YOU MAY BE CONCERNED ABOUT: FREQUENTLY ASKED QUESTIONS

♦ ***Will prenatal treatment prevent my child from having CAH?***

No. Treatment will only prevent or reduce genital masculinization in a girl with CAH. It will not prevent her from having CAH.

♦ ***My CAH son is not a salt-waster. Do I still need prenatal treatment?***

Masculinization of the genitalia in CAH girls can occur even if there is no salt-wasting. To fully assess the pros and cons of treatment, as it applies to your particular situation, it is best to speak with a genetic counselor.

♦ ***Is prenatal treatment effective for all types of CAH?***

Most studies on prenatal dexamethasone treatment have involved infants with 21-hydroxylase deficiency. There is less experience with dexamethasone treatment in 11-hydroxylase deficiency, although some successful outcomes have also been reported. Excess androgen production, leading to masculinization of the female genitalia, is generally associated with these two most common types of CAH.

Other less common types of CAH, such as 3-beta dehydrogenase deficiency, do not involve the excess production of androgens. Because severe masculinization of the genitalia is not a problem with these types of CAH, prenatal treatment is generally not warranted.

♦ ***Because dexamethasone suppresses fetal androgen production, can boys who have been exposed to prenatal treatment end up with under-virilized genitalia?***

Male genital development is mostly dependent on the testosterone that is made by the testicles. Because dexamethasone suppresses the activity of the adrenal glands, not the testicles, the male genitals should develop normally, even if you take dexamethasone during pregnancy.

♦ ***In some types of CAH, such as 3-beta deficiency, male under-virilization occurs because the adrenal glands do not make enough testosterone. What is the difference between that and suppressing testosterone production via prenatal dexamethasone treatment?***

With 3-beta dehydrogenase deficiency, the ability to produce testosterone in the testicles is also compromised. This lack of testosterone from the testicles is what results in male genital under-development.

♦ ***What if it is the mother who has CAH? Will excess testosterone from a mother with CAH result in masculinization of the fetus in the womb?***

If mothers are taking androgens or have androgen-producing conditions, like under-treated CAH or certain forms of ovarian tumors, female infants can be born masculinized.

♦ ***Should women with CAH, who normally take hydrocortisone to treat their own CAH, switch over to dexamethasone when they become pregnant?***

Not necessarily. Dexamethasone is used in prenatal treatment because it crosses the placenta to affect the developing fetus. However, if the baby's father has been genetically tested and found not to be a carrier of CAH, then the child will not have CAH. In that case—because the long-term effects of prenatal treatment are still unknown—the mother who has CAH herself may wish to remain on hydrocortisone, specifically because it does not cross the placenta and will not affect the baby.

♦ ***What should I do if I forget a dose of dexamethasone?***

Take the missed dose as soon as you remember it. Then, take the next dose at the regularly scheduled time. If it is close to the time of your next dose, just take the next scheduled dose.

♦ ***Is it painful to undergo either an amniocentesis or CVS?***

Both these procedures are generally painless. However, you may experience slight cramping and spotting, after either an amniocentesis or CVS.

♦ ***If the amnio or CVS shows that my baby does NOT have CAH, can I switch from dexamethasone to hydrocortisone during the weaning period, so as not to expose the baby to prenatal treatment for any longer than absolutely necessary?***

While theoretically possible, it may be difficult to know what dose of hydrocortisone to substitute for the dexamethasone. Miscalculating the dose can be harmful or result in undesirable side effects. Thus, there may be as much risk in switching medication "midstream" as there is in staying the course with the same medication. This underscores the need to understand all the potential risks and benefits of prenatal therapy prior to undergoing treatment.

♦ ***My doctor is also suggesting a FISH test. Can you tell me what this is?***

FISH stands for "Fluorescent in situ Hybridization." With a FISH test, you will be able to know the sex of your unborn child much more quickly than you will with either an amniocentesis or CVS, usually within a few days. Thus, dexamethasone treatment can be stopped much sooner if it is found that the baby is a boy.

A FISH test is done using the same tissue that is extracted during the amnio or CVS. To determine if the baby has CAH, you will still need to wait for the results of the amnio or CVS.

♦♦♦

# Epilogue

***By C. Y. Hsu***

Parents often ask if their child can lead a normal life with CAH. Are our lives today "normal?" Well, yes and no.

***

Nick was in the first grade when he was diagnosed with CAH. He is now almost twelve years old and in middle school. A lot has happened in the last five years.

The first year after his diagnosis was nothing if not a wild roller-coaster ride. We went through periods of under-suppression where Nick suffered terrible mood swings. His behavior was unpredictable and he often complained of headaches and neck aches. In a span of less than six months, we switched doctors, and then switched back again. Twice, we sought out a child psychologist. The second time, we almost let ourselves be talked into putting Nick on an anti-depressant. In my heart, I felt his erratic behavior had to do with his doses of medication, but I had no way of proving it. I was sure we had entered a purgatory where we would be damned if we treated him and damned if we didn't.

Then, miraculously, the problems with the under-suppression were straightened out, and there followed a period of over-suppression. The signs were subtle, at first, but when I look back at pictures now, I can see the unmistakable roundness in Nick's face and the puffy cheeks. The boy who had always been a slender, lithe natural athlete suddenly started thinking of himself as chubby. It seemed like we were shopping for new clothes every other week.

But somehow we managed to get through that, too. Now, more than five years after starting treatment for CAH, Nick is doing wonderfully. He is extremely healthy and has never had a crisis, and by treading that fine line between under-suppression and over-suppression, his height prognosis has improved significantly since diagnosis.

Sometimes, I find myself trying to understand this strange dichotomy. Nick takes medicine every day. He has a standing order at the hospital for blood and urine tests. He wears a *MedicAlert* bracelet. He was in the hospital twice for fluids after vomitting. Yet, without these clues, it would be impossible to guess that he is anything but completely healthy.

He is a talented athlete, who is well known in youth sports circles around town. In the summer, he is an all-star baseball player; in the winter, an all-star basketball player. His dream is to be a pitcher for the Boston Red Sox when he grows up.

He is an "A" student and in the Academically Talented program at school. He is particularly good in math. When he was nine, he was the chess champion of his fourth-grade class.

He is the class heartthrob. Some days, the phone rings off the hook with giggling admirers. In a racially mixed and economically diverse student body, he gets along well with everyone.

At home, he is spirited and exuberant. He plays the drums and loves rap music. He is kind to babies and small children. He laughs and cries with equal ease. He seems to be a happy child.

***

Five years ago, it seemed that life could never approach normalcy again, but with time, it *has* gotten easier. You *can* learn to co-exist peacefully with CAH, but you need to be your child's advocate and you need to have proper care and treatment. You also need to respect the seriousness of the medical condition without letting it own your child. Admittedly, striking that delicate balance is not always easy.

So, yes, I do think it is possible to have CAH and live a "normal" life. With care, vigilance, and—perhaps—a little bit of luck, it may even be possible to be a little bit extraordinary.

♦♦♦

***I wish to thank my co-author, Dr. Scott Rivkees, for making this book possible and for taking such miraculous care of Nick.***

# Appendix

*The authors do not specifically endorse any organization, website, or publication included in this appendix. They are listed for the reader's convenience only. While every attempt has been made to make sure that the information is up-to-date and accurate, readers should also be aware that names, addresses, and telephone numbers are subject to change, without notice.*

# PATIENT RESOURCES

## SUPPORT GROUPS

- ***Addison's Support Forum***
  <www.healinglight.com/cgi-bin/addisons.pl>

- ***Adrenal Hyperplasia Network (UK)***
  <www.ahn.org.uk/>

- ***Bodies Like Ours***
  <www.bodieslikeours.org>

- ***CAH Sisters***
  <http://health.groups.yahoo.com/group/CAHSISTERS2/>

- ***CARES (Congenital Adrenal Hyperplasia Research and Education) Foundation Inc.***
  1-973-912-3895 (in New Jersey)
  1-866-227-3737 (toll free out-of-state)
  <www.caresfoundation.org>

- ***Climb Congenital Adrenal Hyperplasia UK Support Group***
  <www.cah.org.uk/>

- ***Congenital Adrenal Hyperplasia Education and Support Network***
  <www.congenitaladrenalhyperplasia.org>

- ***Congenital Adrenal Hyperplasia Support Group Australia Inc.***
  <http://home.vicnet.net.au/~cahsga/>

- ***Hope Oasis***
  <http://www.hopeoasis.org>

- ***Magic Foundation***
  1-708-383-0899
  <www.magicfoundation.org>

- ***Intersex Society of North America***
  1-206-663-6077
  <www.isna.org>

- ***Late-onset CAH Message Board***
  <www.members4.boardhost.com/LOCAH/>

## OTHER ORGANIZATIONS

- ***Endocrine Society***
  <http://www.endo-society.org/>

- ***Lawson Wilkins Pediatric Endocrine Society***
  <http://www.lwpes.org/>

- ***National Adrenal Diseases Foundation***
  1-516-487-4992
  <medhelp.org/www/nadf.htm>

- ***National Center for Biotechnology Information***
  <http://www.ncbi.nlm.nih.gov/Omim/>

- ***National Organization of Rare Diseases (NORD)***
  <http://www.rarediseases.org/>

- ***Pediatric Endocrine Nursing Society***
  <http://www.pens.org/>

- ***PENS (Pediatric Endocrine Nursing Society) Bulletin Board***
  <http://www.pens.org/wwwboard/wwwboard.html>

- ***Rare Genetic Diseases in Children***
  <http://www.med.nyu.edu/rgdc/homenew.htm>

## ONLINE PUBLICATIONS

- ***Congenital Adrenal Hyperplasia***
  Emedicine
  <http://www.emedicine.com/ped/topic48.htm>

- ***Congenital Adrenal Hyperplasia: Not Really a Zebra***
  American Family Physicians
  http://www.aafp.org/afp/990301ap/1190.html

- ***Disorders of Puberty***
  American Family Physicians
  http://www.aafp.org/afp/990700ap/209.html

- ***Sick Kids***
  http://www.sickkids.ca/childphysiology/

- ***Technical Report: Congenital Adrenal Hyperplasia***
  American Academy of Pediatrics
  <http://www.aap.org/policy/re0027.html>

- ***Your Child With Congenital Adrenal Hyperplasia***
  Dr. Gary Warne, Royal Children's Hospital
  Victoria, Australia
  <http://www.rch.unimelb.edu.au/cah_book/index.cfm?doc_id=137 5>

## OTHER SOURCES OF ONLINE INFORMATION

- ***BioMedNet***
  <http://www.bmn.com>

- ***Emedicine***
  <http://www.emedicine.com>

- ***PubMed***
  <http://www.ncbi.nlm.nih.gov/entrez/query.fcgi?db=PubMed>

## FINDING A DOCTOR

- ***American Medical Association***
  <http://www.ama-assn.org/aps/amahg.htm>

- ***CARES Foundation***
  1-973-912-3895 (in New Jersey)
  1-866-227-3737 (toll free out-of-state)
  <www.caresfoundation.org>

- ***WebMDHealth***
  <http://my.webmd.com/find_a_phys/doctor>

- ***The Best Doctors in America***
  Woodward/White, Inc., Aiken, SC

- ***Directory of Physicians in the United States***
  American Medical Association, Chicago, IL

- ***Folio Medical Directory***
  Folio Associates, Hyannis, MA

- ***How to Find the Best Doctors***
  Castle Connolly Ltd., New York, NY

- ***Official ABMS Directory of Board Certified Medical Specialists***
  Elsevier Science, St. Louis, MO

## INSTRUCTIONS FOR GIVING A *SOLU-CORTEF* INJECTION

- ***Patient Information Publications***
  Warren Grant Magnuson Clinical Center
  National Institute of Health
  <www.cc.nih.gov/ccc/patient_education/pepubs/mngadrins.pdf>

- ***Pediatric Endocrine Nursing Society***
  <http://www.pens.org/educationmaterial.html>

## MEDICAL ALERT TAGS

- ***Cody Cares ID, Inc.***
  1-317-783-7702
  *<http://www.codycaresid.com/>*

- ***Lauren's Hope***
  1-800-360-8680
  <http://www.laurenshope.com/>

- ***MedicAlert Foundation International***
  1-888-633-4298
  <http://medicalert.com>

- ***Safety Sport ID, Inc.***
  1-866-830-8243
  <http://www.safetysportid.com>

## OTHER USEFUL MEDICAL PRODUCTS

- ***Baxa Corporation***
  1-800-567-2292
  <http://baxa.com>

- ***The Bedwetting Store***
  1-800-214-9605
  <http://www.bedwettingstore.com/watches-diurnalenuresis.htm>

- ***Epill.com***
  1-800-549-0095
  <www.epill.com>

- ***Fifty 50 Pharmacy***
  1-800-746-7505
  <http://www.fifty50.com/>

## GENE TESTING LABS

- ***ARUP Labs***
  500 Chipeta Way
  Salt Lake City, UT 84108
  1-800-242-2787
  http://www.aruplab.com/guides/clt/tests/clt_a164.htm

- ***Center for Genetic Testing***
  6465 S. Yale Avenue
  Tulsa, OK 74136
  1-866-846-0315
  918-502-1725
  www.saintfrancisgenetics.com

- ***Chapman Institute of Medical Genetics***
  4502 E. 41st St.
  Tulsa, OK 74135
  1-800-299-7919
  <http://genetics.hillcrest.com/>

- ***Comprehensive Genetic Services***
  3720 North 124th Street
  Milwaukee, WI 53222
  1-877-COMPGENE
  <http://www.compgene.com>

- ***Mount Sinai Medical Center***
  1 Gustave Levy Place
  Box 1198
  Annenberg, 17th Floor, Rm. 271
  New York, NY 10029
  212-241-7962
  www.marianew.com/Laboratory

- ***Quest Diagnostics***
  33608 Ortega Highway
  San Juan Capistrano, CA 92690
  949-728-4000
  www.questdiagnostics.com

- ***University of Pittsburgh***
  E1651 Genetics Education and Counseling Program
  Biomedical Science Tower
  Pittsburgh, PA 15213
  <http://www.pitt.edu/~edugene/>

## NEWBORN SCREENING LABORATORIES AND INFORMATION

- ***National Newborn Screening and Genetics Resource Center (GNSRUS)***
  1912 West Anderson Lane, Suite 210
  Austin, TX 78757
  1-512-454-6419
  <http://genes-r-us.uthscsa.edu/index.htm>

- ***Pediatrix Screening***
  P.O. Box 219
  Bridgeville, PA 15017
  1-866-463-6436
  <http://www.pediatrixscreening.com>

- ***Save Babies Through Screening***
  <http://www.savebabies.org/>

## BODY SURFACE AREA CALCULATORS

- ***<www.halls.md/body-surface-area/bsa.htm>***

- ***<http://medicine.ucsd.edu/cystinosis/bodysurf.htm>***

- ***<http://www-users.med.cornell.edu/~spon/picu/calc/bsacalc.htm>***

## BLOOD PRESSURE TABLES

- ***<http://www.nhlbi.nih.gov/health/prof/heart/hbp/hbp_ped.pdf>***

## INSTRUCTIONS FOR SCHOOLS AND OTHER CAREGIVERS:

RE: ________________________________ DOB: ______________

The individual named herein has a medical condition called **CONGENITAL ADRENAL HYPERPLASIA (CAH)**. S/he is unable to properly make the stress hormone "cortisol." When ill, special precautions need to be taken to safeguard his/her health (see below). Failure to do so can result in circulatory collapse, coma, shock, or death.

1. **In event of fever:**

   >101° F (38.3° C): Give ______ mg HCT/PRED/DEX orally. Repeat every ____ hrs.
   >102° F (38.9° C): Give ______ mg HCT/PRED/DEX orally. Repeat every ____ hrs.

   Also give OTC fever-reducer (*Tylenol*, *Advil*, etc.).

2. **In event of mild vomiting and/or diarrhea; unexplained dizziness, headache, or excessive tiredness:**

   Give _____ mg HCT/PRED/DEX orally. If symptoms persist, but individual remains alert and is able to take oral medications, repeat dose every _____ hours.

3. **If vomiting and/or diarrhea is severe; if individual cannot retain oral medications; or shows signs of dehydration (e.g., parched lips, lack of urination):**

   Mix and administer 100 mg *Solu-Cortef* (hydrocortisone succinate). Give via intramuscular injection. Phone doctor's office and be prepared to transport individual to hospital Emergency Room.

4. **If symptoms get worse:**

   Call 911 and have individual transported to hospital. Repeat intramuscular injection every 6 hours, until treatment is given at hospital.

5. **In event of serious physical injury or trauma resulting in severe bleeding or loss of consciousness; or if individual is unresponsive or appears dazed and confused:**

   Give *Solu-Cortef* injection *immediately*. Call EMS (911) and have individual transported to hospital. *Note: Do not delay giving Solu-Cortef in anticipation of treatment by EMS.* Give EMS accompanying letter "Guidelines for Stress Treatment in Hospital."

**Doctor Signature:**______________________________**Date:** ____________
**Doctor Name (Printed):** ________________________________________
**Phone:** ____________________________**Beeper:** __________________

## GUIDELINES FOR STRESS TREATMENT IN HOSPITAL

Individuals with CONGENITAL ADRENAL HYPERPLASIA (CAH) can develop adrenal insufficiency with illness and need stress-coverage with illness, trauma, or emergency surgery.

| GUIDELINES FOR STRESS TREATMENT IN HOSPITAL | | |
|---|---|---|
| **Treatment** | **Initial Dose** | **Follow-up Dose** |
| Hydrocortisone: *Solu-Cortef* | <50 lbs: 50 mg<br>>50 lbs: 100 mg<br>>150 lb: 200 mg | 100 $mg/m^2/day$. Give doses every 6 hrs |
| Intravenous fluids | 20-30 ml/kg of normal saline (0.9% NaCl);<br><br>May need to be repeated. | 5% dextrose and ½ normal saline (D5, ½ NS);<br><br>1500-3000 $mg/m^2/day$ |
| *All treatment to be delivered intravenously. Consultation with an endocrinologist is recommended.* | | |

## LETTER FOR AIRLINES AND OTHER SECURITY PERSONNEL

**TO WHOM IT MAY CONCERN:**

**RE:** ________________________________ **DOB:** _______________

The individual named herein has a medical condition called CONGENITAL ADRENAL HYPERPLASIA (CAH). In the event of illness, this patient may require treatment with a medication called *Solu-Cortef*. Failure to give *Solu-Cortef*, in an emergency, can result in circulatory collapse, coma, shock, or death.

*Solu-Cortef* must be given via injection. Thus, it is necessary for this patient to carry supplies, including a hypodermic needle and syringe. As the physician of record, I certify that these items are needed for a medical purpose.

If you have any questions, please do not hesitate to contact me at the numbers listed below. Thank you for your cooperation.

**Doctor Signature:** ________________________ **Date:** ____________

**Doctor Name (Printed):** ____________________________________

**Hospital/Institution Affiliation:** ______________________________

**Doctor Phone:** ___________________ **Beeper:** __________________

## MEDICATION SCHEDULE/ EMERGENCY PHONE NUMBERS

**Name**________________________ **Home Phone**____________________

**Address**____________________________________________

**Directions**__________________________________________

**Work #1** ________________________ **Cell #1**____________________

**Work #2** ________________________ **Cell #2**____________________

| MEDICATION SCHEDULE | | | | |
|---|---|---|---|---|
| **Name** | **D.O.B.** | **Condition Treated** | **Medication Name** | **Dose/Time given** |
| | | | | |
| | | | | |
| | | | | |
| | | | | |

| EMERGENCY PHONE NUMBERS | |
|---|---|
| **Name / Relationship** | **Phone Number** |
| Police/Fire/EMS | **911** |
| Pediatrician | |
| Pediatric Endocrinologist | |
| Dentist | |
| | |
| | |
| | |
| | |

In event of an emergency, I give permission for minor children to be transported to hospital and treated by emergency medical services.

**Parent Signature:** ____________________________ **Date:** _________

## PARENT RIGHTS UNDER SECTION 504

Section 504 of the Rehabilitation Act provides services for students identified as having a disability as defined by the Act, which substantially limits a major life activity. You have the following rights:

1. the right to be informed of your rights under Section 504 of the Rehabilitation Act

2. the right for your child to have equal opportunities to participate in academic, non-academic, and extracurricular activities in your school

3. the right to be notified about referral, evaluation, and programs for your child

4. the right for your child to be evaluated fairly

5. the right, if eligible for services under 504, for your child to receive accommodations, modifications, and related services that will meet his or her needs as well as the needs of students without disabilities are met

6. the right for your child to be educated with peers who do not have disabilities as much as possible

7. the right to an impartial hearing if you disagree with the school regarding your child's educational program

8. the right to review and obtain copies of your child's school records

9. the right to request attorney fees related to securing your rights under Section 504

10. the right to request changes in the educational program of your child

**Parent Signature:** ________________________ **Date:** _______________

**School Representative:** ____________________ **Date:** _______________

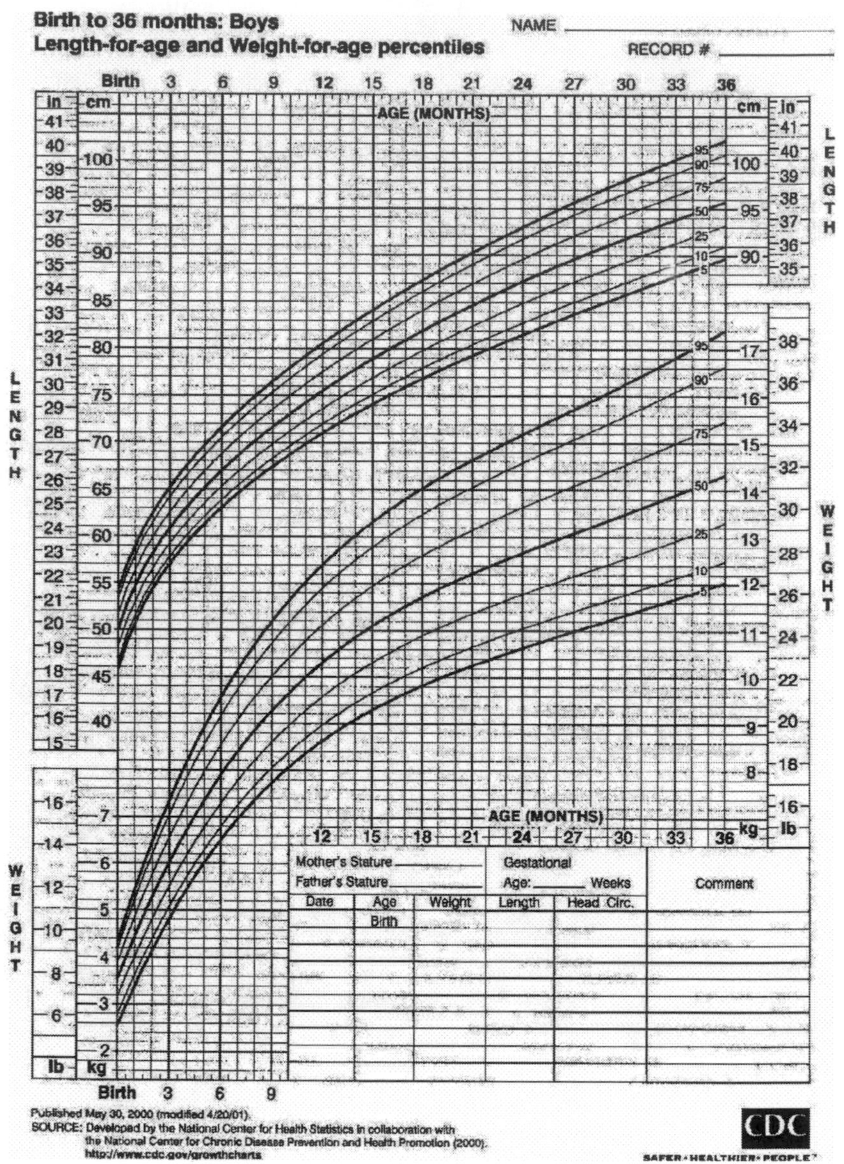
Birth to 36 months: Boys
Length-for-age and Weight-for-age percentiles
NAME
RECORD #
Birth 3 6 9 12 15 18 21 24 27 30 33 36
AGE (MONTHS)
LENGTH
WEIGHT
in
cm
lb
kg
95
90
75
50
25
10
5
Mother's Stature
Father's Stature
Gestational
Age: Weeks
Date
Age
Weight
Length
Head Circ.
Comment
Birth
Published May 30, 2000 (modified 4/20/01).
SOURCE: Developed by the National Center for Health Statistics in collaboration with
the National Center for Chronic Disease Prevention and Health Promotion (2000).
http://www.cdc.gov/growthcharts
CDC
SAFER·HEALTHIER·PEOPLE

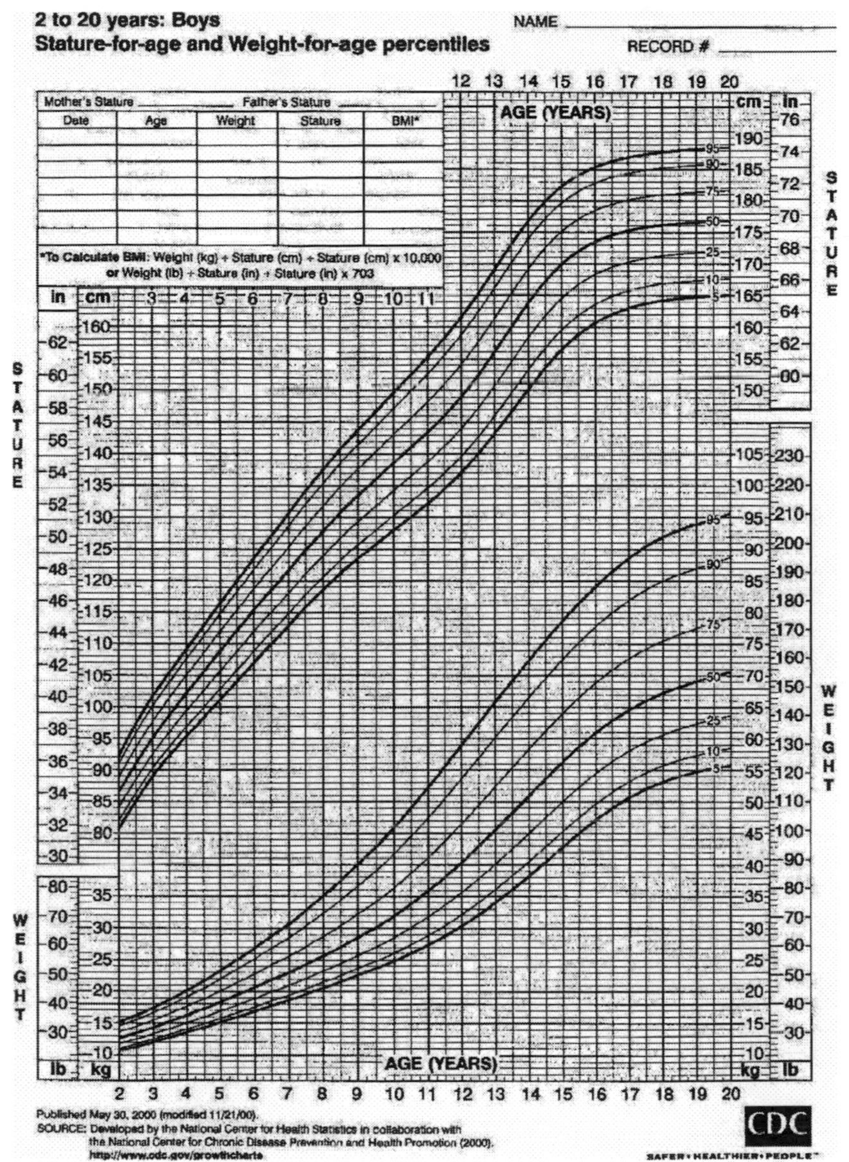
2 to 20 years: Boys
Stature-for-age and Weight-for-age percentiles
NAME
RECORD #
Mother's Stature
Father's Stature
Date
Age
Weight
Stature
BMI*
*To Calculate BMI: Weight (kg) ÷ Stature (cm) ÷ Stature (cm) x 10,000
or Weight (lb) ÷ Stature (in) ÷ Stature (in) x 703
AGE (YEARS)
STATURE
WEIGHT
Published May 30, 2000 (modified 11/21/00).
SOURCE: Developed by the National Center for Health Statistics in collaboration with
the National Center for Chronic Disease Prevention and Health Promotion (2000).
http://www.cdc.gov/growthcharts
CDC
SAFER • HEALTHIER • PEOPLE

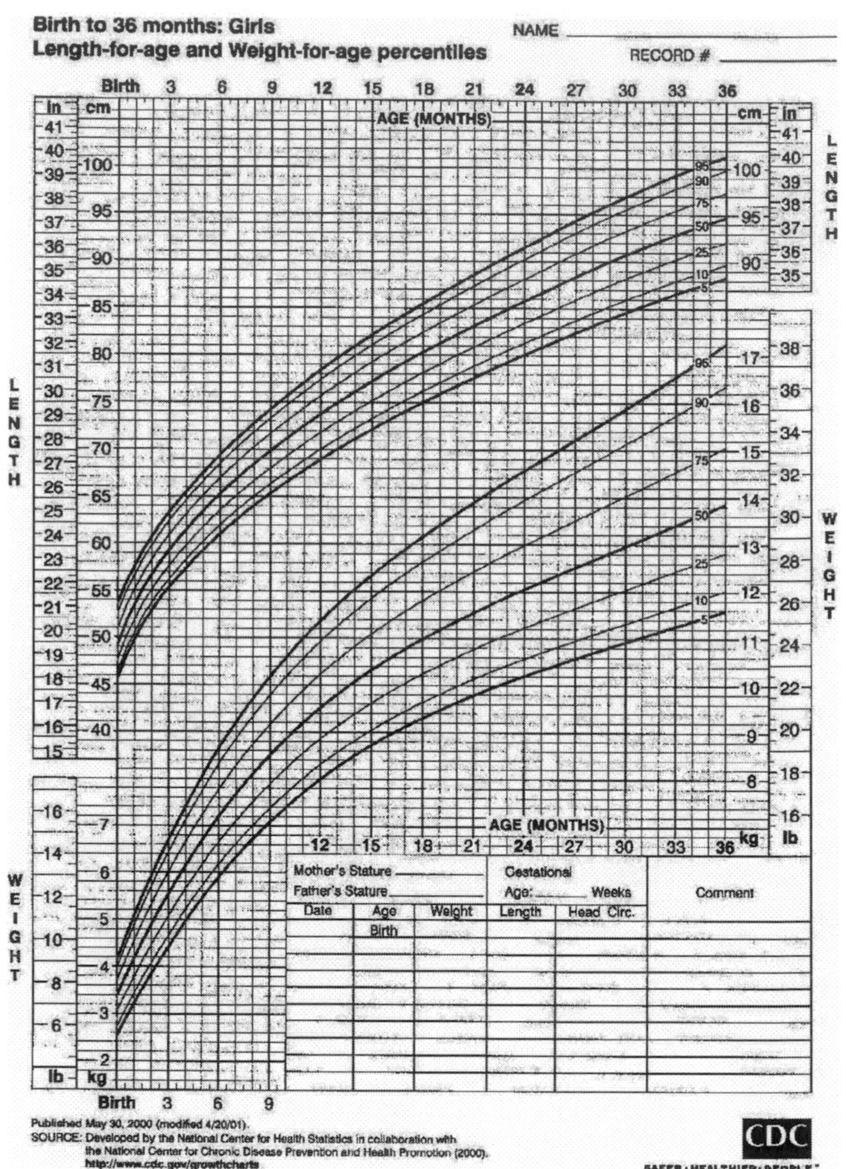
Birth to 36 months: Girls
Length-for-age and Weight-for-age percentiles
NAME
RECORD #
AGE (MONTHS)
LENGTH
WEIGHT
Mother's Stature
Father's Stature
Gestational Age: Weeks
Date
Age
Weight
Length
Head Circ.
Comment
Birth
Published May 30, 2000 (modified 4/20/01).
SOURCE: Developed by the National Center for Health Statistics in collaboration with the National Center for Chronic Disease Prevention and Health Promotion (2000).
http://www.cdc.gov/growthcharts
CDC
SAFER · HEALTHIER · PEOPLE™

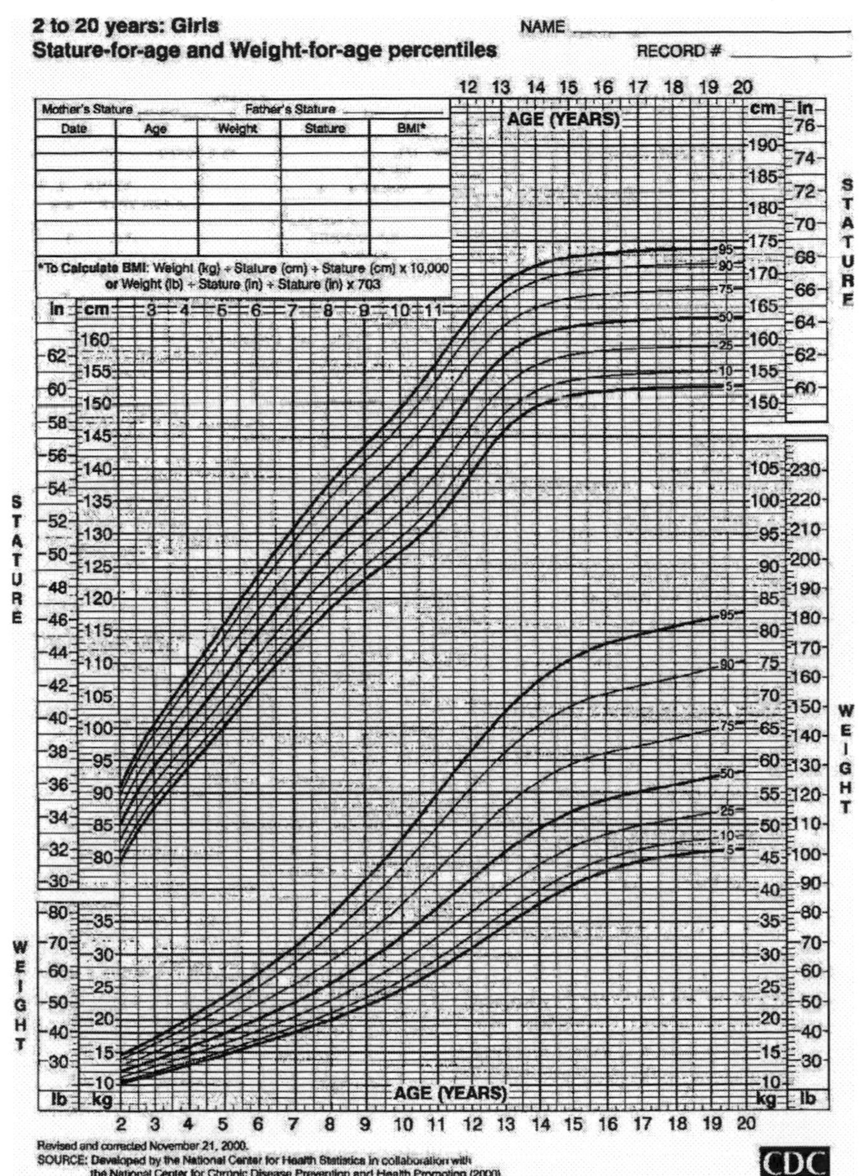
2 to 20 years: Girls
Stature-for-age and Weight-for-age percentiles
NAME
RECORD #
Mother's Stature
Father's Stature
Date
Age
Weight
Stature
BMI*
*To Calculate BMI: Weight (kg) ÷ Stature (cm) ÷ Stature (cm) x 10,000
or Weight (lb) ÷ Stature (in) ÷ Stature (in) x 703
AGE (YEARS)
STATURE
WEIGHT
in
cm
lb
kg
Revised and corrected November 21, 2000.
SOURCE: Developed by the National Center for Health Statistics in collaboration with
the National Center for Chronic Disease Prevention and Health Promotion (2000).
http://www.cdc.gov/growthcharts
CDC

# Glossary

Adapted from <http://www.genome.gov/page.cfm?pageID=10002096>; <http://arbl.cvmbs.colostate.edu/hbooks/glossary.html>; and Mosby's Medical Encyclopedia, Penguin Putnam, Inc., New York, NY.

**17-hydroxyprogesterone:** A steroid hormone that is a precursor to cortisol.

**17-ketosteroids:** The urinary metabolites of androgens.

**acute:** Having a short and relatively severe course.

**Addison's disease:** A life-threatening disease caused by partial or complete failure of the adrenal glands. Addison's disease results in a deficiency of all the adrenal steroids, including mineralocorticoids, glucocorticoids, and androgens.

**adrenal cortex:** The outer part of the adrenal gland. The adrenal cortex produces mineralocorticoids, glucocorticoids, and androgens.

**adrenal crisis:** A sudden life-threatening state brought on by the lack of an adrenal hormone.

**adrenal glands:** A pair of hormone-producing organs located near the kidneys.

**adrenal hyperplasia, congenital:** A group of inherited disorders characterized by the inability to synthesize cortisol. The disorder begins early in gestation and is present at birth.

**adrenal medulla:** The inner part of the adrenal gland. The adrenal medulla produces the hormones *epinephrine* and *norepinephrine*.

**adrenalectomy:** Surgical removal of one or both adrenal glands, or a part of the glands.

**adrenaline:** A trade name for the hormone *epinephrine*.

**adrenocorticotropic hormone (ACTH):** A hormone secreted from the pituitary gland that stimulates secretion of glucocorticoids from the adrenal glands.

**aldosterone:** A steroid hormone produced by the adrenal cortex that participates in control of sodium, potassium, and water balance.

**allele:** One of the variant forms of a gene on a chromosome. Different alleles produce variation in inherited characteristics such as hair color or blood type. In an individual, one form of the allele (the dominant one) may be expressed more than another form (the recessive one).

**amino acid:** A building block of proteins. There are 20 common amino acids found in proteins.

**amniocentesis:** Removal of a small amount of fluid in the womb during pregnancy to test for birth defects and the sex of a fetus.

**androgen:** A class of steroid hormone that increases male physical characteristics.

**androstenedione:** An androgen. The precursor hormone of testosterone.

**angiotensin:** A hormone produced by the kidney that causes blood vessels to tighten.

**autoimmune:** Referring to conditions in which the body attacks itself.

**autosome:** Any chromosome other than a sex chromosome. Humans have twenty-two pairs of autosomes.

**base pair:** Two bases which form a "rung of the DNA ladder." A DNA nucleotide is made of a molecule of sugar, a molecule of phosphoric acid, and a molecule called a base. The bases are the "letters" that spell out the genetic code. In DNA, the code letters are A, T, G, and C, which stand for the chemicals adenine, thymidine, guanine, and cytosine, respectively. In base pairing, adenine always pairs with thymidine, and guanine always pairs with cytosine.

**bioavailability:** The amount of taken medication that is absorbed.

**carrier:** An individual who possesses one copy of a defective allele that causes disease only when two copies are present. Although carriers not affected by the disease, two carriers can produce a child who has the disease.

**catheter:** A thin flexible tube inserted into the body to permit introduction or withdrawal of fluids or to keep a passageway open.

**chorionic villus sampling (CVS):** A procedure used in early pregnancy to obtain fetal tissue. Commonly, a sample of the placenta is withdrawn using a catheter inserted through the uterus.

**chronic:** Persisting over a long period of time.

**circadian:** Pertaining to a period of a day. Circadian rhythms are daily rhythms.

**clitoris:** The female sexual organ that corresponds to the male penis. The clitoris is a pea-shaped projection made up of nerves, blood vessels, and erect tissue.

**clitoroplasty:** Surgery performed on the clitoris.

**confluence:** The coming together of two parts.

**contrast**: A dye used in x-ray studies.

***Cortef*:** Trade name for a synthetic form of hydrocortisone.

**congenital:** Present at birth, as in a congenital defect.

**corticosteroid:** Another name for a glucocorticoid. A type of steroid hormone synthesized and secreted from the adrenal cortex.

**corticotropin:** Another name for adrenocorticotropic hormone (ACTH).

**corticotropin-releasing hormone (CRH):** A hormone secreted by the hypothalamus that stimulates secretion of adrenocorticotropic hormone from the pituitary gland.

**cortisol:** A steroid hormone produced by the adrenal cortex that participates in control of blood glucose concentration as well as several other processes.

**cushingoid:** exhibiting the physical characteristics of someone with hypercortisolism (too much cortisol).

**Cushing's disease:** An endocrine disease also called hyperadrenocorticism, resulting from an excess of glucocorticoids (cortisol).

**cystoscopy:** A procedure in which a tube is used to look into the bladder.

**deletion:** A particular kind of mutation: loss of a piece of DNA from a chromosome. Deletion of a gene or part of a gene can lead to a disease or abnormality.

**deoxyribonucleic acid (DNA):** The chemical inside the nucleus of a cell that carries the genetic instructions for making living organisms.

**dexamethasone:** A synthetic substitute for cortisol. Dexamethasone is more potent and has a longer duration of action than cortisol.

**dilation**: Expanding the size of an opening.

**distal:** The far part of a structure.

**diurnal:** Occurring during the day.

**DNA sequencing:** Determining the exact order of the base pairs in a segment of DNA.

**DNA testing:** The technology of using DNA to differentiate one individual from another.

**efficacy:** Capacity for producing the desired result or effect. A drug that cures a particular disease has efficacy for treating that disease and is efficacious.

**emulsion:** A preparation of one liquid distributed as small globules in another liquid; for example, oil droplets in water.

**endocrine:** The activity of a hormone or growth factors that circulates in blood, and binds to and affect cells distant from the source of secretion.

**endocrinology:** The study of the endocrine system or hormones.

**endoscope:** A tube used to look inside the body.

**enzyme:** A protein that causes a biochemical reaction.

**epinephrine:** A hormone secreted from the adrenal medulla in response to various stressors.

**epiphyses:** The growth center of bones.

**exon:** The region of a gene responsible for producing the gene's protein. Each exon codes for a specific portion of the complete protein.

**fistula**: An abnormal passage or connection leading from inside the body to the skin.

***Florinef*:** A trade name for fludrocortisone.

**fludrocortisone:** A synthetic aldosterone.

**follicle-stimulating hormone (FSH):** A hormone secreted from the pituitary gland that controls several aspects of reproductive function.

**fusion**: The joining of two structures.

**gene:** The functional and physical unit of heredity passed from parent to offspring. Genes are pieces of DNA that contain the information for making a specific protein.

**gene therapy**: An evolving technique used to treat inherited diseases. The medical procedure involves either replacing, manipulating, or supplementing nonfunctional genes with healthy genes.

**genitogram**: An x-ray study to look at the reproductive system.

**genome:** All the DNA contained in an organism or a cell.

**glucocorticoid:** A type of steroid hormone synthesized and secreted from the adrenal cortex. The major glucocorticoid in most animals is cortisol.

**gluconeogenesis:** A metabolic process in which proteins and fats are converted to glucose. Occurs predominantly in the liver and, to a lesser extent, in the kidney.

**glucose:** A simple sugar that serves as a major fuel source for cells.

**gonad:** A gland that releases ovum or sperm, such as the ovary or testis.

**gonadotropin:** A term used to describe luteinizing and follicle-stimulating hormones, hormones secreted from the pituitary gland that control several aspects of reproductive function.

**gonadotropin-releasing hormone:** A hormone secreted from the hypothalamus that stimulates secretion of the gonadotropins luteinizing hormone and follicle-stimulating hormone from the anterior pituitary gland.

**growth hormone:** A protein hormone secreted from the anterior pituitary that has potent metabolic and growth-promoting activities.

**heterozygous:** Possessing two different forms of a particular gene, one inherited from each parent.

**homozygous:** Possessing two identical forms of a particular gene, one inherited from each parent.

**hormone:** A chemical messenger that binds to receptors on target cells, which leads to some change in that cells physiologic state.

**hydrocortisone:** A synonym for the hormone cortisol.

**hyperglycemia:** Abnormally high level of glucose in the blood.

**hyperkalemia:** Abnormally high level of potassium in the blood.

**hypernatremia:** Abnormally high level of sodium in the blood.

**hyperplasia:** An increase in number of cells (rather than cell size); often associated with an increase in organ size.

**hypo-:** Prefix meaning *below* or *deficient*. Hypotension is the condition of blood pressure below normal.

**hypoglycemia:** Abnormally low level of glucose in the blood.

**hypokalemia:** Abnormally low level of potassium in the blood.

**hyponatremia:** Abnormally low level of sodium in the blood.

**hypospadias:** An inherited defect in which the urinary opening is on the underside of the penis.

**hypothalamus:** A portion of the brain that activates, controls, and integrates part of the nervous system, endocrine processes, and many bodily functions.

**hypothermia:** A condition in which body temperature becomes dangerously low.

**hypovolemic:** Having an abnormally low circulating blood volume.

**idiopathic:** Of unknown cause. An idiopathic disease is one for which the cause has not been determined.

**implantation:** The first intimate association of the embryo with maternal tissue. The first step in the process of placentation.

**in vitro:** Outside of a living system. Literally means *in glass*, although in most laboratories today, in vitro reactions take place in plastic vessels. For example, in vitro fertilization is fertilization outside the body or test tube fertilization. Opposite of in vivo.

**in vivo:** Within the living body. An in vivo reaction occurs within a living organism. Opposite of in vitro.

**ingestion:** The act of taking food or other materials into the mouth.

**inherited:** Transmitted through genes from parents to offspring.

**insertion:** A type of chromosomal abnormality in which a DNA sequence is inserted into a gene, disrupting the normal structure and function of that gene.

**insulin:** A protein hormone produced by the pancreas that has important effects in regulation of carbohydrate and lipid metabolism.

**inter-:** Prefix meaning *between*. An intercellular substance is between cells.

**intersex:** A term used to describe conditions in which the reproductive structures are not typically male or female.

**intra-:** Prefix meaning *within* or *inside*. An intracellular structure is inside a cell.

**intramuscular:** In a muscle.

**intravenous:** In a vein.

**intron:** A piece of DNA that has no function.

**jaundice:** A yellow discoloration of mucous membranes and skin due to high concentrations of bilirubin in blood and tissues. The same as icterus.

**jaundice, neonatal:** A type of jaundice commonly seen in infants.

**karyotype:** A systematized arrangement of the chromosomes from a cell, including the number of chromosomes and any abnormalities.

The term is also used to refer to a photograph of an individual's chromosomes.

**labia majora**: The outer skin folds of the female genitals.

**labia minora**: The inner skin folds of the female genitals.

**labioplasty**: Surgery on the labia.

**labioscrotal folds**: Masculinized labial skin.

**liver:** A large abdominal organ that plays a critical role in digestion and metabolism.

**luteinizing hormone (LH):** A hormone secreted from the pituitary gland that controls several aspects of reproductive function.

**masculinization:** To acquire more male-like characteristics. Synonymous with "virilization."

**maternal:** Pertaining to the mother.

**mEq/l (milliequivalents per liter):** A measure of the number of charged molecules in a liter of water.

**metabolism:** The process of converting one substance into another within a living organism.

**mineralocorticoid:** A type of steroid hormone synthesized and secreted from the adrenal cortex. The major mineralocorticoid is aldosterone.

**mosaic (mosaicism):** In genetics, an animal that has more than one genetically-distinct population of cells derived from a single zygote; as most commonly used, the different populations of cells have differing numbers of chromosomes.

**mutation:** A permanent structural alteration in DNA. In most cases, DNA changes either have no effect or cause harm, but occasionally a mutation can improve an organism's chance of surviving and passing the beneficial change on to its descendants.

**non-coding DNA:** The strand of DNA that does not carry the information necessary to make a protein. The non-coding strand is the mirror image of the coding strand and is also known as the antisense strand.

**norepinephrine:** A catecholamine secreted from the adrenal medulla and from certain sympathetic neurons

**oral administration of medication:** Giving tablet, capsule, or liquid medication by mouth.

**ovary:** One of the pair of female reproductive organs that produce ovum.

**pancreas:** An abdominal organ that is a source of the hormones *insulin* and *glucagons,* which are important for in regulating fuel metabolism.

**paternal:** Pertaining to the father.

**PCR (Polymerase Chain Reaction):** A test for amplifying pieces of DNA.

**perineum**: The region between the anus and the genital organs.

**phenotype:** The observable traits or characteristics of an organism; for example, hair color, weight, or the presence or absence of a disease. Phenotypic traits are not necessarily genetic.

**pituitary gland:** A major endocrine organ located immediately below the brain. Produces a large number of protein and peptide hormones.

**placenta:** A tissue formed from cells of the mother and fetus that forms an interface between the vascular systems of those two individuals.

**polymorphism:** A common variation in the sequence of DNA among individuals.

**postnatal**: Occurring after birth.

**Prader Scale**: A scoring system for grading the degrees of genital masculinization.

**prenatal**: Occurring before birth.

**prednisolone:** A synthetic substitute for cortisol, closely related to prednisone.

**prednisone:** A synthetic substitute for cortisol. Prednisone is more potent and has a longer duration of action than cortisol.

**pregnantriol:** The urinary metabolite of 17-hydroxyprogesterone.

**pregnelolone:** A steroid hormone produced in the adrenal cortex.

**progesterone:** A steroid hormone produced in the adrenal cortex.

**protein:** A large complex molecule made up of one or more chains of amino acids. Proteins perform a wide variety of activities in the cell.

**pseudo-:** Prefix meaning "false."

**pseudogene:** A sequence of DNA that is very similar to a normal gene but that has been altered slightly so it is not expressed. Such genes were probably once functional but over time acquired one or more mutations that rendered them incapable of producing a protein product.

**recessive:** A genetic disorder that appears only in patients who have received two copies of a mutant gene, one from each parent.

**recombination:** Exchange of DNA material.

**renal:** Pertaining to the kidneys.

**renin:** A hormone secreted by the kidneys in response to drop in blood pressure and blood volume.

**ribonucleic acid (RNA):** A chemical similar to a single strand of DNA. In RNA, the letter U, which stands for uracil, is substituted for T in the genetic code. RNA delivers DNA's genetic message to the cytoplasm of a cell, where proteins are made.

**rugation:** The wrinkling of skin.

**scrotum**: The skin sac that contains the testicles.

**sex chromosome:** One of the two chromosomes that specify an organism's genetic sex. Humans have two kinds of sex chromosomes, one called X and the other Y. Normal females possess two X chromosomes, and normal males one X and one Y.

**sex-linked:** Located on the X chromosome. Sex-linked (or x- linked) diseases are generally seen only in males.

**shock:** The collapse of blood circulation.

**sinogram**: An X-ray study to examine where a passage in the body leads.

**sinus:** Abnormal opening.

**Southern Blot Analysis:** A technique used to identify and locate DNA sequences, which are complementary to another piece of DNA called a probe.

**stenosis**: Abnormal narrowing of a body cavity or passageway.

**steroid:** Any hormone derived from *cholesterol*, which itself is a steroid. Many steroids function as hormones.

**subcutaneous:** Under the skin.

**synthesize:** To make or produce.

**target cell:** A cell that is responsive to a particular hormone because it bears the receptor for that hormone.

**testicles:** One of the pair of male gonads that produces semen.

**testosterone:** A potent androgen.

**thyroid gland:** An endocrine organ located in the neck that secretes thyroid hormones and calcitonin.

**ureter:** The tube connecting the kidney to the bladder.

**urethra:** The tube that drains urine from the bladder.

**urinary tract infection (UTI)**: An infection of the urinary tract, mostly caused by bacteria.

**urogenital**: Referring to the urinary and reproductive systems.

**urogenital sinus**: A common passageway for the reproductive and urinary systems.

**urologist**: A physician specializing in the urinary and reproductive systems.

**uterus**: The hollow, pear-shaped inner female organ of reproduction in which the fertilized ovum is implanted and the fetus grows.

**vagina:** The part of the female genitalia that forms a canal from the opening to the passageway to the cervix.

**vaginoplasty:** An operation on the vagina.

**vaginoscopy:** Using a tube to look inside the vagina.

**villus** (pl. **villi**)**:** Fingerlike projections of capillaries, usually covered with epithelial cells. Examples are seen in the lining of the small intestine and chorionic villi of the placenta.

**virilization:** To acquire more male-like characteristics. Synonymous with “masculinization.”

**zona fasciculata:** the middle layer of the adrenal cortex, which produces glucocorticoids.

**zona glomerulosa:** the outer layer of the adrenal cortex, which produces mineralocorticoids.

**zona reticularis:** the inner layer of the adrenal cortex, which produces androgens.

# Selected References


2000. "Technical report: congenital adrenal hyperplasia. Section on Endocrinology and Committee on Genetics." *Pediatrics* 106(6): 1511-18.

The Section on Endocrinology and the Committee on Genetics of the American Academy of Pediatrics, in collaboration with experts from the fields of pediatric endocrinology and genetics, developed this policy statement as a means of providing up-to-date information for the practicing pediatrician about current practice and controversial issues in congenital adrenal hyperplasia (CAH), including the current status of prenatal diagnosis and treatment, the benefits and problem areas of neonatal screening programs, and the management of children with non-classic CAH. The reference list is designed to allow physicians who wish more information to research the topic more thoroughly.

2002. "Consensus statement on 21-hydroxylase deficiency from the Lawson Wilkins Pediatric Endocrine Society and the European Society for Paediatric Endocrinology." *Journal of Clinical Endocrinology and Metabolism* 87(9): 4048-53.

Appan, S., P. C. Hindmarsh, et al. 1989. "Monitoring treatment in congenital adrenal hyperplasia." *Archives of Disease in Childhood* 64(9): 1235-9.

We report results of monitoring treatment in 41 patients with congenital adrenal hyperplasia controlled over 0.3-13.1 years using standard auxological techniques alone. Doses of glucocorticoid (15-25 mg/m2/day) and mineralocorticoid (0.15 mg/m2/day) replacement were determined initially using biochemical indices and thereafter adjusted according to surface area. Monitoring was solely directed at maintaining a 50th percentile height velocity for chronological age. Of 41 patients, 32 were referred after the newborn period. Nearly half of these patients were either overtreated or undertreated before their referral. Of the nine treated from birth, all but one were in good control and only two have had a second hospital admission. Present height standard deviation scores (SDS) for chronological age range from -1.60 to -0.26. Height SDS for bone age were compared with midparental heights in 33 patients: 15 treated with early emphasis on growth had a height prognosis exceeding midparental values; patients who had experienced appreciable prior over-treatment or under-treatment fared less well. In the long-term management of congenital adrenal hyperplasia correction of salt loss is of primary importance. Doses of glucocorticoid required in addition to mineralcorticoid replacement should be continuously assessed and adjusted to maintain a normal growth velocity. This is most conveniently achieved by standardising replacement doses on surface area.

Bailey, C. C., G. M. Komrower, et al. 1978. "Management of congenital adrenal hyperplasia. Urinary steroid estimations—review of their value." *Archives of Disease in Childhood* 53(2): 132-35.

A retrospective study was made of 16 children with 21-hydroxylase-deficient congenital adrenal hyperplasia of the salt-losing variety, who were treated with fludrocortisone and prednisone and were in good health during the period under review. The height velocity of the children was subnormal, height achievement was poor, and their bone ages retarded. Urinary 17-oxosteroid and pregnanetriol excretion were used to monitor the therapy of the children and these data have been related to growth velocities. In spite of urinary steroid figures in excess of those published as desirable for monitoring therapy, the children failed to grow properly, probably as a result of glucocorticoid overdosage. Published urinary steroid criteria are considered too strict and in order to achieve them one would need to give unnecessarily high doses of steroid. Regular measurement of height velocity and skeletal maturation rate are better indicators of therapeutic control and should lead to more satisfactory growth and ultimate height.

Bartter, F. C., A. P. Forbes, et al. 1950. "Congenital adrenal hyperplasia associated with the adrenogenital syndrome: an attempt to correct its disordered pattern." *Journal of Clinical Investigation* 29: 797.

Berenbaum, S. A. 2001. "Cognitive function in congenital adrenal hyperplasia." *Endocrinology and Metabolism Clinics of North America* 30(1): 173-92.

Cognition in patients with CAH has not been as well studied as other aspects of psychologic function. Nevertheless, it is possible to make some conclusions and to offer a number of hypotheses for further study (Table 1). First, patients with CAH do not seem to have an overall intellectual advantage as a direct consequence of the disease. The high IQs reported in some groups of patients with CAH are also reported in their siblings and probably reflect sampling bias. Second, it is possible that, on average, patients with salt-wasting CAH have lower overall ability than patients with the simple-virilizing form, but both groups are well within the normal range, and there is considerable variability among both groups. Third, the evidence to date does not confirm that patients with CAH are more likely to have diagnosable learning disabilities when compared with their unaffected relatives, but this issue has not been well studied with the appropriate psychoeducational assessments. It is unlikely that patients with CAH are at substantially increased risk for frank learning disabilities, but they may be likely to have problems in specific areas. Fourth, females with CAH seem to have enhanced spatial ability as a result of exposure to high levels of androgens early in development. The neural substrate of this advantage is unknown but a subject of active research. It is unclear whether when compared with their unaffected siblings, females with CAH are better in other abilities that are typically performed best by males or worse in abilities typically performed best by females. Fifth, it is likely that patients with CAH have other cognitive changes as a consequence of disease characteristics (besides androgens) and of the treatment of the disease. Some evidence suggests that patients with CAH are more likely to have white-matter brain changes produced by the disease and its treatment. This has not been well studied but should be because of the potential clinical implications. It is reasonable to hypothesize that there will be cognitive changes that reflect effects of under-treatment (e.g., ACTH effects on attention) and other changes that reflect effects of over-treatment (e.g., glucocorticoid effects on memory). Some of these effects may be transient, reflecting acute brain changes, whereas others may become chronic as a result of permanent brain changes with repeated exposure. There is need for continuing study of cognition in patients with CAH. Such studies will provide basic information about hormonal effects on cognition and the neural mechanisms that mediate those effects. They will also provide important clinical information to guide psychologic and medical treatment of patients.

Berenbaum, S. A., K. Korman Bryk, et al. 2004. "Psychological adjustment in children and adults with congenital adrenal hyperplasia." *Journal of Pediatrics* 144(6): 741-46.

OBJECTIVE: To determine psychological health in individuals with one form of intersexuality, congenital adrenal hyperplasia (CAH), and its relation to characteristics of the disease and treatment. STUDY DESIGN: Participants (ages 3-31 years) included 72 females and 42 males with CAH, and unaffected relatives (44 females and 69 males). Psychological adjustment was assessed with parent-reports on the Child Behavior Checklist (CBCL) and subject self-reports on the Self-Image Questionnaire for Young Adolescents (SIQYA) or the

Multidimensional Personality Questionnaire (MPQ). Information about disease characteristics and genital surgery was obtained from medical records. RESULTS: There were no significant differences between females with CAH and unaffected females on any measure. Psychological adjustment was not significantly associated with genital virilization or age at genital surgery. Males with CAH were not significantly different from unaffected males in childhood, but they showed more negative affect at older ages. CONCLUSIONS: Psychological adjustment is not compromised in females with virilized genitalia who are treated early in life and reared as females. Adjustment does not appear to depend on the characteristics of the disease or its treatment, but sample size and restricted range limit generalizability about adjustment-disease associations.

Bode, H. H., S. A. Rivkees, et al. 1999. "Home monitoring of 17-hydroxyprogesterone levels in congenital adrenal hyperplasia with filter paper blood samples." *Journal of Pediatrics* 134(2): 185-89.

OBJECTIVE: The purpose of this study was to evaluate the usefulness of 17-hydroxyprogesterone (17-OHP) determination in dried filter paper blood samples from patients with congenital adrenal hyperplasia caused by 21-hydroxylase deficiency. It was hypothesized that these home samples would enhance patient treatment. STUDY DESIGN: Results of 17-OHP determination in simultaneously collected venous and dried filter paper blood samples were compared to establish assay reliability. Thereafter, parents mailed dried filter paper blood samples collected before each hydrocortisone dose. RESULTS: The 17-OHP levels in wet and dried blood samples correlated well ($r = 0.98$). Results did not change when stored for 2 weeks under various conditions. Blood sampling at different times of the day provided insights into the patterns of 17-OHP secretion and identified times of inadequate adrenal suppression. Dose adjustments were then made considering the time of day when adrenal suppression was inadequate. CONCLUSION: Home monitoring of 17-OHP is a reliable and practical approach for assessing adrenal steroid activity in patients with congenital adrenal hyperplasia. Considering the time of day of 17-OHP elevations also facilitates hydrocortisone dosing adjustment.

Brook, C. G., M. Zachmann, et al. 1974. "Experience with long-term therapy in congenital adrenal hyperplasia." *Journal of Pediatrics* 85(1): 12-19.

Charmandari, E., A. Johnston, et al. 2001. "Bioavailability of oral hydrocortisone in patients with congenital adrenal hyperplasia due to 21-hydroxylase deficiency." *Journal of Endocrinology* 169(1): 65-70.

The management of congenital adrenal hyperplasia due to 21-hydroxylase (CYP21) deficiency requires glucocorticoid substitution with oral hydrocortisone given twice or thrice daily. In paediatric practice little is known of the bioavailability of oral hydrocortisone tablets used in these patients. The aim of this study was to assess the bioavailability of oral hydrocortisone and to evaluate current replacement therapy in the light of cortisol pharmacokinetic properties. We determined the bioavailability of hydrocortisone following oral and intravenous administration in sixteen (median age: 10.9 years, range: 6.0-18.4 years) adequately controlled CYP21 deficient patients. Serum total cortisol concentrations were measured at 20-min intervals for 24 h while patients were on oral substitution therapy, and at 10-min intervals for 6 h following an intravenous bolus of hydrocortisone in a dose of 15 mg/m(2) body surface area. The area under the serum total cortisol concentration versus time curve (AUC) following oral and intravenous administration of hydrocortisone was calculated using the trapezoid method. The bioavailability was estimated by dividing the corrected for dose AUC after oral hydrocortisone administration by the corrected for dose AUC after the intravenous hydrocortisone administration and was exemplified as a percentage. After oral administration of hydrocortisone in the morning, median serum total cortisol concentrations reached a peak of 729.5 nmol/l (range: 492-2520 nmol/l) at 1.2 h (range: 0.3-3.3 h) and declined monoexponentially thereafter to reach undetectable concentrations 7 h (range: 5-12 h) after administration. Following administration of the evening hydrocortisone dose, median peak cortisol concentration of 499 nmol/l (range: 333-736 nmol/l) was attained also at 1.2 h (range: 0.3-3.0 h) and subsequently declined gradually, reaching undetectable concentrations at 9 h (5-12 h) after administration of the oral dose. After the intravenous hydrocortisone bolus a median peak serum total cortisol concentration of 1930 nmol/l (range: 1124-2700 nmol/l) was observed at 10 min (range: 10-20 min). Serum cortisol concentrations fell rapidly and reached undetectable levels 6 h after the hydrocortisone bolus. The absolute bioavailability of oral hydrocortisone in the morning was 94.2% (90% confidence interval (CI): 82.8-105.5%) whereas the apparent bioavailability in the evening was estimated to be 128.0% (90% CI: 119.0-138.0%). We conclude that the bioavailability of oral hydrocortisone is high and may result in supraphysiological cortisol concentrations within 1-2 h after administration of high doses. The even higher bioavailability in the evening, estimated using as reference the data derived from the intravenous administration of hydrocortisone bolus in the morning, is likely to reflect a decrease in the hydrocortisone clearance in the evening. Decisions on the schedule and frequency of administration in patients with congenital adrenal hyperplasia should be based on the knowledge of the bioavailability and other pharmacokinetic parameters of the hydrocortisone formulations currently available.

Charmandari, E., E. J. Lichtarowicz-Krynska, et al. 2001. "Congenital adrenal hyperplasia: management during critical illness." *Archives of Disease in Childhood* 85(1): 26-28.

BACKGROUND: Little is known of the optimal dose and administration schedule of hydrocortisone in critically ill patients with congenital adrenal hyperplasia (CAH) caused by 21-hydroxylase deficiency. AIM: To determine plasma cortisol concentrations after intravenous administration of hydrocortisone in children with CAH and to relate these to plasma cortisol concentrations achieved by endogenous secretion in the stress of critical illness in previously healthy children. METHODS: Plasma cortisol concentrations were measured in 20 patients with classical CAH (median age 11.2 years, range 6.1-16.4) following intravenous administration of hydrocortisone 15 mg/m(2); and in 60 critically ill mechanically ventilated children (median age 2.5 years, range 0.25-16.3) on admission to the paediatric intensive care unit and for 24 hours thereafter. RESULTS: In the CAH patients, plasma cortisol reached a mean peak of 1648.3 nmol/l (SD 511.9) within 10 minutes of the intravenous bolus, and fell rapidly thereafter; levels remained greater than 450 nmol/l for 2.5 hours only. In critically ill children, mean plasma cortisol on admission to the intensive care unit was 727 nmol/l (SD 426.1). Cortisol concentrations remained raised during the first 24 hours. CONCLUSIONS: Critically ill patients with classical CAH may be best managed with a single intravenous hydrocortisone bolus followed by a constant rate infusion of hydrocortisone.

Charmandari, E., D. R. Matthews, et al. 2001. "Serum cortisol and 17-hydroxyprogesterone interrelation in classic 21-hydroxylase deficiency: is current replacement therapy satisfactory?" *Journal of Clinical Endocrinology and Metabolism* 86(10): 4679-85.

One of the main aims in the management of patients with congenital adrenal hyperplasia due to 21-hydroxylase deficiency is to achieve adequate suppression of the adrenal cortex with the smallest possible dose of glucocorticoid substitution. To evaluate the administration schedule of current replacement therapy regimens, we investigated the cortisol-17-hydroxyprogesterone interrelation in 36 patients (13 males and 23 females; median age, 12.3 yr; range, 6.1-18.8 yr) with salt-wasting congenital adrenal hyperplasia. As sufficient variation in 17-hydroxyprogesterone concentrations was required to allow analysis of the cortisol-17-hydroxyprogesterone interrelation, patients were divided into 2 groups depending on the adequacy of hypothalamic-pituitary-adrenal axis suppression. The first group consisted of 17 patients with suppressed 17-hydroxyprogesterone concentrations (group 1), and the second group consisted of 19 patients with nonsuppressed 17-hydroxyprogesterone concentrations (group 2). We determined serum cortisol and 17-hydroxyprogesterone concentrations at 20-min intervals for a total of 24 h while patients were receiving their usual replacement treatment with hydrocortisone and 9alpha-fludrocortisone. We also determined the lowest dose of dexamethasone required to suppress the 0800 h serum ACTH concentrations when administered as a single dose (0.3 or 0.5 mg/m(2)) the night before. Mean 24-h cortisol and 17-hydroxyprogesterone concentrations were 3.9 microg/dl (SD = 2.1) and 66.2 ng/dl (SD = 92.7), respectively, in group 1 and 4.1 microg/dl (SD = 2.5) and 4865.7 ng/dl (SD = 6951) in group 2. The 24-h 17-hydroxyprogesterone concentrations demonstrated circadian variation, with peak values observed between 0400-0900 h. In group 2, 17-hydroxyprogesterone concentrations decreased gradually in response to the rise in cortisol concentrations during the day, but remained low during the night despite the almost undetectable cortisol concentrations between 1600-2000 h. Mean 0800 h androstenedione concentrations correlated strongly with integrated 17-hydroxyprogesterone concentrations ($r = 0.81$; $P < 0.0001$), but not with integrated cortisol concentrations. There was a significant negative correlation between cortisol and 17-hydroxyprogesterone at lag time 0 min ($r = -0.187$; $P < 0.0001$), peaking at lag time 60 min ($r = -0.302$; $P < 0.0001$), with cortisol leading 17-hydroxyprogesterone by these time intervals. Finally, 0800 h serum ACTH concentrations were sufficiently suppressed after a dexamethasone dose of 0.3 mg/m(2) in all but three patients. These findings indicate that in classic 21-hydroxylase deficiency, hydrocortisone should be administered during the period of increased hypothalamic-pituitary-adrenal axis activity, between 0400-1600 h, with the biggest dose given in the morning. Blood investigations performed as part of monitoring of congenital adrenal hyperplasia patients should include androstenedione and 17-hydroxyprogesterone concentrations determined in the morning before the administration of hydrocortisone. It should also be emphasized that blood investigations are only complementary to the overall assessment of these patients, which is primarily based on the evaluation of growth and pubertal progress.

Charmandari, E., S. M. Pincus, et al. 2002. "Oral hydrocortisone administration in children with classic 21-hydroxylase deficiency leads to more synchronous joint GH and cortisol secretion." *Journal of Clinical Endocrinology and Metabolism* 87(5): 2238-44.

In humans, GH and cortisol are secreted in a pulsatile fashion and a mutual bidirectional interaction between the GH/IGF-I axis and hypothalamic-pituitary-adrenal axis has been established. Classic congenital adrenal hyperplasia (CAH) is characterized by a defect in the synthesis of glucocorticoids and often mineralocorticoids, and adrenal hyperandrogenism. Substitution therapy is given to prevent adrenal crises and to suppress the abnormal secretion of androgens and steroid precursors from the adrenal cortex. However, treatment with twice or three times daily oral hydrocortisone does not mimic physiological adrenal rhythms and may influence the activity of the GH/IGF-I axis. We investigated the pattern of GH and cortisol secretion and the synchrony of joint GH-cortisol secretory dynamics in 15 children with classic 21-hydroxylase deficiency (5 males and 10 females; median age 9.5 yr, range 6.1-11.0 yr) and 28 short normal children (23 males and 5 females; median age 7.7 yr, range 4.9-9.3 yr). All subjects were prepubertal. Serum GH and cortisol concentrations were determined at 20-min intervals for 24 h. The irregularity of GH and cortisol secretion was assessed using approximate entropy (ApEn), a scale- and model-independent statistic. The synchrony of joint GH-cortisol secretion was quantified using the cross-ApEn statistic. Cross-correlation analysis of GH and cortisol secretory patterns was computed at various time lags covering the 24-h period. Children with CAH had significantly lower mean 24-h serum cortisol concentrations (6.4 +/- 2.2 vs. 10.4 +/- 2.6 microg/dl, $P < 0.001$), ApEn (GH) (0.64 +/- 0.13 vs. 0.74 +/- 0.17, $P = 0.04$), ApEn (cortisol) (0.54 +/- 0.13 vs. 1.08 +/- 0.18, $P < 0.001$) and cross-ApEn values of paired GH-cortisol secretion (0.78 +/- 0.19 vs. 1.05 +/- 0.12, $P < 0.001$) than normal children. There was no difference in mean 24-h GH concentrations between the two groups (4.5 +/- 2.9 vs. 4.5 +/- 1.9 mU/liter). In children with CAH, a significant positive correlation between GH and cortisol was noted at lag time 0 min (r = 0.299, P < 0.01), peaking at 20 min (r = 0.406, P < 0.0001), whereas in normal children, a significant negative correlation between the two hormones was noted at lag time 0 min (r = -0.312, P < 0.01). The above findings suggest that children with classic CAH have a more regular pattern of GH secretion and a more synchronous joint GH-cortisol secretory dynamics than their normal counterparts. These differences reflect bidirectional interactions between the GH/IGF-I axis and hypothalamic-pituitary-adrenal axis in humans, and are likely to evolve as a result of the exogenous administration of hydrocortisone at fixed doses and at specific time intervals, which leads to a more regular pattern in circulating cortisol concentrations, independent of variations in CRH and ACTH concentrations.

Charmandari, E., C. G. Brook, et al. 2002. "Why is management of patients with classical congenital adrenal hyperplasia more difficult at puberty?" *Archives of Disease in Childhood* 86(4): 266-69.

Congenital adrenal hyperplasia (CAH) due to 21-hydroxylase deficiency is an autosomal recessive condition in which deletions or mutations of the cytochrome P450 21-hydroxylase gene cause glucocorticoid and often mineralocorticoid deficiency. Despite optimal substitution therapy, control of classical CAH is often inadequate at puberty, and the problems encountered relate to hypocortisolism and/or hyperandrogenism. A number of physiological alterations in the endocrine milieu at puberty, which include alterations in the growth hormone/insulin-like growth factor axis, insulin sensitivity, as well as the activity of enzymes participating in cortisol metabolism and adrenal steroidogenesis, may account for the documented hypocortisolism and elevated androgen production, and may explain the difficulty in maintaining adequate adrenocortical suppression in pubertal patients with classical 21-hydroxylase deficiency.

Clayton, P. E., W. L. Miller, et al. 2002. "Consensus statement on 21-hydroxylase deficiency from the European Society for Paediatric Endocrinology and the Lawson Wilkins Pediatric Endocrine Society." *Journal of Clinical Endocrinology and Metabolism* 87: 4048-53.

Collett-Solberg, P. F. 2001. "Congenital adrenal hyperplasia: from genetics and biochemistry to clinical practice, part 2." *Clinical Pediatrics (Philadelphia)* 40(3): 125-32.

Congenital adrenal hyperplasia (CAH) refers to a group of genetic disorders with defects in the synthesis of cortisol. The synthesis of other steroids such as mineralocorticoids and adrenal/ gonadal sex steroids may also be affected. The clinical presentation of the various forms of CAH depend on the following: (1) the affected enzyme, (2) the residual enzymatic activity, (3) the physiologic consequences of deficiencies of the end-products and excess of precursors. The second part of this two-part review discusses the diagnosis and the management of CAH. Although methods for the diagnosis of CAH have not changed over the past few years, new therapeutic approaches are changing the management of CAH. In particular, new drugs and new drug combinations are being tested and old dogmas are being questioned. Early diagnosis, careful discussion with family members of newborns with CAH during the early decision-making process, and close management will decrease the mortality rate and improve the long-term psychological/physical outcome of these children.

Donahoe, P. K. and W. H. Hendren, 3rd 1984. "Perineal reconstruction in ambiguous genitalia infants raised as females." *Annals of Surgery* 200(3): 363-71.

Sixty-six patients with ambiguous genitalia, representing a combined experience, underwent reconstruction of the perineum to achieve a feminine phenotype. These patients represent four major etiologic groups, adrenogenital syndrome, male pseudohermaphroditism, mixed gonadal dysgenesis, and true hermaphroditism. If the patient is to be raised as a female, the perineum is reconstructed early in the neonatal period by doing a clitoral recession, labial reduction, and vaginal exteriorization. The latter is delayed if the vagina enters the urogenital sinus high, until 2 years. The factors affecting the choice of gender and the details and the timing of the surgical techniques are described.

Esoterix. 2002. "Endocrinology expected values." *<http://www.esoterix.com/endocrinology/related/expected_values.pdf>*.

Eugster, E. A., L. A. Dimeglio, et al. 2001. "Height outcome in congenital adrenal hyperplasia caused by 21-hydroxylase deficiency: a meta-analysis." *Journal of Pediatrics* 138(1): 26-32.

OBJECTIVE: To investigate adult heights attained by patients with 21-hydroxylase deficiency and to perform a meta-analysis of height outcomes reported in this population.Study design: A retrospective chart review of our patients >5 years of age (n = 65) who were followed up from 1978 to 1998 for 21-hydroxylase deficiency was conducted. Final height (FH) SD scores and target height (TH) SD scores were determined. The impact of sex, time of diagnosis, and compliance was assessed. Meta-analysis of results from 18 studies was performed; TH was available for 204 of 561 patients. RESULTS: Mean FH SD score-TH SD score for our 65 patients was -1.03. For the meta-analysis, mean weighted FH SD score for all 561 patients was -1.37, whereas weighted mean FH SD score-TH SD score for the 204 patients for whom TH was available was -1.21. No difference in outcome was seen for males compared with females, although a statistically significant difference was seen for patients identified early versus late. CONCLUSIONS: Adult height in patients with 21-hydroxylase deficiency is often within 1 SD of TH. Early diagnosis and good compliance appear to improve the outcome. Rather than pursuing alternate therapies for congenital adrenal hyperplasia, efforts may instead be focused on early detection and improved compliance with traditional medical therapy.

Gmyrek, G. A., M. I. New, et al. 2002. "Bilateral laparoscopic adrenalectomy as a treatment for classic congenital adrenal hyperplasia attributable to 21-hydroxylase deficiency." *Pediatrics* 109(2): E28.

OBJECTIVE: Current medical therapy for congenital adrenal hyperplasia (CAH) attributable to a complete 21-hydroxylase deficiency is not optimal. Difficulties in adequate adrenal androgen suppression are common, causing short adult stature, infertility, and hyperandrogenism. We report the use of laparoscopic bilateral adrenalectomy as a definitive therapy for this condition and argue that it is superior to conventional medical therapy in selected patients. METHODS: Participants were 2 adult females with classic, salt-wasting CAH and a history of poor adrenal control were selected for adrenalectomy: case 1 was a 22-year-old woman with mild hirsutism and primary amenorrhea; case 2 was a 28-year-old woman with severe hirsutism, acne, and amenorrhea. Preoperative and postoperative hormonal profiles were performed. Both underwent laparoscopic bilateral adrenalectomy with a mean follow-up of 37 months. RESULTS: Bilateral laparoscopic adrenalectomy was performed in both patients with no complications and an uneventful recovery. Maintenance medications of glucocorticoid and mineralocorticoid replacement were reduced compared with preoperative doses. Three years postoperatively, however, rising adrenal steroid precursor levels in case 1, presumably caused by adrenal rests, prompted an increase in replacement therapy dose. Hirsutism and acne improved in both patients, and regular menstruation began 5 months (case 1) and 2 months (case 2) postoperatively. Pregnancy 3 years postoperatively was successful in case 2, who delivered a unaffected infant, full-term via Cesarian section. CONCLUSIONS: Surgical adrenalectomy should be considered in females with classic CAH attributable to 21-hydroxylase deficiency and a history of poor hormonal control. Adrenalectomy may prove to be superior to current medical therapy for these patients.

Greulich, W. W., and S. I. Pyle. 1959. *Radiographic Atlas of Skeletal Development of the Hands and Wrists,* Stanford: Stanford University Press.

Hargitai, G., J. Solyom, et al. 2001. "Growth patterns and final height in congenital adrenal hyperplasia due to classical 21-hydroxylase deficiency. Results of a multicenter study." *Hormone Research* 55(4): 161-71.

BACKGROUND: Longitudinal growth and bone age (BA) development are the most important clinical parameters for monitoring adequate glucocorticoid replacement in children with congenital adrenal hyperplasia (CAH). AIM OF THE STUDY: To analyze the growth pattern of patients treated for CAH of the salt wasting (SW) and simple virilizing (SV) clinical forms; to evaluate final height as compared to reference data and individual target height; to evaluate the course of BA development. PATIENTS AND METHODS: A large database of 598 patients with CAH was created in 5 Central European countries and growth data of 341 treated patients with 21-hydroxylase deficiency were analyzed retrospectively. The patients were of Caucasian origin. Centiles were constructed in a cross-sectional manner and an additional longitudinal analysis was performed in order to evaluate the pubertal growth spurt by applying particular statistical methods (Preece-Baines model). RESULTS: The growth of SW CAH patients was impaired in infancy and early childhood (0-3 years of age), but followed normal patterns in childhood until puberty. In contrast, children with SV CAH had normal patterns of growth in infancy and early childhood and were considerably taller than healthy references during childhood. In the longitudinal study, peak height velocity in both boys and girls was normal, but it occurred at an earlier age than in the standard population. The final height of patients with CAH was reduced in comparison to both the reference and the individual target height. No correlations were found between final height and age at the start of the therapy in SV patients or between final height and year of birth. BA was advanced in both types of CAH, but more accelerated in SV patients. CONCLUSION: Characteristic growth patterns for treated SV and SW CAH children were identified, with a normal pubertal growth spurt and reduced final height being observed.

Hayek, A., J. D. Crawford, et al. 1971. "Single dose dexamethasone in treatment of congenital adrenocortical hyperplasia." *Metabolism* 20(9): 897-901.

Horrocks, P. M., and D. R. London. 1982. "A comparison of three glucocorticoid suppressive regimes in adults with congenital adrenal hyperplasia." *Clinical Endocrinology (Oxford)* 17(6): 547-56.

We have compared three glucocorticoids, hydrocortisone (HC) (20 mg mane & 10 mg nocte), cortisone acetate (CA) (25 mg mane & 12.5 mg nocte), dexamethasone (DXM) (0.5 mg mane & 0.25 mg nocte), for their effect on the biochemical control of adult patients with congenital adrenal hyperplasia (CAH). Twenty-four-hour profiles of plasma concentrations of ACTH, 17-hydroxyprogesterone (17-OHP) and androstenedione (delta 4A), and 09.00 h dehydroepiandrosterone sulphate (DHAS) plasma concentrations were used to assess control. The patients were studied after 2 weeks on each glucocorticoid. The areas under the curves, the heights of the morning peaks of each hormone, the midnight concentrations, and the concentrations of hormones just before the evening dose were analysed. The results show that all the indices, except the midnight concentrations which were uniformly low, were significantly lower on DXM than on either HC or CA. There were no significant differences between HC and CA for any of the indices. The DHAS concentrations were low on all three glucocorticoids but again significantly lower on DXM. DXM (0.5 mg mane & 0.25 mg nocte) is therefore, in the short term, a better suppressor of the pituitary- adrenal axis in adults with CAH than either HC or CA, and in the dose used did not suppress ACTH to undetectable levels, nor the steroids to below levels found in normal subjects.

Hughes, I. 2002. "Congenital adrenal hyperplasia: phenotype and genotype." *Journal of Pediatric Endocrinology and Metabolism* 15 Suppl 5: 1329-40.

Congenital adrenal hyperplasia (CAH) is a monogenic autosomal recessive condition manifested as a heterogeneous phenotype and caused by mutations in the CYP21 gene on chromosome 6p21.3. More than 50 mutations have been described, of which about 10 types account for >90% of affected alleles. Concordance between genotype and phenotype is sufficiently robust to be of significant value in the diagnosis and management of the adrenal disorder. Knowledge of the genotype is essential in planning a strategy for prenatal treatment and useful in resolving diagnostic dilemmas in newborn screening programs, identifying nonclassic CAH in hyperandrogenic women with elevated 17-hydroxyprogesterone levels, and studying the role of 21-hydroxylase deficiency in adrenal 'incidentalomas'. CYP21 genotyping is also valuable in defining the requirement for glucocorticoid and mineralocorticoid replacement from infancy to adulthood. More detailed gene sequencing of the noncoding as well as the coding regions, together with analysis of other genes involved in steroid hormone production and action, will potentially be a significant step toward the goal of tailoring treatment to each individual.

Hughes, I. A. 1988. "Management of congenital adrenal hyperplasia." *Archives of Disease in Childhood* 63(11): 1399-404.

Hughes, I. A., J. Dyas, et al. 1985. "Monitoring treatment in congenital adrenal hyperplasia. Use of serial measurements of 17-OH-progesterone in plasma, capillary blood, and saliva." *Annals of the New York Academy of Sciences* 458: 193-202.

Kaplowitz, P. B., and S. E. Oberfield. 1999. "Reexamination of the age limit for defining when puberty is precocious in girls in the United States: implications for evaluation and treatment. Drug and Therapeutics and Executive Committees of the Lawson Wilkins Pediatric Endocrine Society." *Pediatrics* 104(4 Pt. 1): 936-41.

In 1997 a study from the Pediatric Research in Office Settings network, based on pubertal staging of >17,000 girls between 3 and 12 years of age, indicated that breast and pubic hair development are occurring significantly earlier than suggested by our current guidelines, especially in African-American girls. In response to this article, the Lawson Wilkins Pediatric Endocrine Society undertook a comprehensive review of this topic. The primary conclusions of this review are: 1. The current recommendation that breast development before age 8 is precocious is based on outdated studies. Until 1997, no data were available on pubertal staging in US girls that could have documented a trend to earlier maturation. 2. The 1997 study indicates that stage 2 of breast and pubic hair development is being achieved ~1 year earlier in white girls and 2 years earlier in African-American girls than previous studies have shown. 3. Concerns that girls with moderately precocious puberty will be significantly short adults are overstated; most have adult height within the normal range. 4. Therapy with gonadotropin-releasing hormone agonists has not been proven to have a substantial effect on adult height in most girls whose puberty starts between 6 and 8 years of age. 5. New guidelines propose that girls with either breast development or pubic hair should be evaluated if this occurs before age 7 in white girls and before age 6 in African-American girls. No changes in the current guidelines for evaluating boys (signs of puberty at younger than 9 years) can be made at this time.normal puberty, breast development, pubic hair.

Kaplowitz, P. B., E. J. Slora, et al. 2001. "Earlier onset of puberty in girls: relation to increased body mass index and race." *Pediatrics* 108(2): 347-53.

OBJECTIVE: A recent study conducted by the Pediatric Research in Office Settings network provided evidence that girls in the United States, especially black girls, are starting puberty at a younger age than earlier studies had found, but the reasons for this are not known. Because nutritional status is known to affect timing of puberty and there is a clear trend for increasing obesity in US children during the past 25 years, it was hypothesized that the earlier onset of puberty could be attributable to the increasing prevalence of obesity in young girls. Therefore, the objective of this study was to reexamine the Pediatric Research in Office Settings puberty data by comparing the age-normalized body mass index (BMI-ZS; a crude estimate of fatness) of girls who had breast or pubic hair development versus those who were still prepubertal, looking at the effects of age and race. RESULTS: For white girls, the BMI-ZS were markedly higher in pubertal versus prepubertal 6- to 9-year-olds; for black girls, a smaller difference was seen, which was significant only for 9-year-olds. Higher BMI-ZS also were found in girls who had pubic hair but no breast development versus girls who had neither pubic hair nor breast development. A multivariate analysis confirms that obesity (as measured by BMI) is significantly associated with early puberty in white girls and is associated with early puberty in black girls as well, but to a lesser extent. CONCLUSIONS: The results are consistent with obesity's being an important contributing factor to the earlier onset of puberty in girls. Factors other than obesity, however, perhaps genetic and/or environmental ones, are needed to explain the higher prevalence of early puberty in black versus white girls.

Lee, P. A., M. D. Urban, et al. 1980. "Plasma progesterone, 17-hydroxyprogesterone, androstenedione and testosterone in prepubertal, pubertal and adult subjects with congenital virilizing adrenal hyperplasia as indicators of adrenal suppression." *Hormone Research* 13(6): 347-57.

To determine whether a single morning plasma level of 17-hydroxyprogesterone (17-OHP), androstenedione, testosterone and progesterone reflected the degree of control of 21-hydroxylase congenital virilizing adrenal hyperplasia (CVAH) as indicated by 24-hour urinary 17-ketosteroid and pregnanetriol excretion, 142 simultaneous 24-hour urine and morning blood collections were made from 65 patients with CVAH. Patients were grouped into five categories on the basis of age, skeletal age, and sex. Paired blood and urinary data were analyzed. The results suggest that androstenedione is the most reliable indicator for all patient categories. Testosterone is an excellent indicator for children of both sexes and for adolescent and adult females. Levels of 17-OHP are difficult to interpret, as they can be several fold higher than the normal values when adrenal suppression appears adequate on the basis of urinary data. In general, progesterone is a poor indicator.

Meier, U., C. Schnabel, et al. 2004. "Comparison of three commercial assays for the measurement of 17alpha-hydroxyprogesterone (17alpha-OHPR): limitations of the quality control system." *Clinical Chemistry and Laborotory Medicine* 42(4): 450-4.

The measurement of 17alpha-hydroxyprogesterone (17alpha-OHPR) is of value for the diagnosis and management of congenital adrenal hyperplasia (CAH) due to 21-hydroxylase deficiency. In the central laboratory from 2000 to 2002, we observed, using the assay from the manufacturer DSL, an elevation of the moving average of 17alpha-OHPR concentrations and a number of adrenocorticotropic hormone (ACTH) stimulation tests despite the lack of any changes to the internal and external quality control, of which the criteria were continuously fulfilled. We studied a population of n=49 patients for the measurement of 17alpha-OHPR, with and without extraction, to evaluate the quality of different commercially available radioimmunoassays. The internal and external quality controls were successful in determining 17alpha-

OHPR. An excellent measurement and correlation of 17alpha-OHPR was expressed with the assay from the manufacturer IBL without extraction and from the manufacturer DSL with extraction. The quantitative determination of 17alpha-OHPR requires adequate specificity and accuracy of the 17alpha-OHPR radioimmunoassays. The results show that internal and external quality control systems are not sufficient to resolve analytical problems described in this study.

Merke, D. P., S. R. Bornstein, et al. 2002. "NIH conference. Future directions in the study and management of congenital adrenal hyperplasia due to 21-hydroxylase deficiency." *Annals Internal Medicine* 136(4): 320-34.

Congenital adrenal hyperplasia describes a group of inherited autosomal recessive disorders characterized by an enzymatic defect in cortisol biosynthesis, compensatory increases in corticotropin secretion, and adrenocortical hyperplasia. 21-Hydroxylase deficiency is responsible for more than 95% of cases and is one of the most common known autosomal recessive disorders. The classic or severe type presents in the newborn period or early childhood with virilization and adrenal insufficiency, with or without salt loss; the mild or non-classic form presents in late childhood or early adulthood with mild hyperandrogenism and is an important cause of masculinization and infertility in women. This wide range of phenotypic expression is mostly explained by genetic variation, although genotype-phenotype discrepancies have been described. Reproductive, metabolic, and other comorbid conditions, including risk for tumors, are currently under investigation in both forms of the disease. A high proportion of patients with adrenal incidentalomas may be homozygous or heterozygous for 21-hydroxylase deficiency. Women with congenital adrenal hyperplasia often develop the polycystic ovary syndrome. Ectopic adrenal rest tissue is often found in the testes of men with congenital adrenal hyperplasia; characteristic clinical and radiologic findings help differentiate this tissue from other tumors. Levels of corticotropin-releasing hormone are elevated in patients with depression and anxiety and are expected to be elevated in patients with congenital adrenal hyperplasia; it is unknown whether patients with 21-hydroxylase deficiency have an increased incidence of these psychiatric disorders. Abnormalities in both the structure and function of the adrenal medulla have been shown in patients with classic congenital adrenal hyperplasia, and the degree of adrenomedullary impairment may be a biomarker of disease severity. The 21-hydroxylase-deficient mouse has provided a useful model with which to examine disease mechanisms and test new therapeutic interventions in classic disease, including gene therapy. Treatment of this condition is intended to reduce excessive corticotropin secretion and replace both glucocorticoids and mineralocorticoids. However, clinical management is often complicated by inadequately treated hyperandrogenism, iatrogenic hypercortisolism, or both. New treatment approaches currently under investigation include combination therapy to block androgen action and inhibit estrogen production, and bilateral adrenalectomy in the most severely affected patients. Other approaches, which are in a preclinical stage of investigation, include treatment with a corticotropin-releasing hormone antagonist and gene therapy.

Merke, D. P., and C. A. Camacho. 2001. "Novel basic and clinical aspects of congenital adrenal hyperplasia." *Reviews in Endocrine and Metabolism Disorders* 2(3): 289-96.

Merke, D. P., and G. B. Cutler, Jr. 2001. "New ideas for medical treatment of congenital adrenal hyperplasia." *Endocrinology and Metabolism Clinics of North America* 30(1): 121-35.

During the past 50 years since the discovery of cortisone therapy as an effective treatment for CAH, many advances have been made in the management of 21-hydroxylase deficiency. Despite these advances, the clinical management of patients with CAH is often complicated by abnormal growth and development, iatrogenic Cushing's syndrome, inadequately treated hyperandrogenism, and infertility. New treatment approaches to classic CAH represent potential solutions to these unresolved issues. At the National Institutes of Health, a long-term randomized clinical trial is investigating a new treatment regimen: a reduced hydrocortisone dose, an antiandrogen, and an aromatase inhibitor. Peripheral blockade of androgens may also be helpful in the adult woman with CAH and PCOS. Other promising new treatment approaches include LHRH agonist-induced pubertal delay with or without growth hormone therapy, alternative glucocorticoid preparations or dose schedules, CRH antagonist treatment, and gene therapy. The applicability and success of these new approaches await the results of current research.

Meyer-Bahlburg, H. F., C. Dolezal, et al. 2004. "Cognitive and motor development of children with and without congenital adrenal hyperplasia after early-prenatal dexamethasone." *Journal of Clinical Endocrinology and Metabolism* 89(2): 610-4.

Dexamethasone (DEX) administration to the pregnant woman has become the treatment of choice for the prevention of genital masculinization in female fetuses affected with congenital adrenal hyperplasia (CAH). Although no somatic teratological side effects have been found to date, recent animal research has shown adverse effects of glucocorticoids on brain structures such as the hippocampus, raising concerns about possible functional side effects of DEX on human development. The current survey of 487 children, 1 month to 12 yr of age, focused on cognitive and motor development. The mothers of 174 prenatally DEX-exposed children (including 48 with CAH) and 313 unexposed children (including 195 with CAH) completed four standardized developmental questionnaires about their children. None of the comparisons of prenatally DEX-exposed children and unexposed controls was significant. Among the DEX-exposed children, increased duration of DEX exposure was correlated with significantly fewer developmental delays on three variables of one of the questionnaires, but none of the correlations reached significance, when Bonferroni corrections for multiple correlations were used. With the methods used, we were unable to document any adverse effects of early-prenatal DEX treatment in the doses recommended for the treatment of pregnancies at risk for CAH on motor and cognitive development.

Meyer-Bahlburg, H. F., C. Dolezal, et al. (2004). "Prenatal androgenization affects gender-related behavior but not gender identity in 5-12-year-old girls with congenital adrenal hyperplasia." *Archives of Sexual Behavior* 33(2): 97-104.

Gender assignment of children with intersexuality and related conditions has recently become highly controversial. On the basis of extensive animal research and a few human case reports, some authors have proposed the putative masculinization of the brain by prenatal hormones-indicated by the degree of genital masculinization-as the decisive criterion of gender assignment and have derived the recommendation that 46,XX newborns with congenital adrenal hyperplasia (CAH) and full genital masculinization should be assigned to the male gender. The purpose of this study was to test in CAH girls of middle childhood the assumption that prenatal androgens determine the development of gender identity. Fifteen girls with CAH (range of genital Prader stage, 2-4/5), 30 control girls, and 16 control boys (age range, 5-12 years) underwent 2 gender-play observation sessions, and a gender identity interview yielding scales of gender confusion/dysphoria. About half a year earlier, mothers had completed 2 questionnaires concerning their children's gender-related behavior. The results showed that, as expected, CAH girls scored more masculine than control girls on all scales measuring gender-related behavior, with robust effect sizes. By contrast, neither conventionally significant differences nor trends were found on the 3 scales of the gender identity interview. We conclude that prenatal androgenization of 46,XX fetuses leads to marked masculinization of later gender-related behavior, but the absence of any increased gender-identity confusion/dysphoria does not indicate a direct determination of gender identity by prenatal androgens and does not, therefore, support a male gender assignment at birth of the most markedly masculinized girls.Migeon, C. J., and R. L. Lanes. 1995. "Adrenal cortex; hypofunction and hyperfunction." *Pediatric Endocrinology*. L. F. New York, Marcel Dekker: 333-352.

Migeon, C. J., and A. B. Wisniewski. 2001. "Congenital adrenal hyperplasia owing to 21-hydroxylase deficiency. Growth, development, and therapeutic considerations." *Endocrinology and Metabolism Clinics of North America* 30(1): 193-206.

In the absence of long-term results of experimental therapies, a common sense approach toward dealing with the growth of patients who have CAH is desirable. First, an effort can be made to decrease the replacement cortisol dose during the first year of life. Doubling, rather than tripling, the basal dose at times of stress could be helpful. The use of adjunctive therapy for infections could result in fewer fevers. After 1 year of age, mean parental height could be used to establish at which centile the child should theoretically grow. The dose of cortisol could be adjusted to maintain the bone age between +/- 1 SD. Plasma androstenedione levels should not rise above 50 ng/dL, and 17-hydroxyprogesterone should not be totally suppressed but be maintained between 500 and 1000 ng/dL. Compliance with therapy should be encouraged, particularly for adolescent patients. In the final analysis, a realistic expectation for patients would be a height between the 50th and third percentile of the normal growth curve and, in some cases, slightly below the third percentile when the genetic potential is slight.

Miller, W. L. 1994. "Clinical review 54: Genetics, diagnosis, and management of 21-hydroxylase deficiency." *Journal of Clinical Endocrinology and Metabolism* 78(2): 241-46.

Mullis, P. E., P. C. Hindmarsh, et al. 1990. "Sodium chloride supplement at diagnosis and during infancy in children with salt-losing 21-hydroxylase deficiency." *European Journal of Pediatrics* 150(1): 22-25.

Eight infants (6 female, 2 male) with salt-losing congenital adrenal hyperplasia (CAH) due to 21-hydroxylase deficiency were studied to determine the sodium deficit at diagnosis and the level of salt supplement required in addition to subsequent hormone replacement. The median sodium deficit at diagnosis was 34 mmol (range 16-78) or 10.5 mmol/kg (range 4-24). A mean sodium supplement of 2.2 mmol/kg per day (range 0.5-4.9), double the amount provided with feeds, was required to maintain plasma sodium concentration and plasma renin activity (PRA) in the normal range for age. We present an equation based on sodium output (urine), sodium input (feeding plus supplement) and plasma sodium concentration to calculate the sodium supplement needed to maintain sodium balance on hormone replacement in this condition and some practical management suggestions. The necessity for salt supplements is often underestimated and the salt-losing tendency exacerbated by infection remains an unnecessary reason for hospitalization during the first months of life. In patients with salt-losing CAH life-long mineralocorticoid treatment is necessary but additional salt supplements are needed to maintain plasma sodium concentration and PRA in the normal range during infancy.

New, M. I. 2001. "Antenatal diagnosis and treatment of congenital adrenal hyperplasia." *Current Urology Reports* 2(1): 11-18.

Congenital adrenal hyperplasia (CAH) is a family of monogenic autosomal recessive disorders of steroidogenesis in which enzymatic defects result in impaired synthesis of cortisol by the adrenal cortex. The adrenal 21-hydroxylase (21-OH) enzyme is one of five enzymes necessary for the synthesis of cortisol from cholesterol, and its deficiency is the most common enzymatic defect causing CAH. 21-OH deficiency (21-OHD) occurs in a classical form that can cause genital ambiguity at birth in genetic females. Newborn males have normal genitalia. Prenatal treatment of 21-hydroxylase deficiency with dexamethasone has been used for approximately 15 years. An algorithm was developed for prenatal diagnosis and treatment.

New, M. I. 2001. "Factors determining final height in congenital adrenal hyperplasia." *Journal of Pediatric Endocrinology and Metabolism* 14 Suppl 2: 933-37.

Congenital adrenal hyperplasia (CAH) is a family of adrenal disorders whereby cortisol biosynthesis is impaired or abolished. In most cases, CAH is caused by a deficiency of the enzyme 21-hydroxylase causing a massive buildup of adrenal precursors. In addition to prenatal virilisation of genetic females and postnatal virilisation of both males and females, short adult stature is characteristic of the disorder. The inadequate final height in CAH patients is often attributed to over-treatment with glucocorticoid replacement and poor control of adrenal androgen levels. In a recent study, the use of growth hormone alone and in combination with gonadotropin releasing hormone analogue in children with CAH and poor predicted final height was found to decrease height deficit after one and two years of treatment.

New, M. I. 2003. "Inborn errors of adrenal steroidogenesis." *Molecular and Cellular Endocrinology* 211(1-2): 75-83.

Congenital adrenal hyperplasia (CAH) refers to a family of inherited disorders of adrenal steroidogenesis in which each disorder is characterized by a specific enzyme deficiency that impairs cortisol production by the adrenal cortex. The enzymes most commonly affected are 21-hydroxylase (21-OH), 11beta-hydroxylase, 3beta-hydroxysteroid dehydrogenase, and less often, 17alpha-hydroxylase/17,20-lyase and cholesterol desmolase. Many of the corresponding genes for the described enzymes have been isolated and characterized, and specific mutations causing CAH have been identified. In classical CAH (simple-virilizing and salt-wasting forms), androgen excess causes external genital ambiguity in newborn females and progressive postnatal virilization in both sexes. In non-classical CAH, 21-OHD is partial and occurs with milder symptoms. A deficiency of 11beta-Hydroxylase deficiency results in ambiguous genitalia in the newborn genetic female and androgen excess and hypertension in both males and females. In 3beta-hydroxysteroid deficiency adrenal and gonadal androgen production is deficient resulting in incomplete genital development in genetic males and limited androgen affect in females. Two less frequent causes of CAH 17alpha-Hydroxylase/17,20-lyase and cholesterol desmolase result in external female genitalia in both sexes. Hormonal diagnosis is described for each disorder.

Paganini, C., G. Radetti, et al. 2000. "Height, bone mineral density and bone markers in congenital adrenal hyperplasia." *Hormone Research* 54(4): 164-68.

AIM: To evaluate height, bone growth, areal bone mineral density (aBMD), volumetric bone mineral density (vBMD) and markers of bone turnover in a group of patients affected by congenital adrenal hyperplasia (CAH). PATIENTS: There were 50 patients (23 males, 27 females), aged 1-28 years, affected by CAH due to 21-hydroxylase deficiency: 27 with the salt-wasting (SW); 14 with the simple-virilizing (SV), and 9 with the non-classical (NC) forms. METHODS: Bone morphometry was evaluated with the metacarpal index (MI) and lumbar aBMD and vBMD (L2-L4) by dual energy X-ray absorptiometry. Serum osteocalcin was used as a marker of bone formation, while urinary cross-linked N-telopeptides of type-I collagen and free deoxypyridinoline levels were evaluated as indexes of bone resorption. RESULTS: The height standard deviation score (SDS) was -0.41 +/- 1.4 in SW patients, -0.01 +/- 1.9 in SV patients, and -0.01 +/- 2.3 in NC patients. There was no significant difference among groups and against zero. The MI SDS was also not different between groups and against zero. aBMD was significantly lower in the pubertal patients compared with normal values, but only when patients with the SW and SV forms were considered together ($p < 0.05$). vBMD was significantly reduced in all patients with the classical form. Bone markers were not different in patients and controls. CONCLUSION: Our study shows that normal height can be attained in CAH patients; however, an impairment in bone growth and mineralization may be found in adolescents and young adults affected by the classical form.

Pang, S. 2003. "Newborn screening for congenital adrenal hyperplasia." *Pediatric Annals* 32(8): 516-23.

Parker, K. L. and B. P. Schimmer. 2001. "Genetics of the development and function of the adrenal cortex." *Reviews in Endocrine and Metabolism Disorders* 2(3): 245-52.

Pescovitz, O. H., F. Comite, et al. 1986. "The NIH experience with precocious puberty: diagnostic subgroups and response to short-term luteinizing hormone releasing hormone analogue therapy." *Journal of Pediatrics* 108(1): 47-54.

Between 1979 and 1983, 129 children (95 girls) with precocious puberty were referred to the National Institutes of Health and received treatment for at least 6 months with the long-acting LHRH analogue D-Trp6-Pro9-NEt-LHRH. The majority (107 of 129) of the children had central precocious puberty mediated by activation of the hypothalamic-pituitary-gonadal axis in association with hypothalamic hamartomas (24 of 107) or other central nervous system lesions (21 of 107), or idiopathic precocious puberty (62 of 107). Hypothalamic hamartomas or other central nervous system lesions were a frequent cause of central precocious puberty in girls (27 of 87), but idiopathic precocious puberty was still the most frequent diagnosis (63 percent). Idiopathic precocious puberty was uncommon in boys (6 percent). The patients with peripheral precocious puberty included six girls with McCune-Albright syndrome and six boys with familial male precocious puberty. These children had peripheral sex steroid secretion in the absence of hypothalamic-pituitary-gonadal axis maturation. The children with combined peripheral and central precocious puberty included nine children with congenital adrenal hyperplasia and one girl with a virilizing adrenal tumor. In the patients with central precocious puberty or combined peripheral and central precocious puberty, LHRHa therapy caused suppression of gonadotropin and sex steroid levels (P less than 0.001), stabilization or regression of secondary sexual characteristics, and decreases in growth rate and in the rate of bone age maturation (P less than 0.005). Patients with peripheral precocious puberty, however, had no significant change in gonadotropin or sex steroid levels, growth rate, or the rate of bone-age maturation, and no improvement in secondary sexual characteristics. Thus, LHRHa is an effective treatment of central precocious puberty and combined peripheral and central precocious puberty, but is ineffective in the therapy of peripheral precocious puberty.

Pinto, G., V. Tardy, et al. (2003). "Follow-up of 68 children with congenital adrenal hyperplasia due to 21-hydroxylase deficiency: relevance of genotype for management." *Journal of Clinical Endocrinology and Metabolism* 88(6): 2624-33.

The phenotype of congenital adrenal hyperplasia (CAH) varies greatly. The purpose of this study was to optimize diagnosis and follow-up by comparing phenotype with genotype. Sixty-eight patients with CAH due to 21-hydroxylase deficiency were studied by clinical, hormonal, and molecular genetic methods. Patients were classified according to predicted mutation severity: group 0, null mutation (17.6%); group A, homozygous for IVS2 splice mutation or compound heterozygous for IVS2 and null mutations (33.8%); group B, homozygous or compound heterozygous for I172N mutation (14.7%); group C, homozygous or compound heterozygous for V281L or P30L mutations (26.5%); and group D, mutations with unknown enzyme activity (7.4%). All group 0 and A patients had the salt-wasting form, and group C had nonclassical forms. Group B included five salt-wasting and five simple virilizing forms. Groups 0 and A were younger at diagnosis ($P < 0.02$), and females were more virilized than those in group B. Group B had higher basal plasma 17-hydroxyprogesterone (564 +/- 162 nmol/liter) and testosterone (11 +/- 3 nmol/liter) levels than group C [59 +/- 13 nmol/liter ($P < 0.001$) and 1.4 +/- 0.2 nmol/liter ($P < 0.005$), respectively]. Hydrocortisone doses given to groups 0, A, and B were similar at all ages, but lower in group C ($P < 0.01$). Final height was below target height in classical (n = 16; -2 +/- 0.2 SD score; $P < 0.02$) and nonclassical (n = 11; -1.2 +/- 0.4 SD score; $P < 0.03$) forms. The severity of the genetic defects and the clinical-laboratory features are well correlated. Genotyping, combined with neonatal screening and optimal medical and surgical treatment, can help in the management of CAH.

Punthakee, Z., L. Legault, et al. 2003. "Prednisolone in the treatment of adrenal insufficiency: a re-evaluation of relative potency." *Journal of Pediatrics* 143(3): 402-5.

Ritzen, E. M. 2001. "Prenatal dexamethasone treatment of fetuses at risk for congenital adrenal hyperplasia: benefits and concerns." *Seminal Neonatology* 6(4): 357-62.

Virilization due to congenital adrenal hyperplasia (CAH) can effectively be prevented or diminished by prenatal dexamethasone given to the mother. This treatment, which should only be considered in families with a previous child with a virilizing form of the disease, has to start already at 6-7 weeks of gestation. Thus, the treatment has to be given 'blindly' to all mothers at risk until the diagnosis of an affected female can be ascertained by analysis of DNA from a chorionic villous biopsy, which cannot be performed until the 10th week. Since CAH is inherited as an autosomal recessive disease and only affected girls benefit from the treatment, seven out of eight fetuses are treated unnecessarily. This makes it especially important to monitor possible side effects. Adverse effects on brain and kidneys have been shown in animals exposed to large doses of dexamethasone during the second trimester. Too few follow-up human studies are reported to date to allow definite conclusions on possible side effects in man. Therefore, treatment should be done within controlled clinical studies.

Ritzen, E. M. 2003. "Early puberty: what is normal and when is treatment indicated?" *Hormone Research* 60 Suppl 3: 31-4.

Girls and boys who enter puberty before 8 and 9 years of age, respectively (corresponding to about -3 SDS), are arbitrarily considered to need referral for endocrine investigation. A recent report from the Lawson Wilkins Pediatric Endocrine Society suggested that the limit for investigation of girls and boys should be lowered to 7 and 8 years, respectively. For African-American girls, 6 years is the suggested age. This recommendation has been criticized. Although short stature is a common end result of precocious puberty, short- and long-term psychological symptoms may be more important, since several studies have indicated psychopathology in this patient group. Whether this can be prevented by gonadotropin releasing hormone agonist treatment remains to be shown. This review will highlight the psychological aspects of early puberty. In short, aspects other than height should also be evaluated when considering treatment of the early maturing child.

Rivkees, S. A., and J. D. Crawford. 2000. "Dexamethasone treatment of virilizing congenital adrenal hyperplasia: the ability to achieve normal growth." *Pediatrics* 106(4): 767-73.

OBJECTIVE: To assess whether treatment of virilizing congenital adrenal hyperplasia (CAH) with long-acting glucocorticoids is associated with favorable growth outcomes. METHOD: We examined the long-term growth of 17 boys and 9 girls with CAH treated with dexamethasone (.27 +/-.01 mg/m(2)/day). RESULTS: For individuals with comparable bone age (BA) and chronological age (CA) at the onset of dexamethasone therapy, males were 2.8 +/-.8 years (mean +/- standard error of the mean; n = 13) and females were 2.4 +/- 1.0 years (n = 6). Males were treated for 7.3 +/- 1.1 years (DeltaCA) over which time the change in BA (DeltaBA) was 7.0 +/- 1.3 years, and the change in height age (DeltaHA) was 6.9 +/- 1.1 years. Females were treated for 6.8 +/- 1.3 years, over which time the DeltaBA was 6.5 +/- 1.0 years, and the DeltaHA was 6.3 +/-.8 years. During treatment 17 ketosteroid excretion rates were normal for age and 17-hydroxyprogesterone values were 69.6 +/- 18 ng/dL. Testicular enlargement was first detected at 10.7 +/-.8 years and breast tissue at 9.9 +/- 1.2 years. Three boys and 1 girl had final heights of 171. 8 +/- 6 cm and 161 cm, respectively, compared with midparental heights of

176.1 +/- 4.1 cm and 160 cm. Predicted adult heights for 6 other boys and 5 girls were 176.8 +/- 2.0 cm and 161.4 +/- 2.8 cm, respectively, compared with midparental heights of 174.6 +/- 1.4 cm and 158.2 +/- 2.0 cm. Statural outcomes were less favorable for 7 children started on dexamethasone when BAs were considerably advanced, although height predictions increased during therapy. CONCLUSIONS: These observations show that children treated with dexamethasone for CAH can achieve normal growth with the convenience of once-a-day dosing in most cases.congenital adrenal hyperplasia, dexamethasone, growth.

Silverman, M. L., and A. K. Lee. 1989. "Anatomy and pathology of the adrenal glands." *Urologic Clinics of North America* 16(3): 417-32.

The adrenals are paired glands that lie in the retroperitoneum and have a close anatomic relation to the kidneys. Each gland has a cortex and a medulla, which act as separate entities. The adrenals are affected by various pathologic conditions, including congenital abnormalities, hypofunction, nodular enlargement, hyperplasia, and malignant and benign tumors. Newer developments in pathologic evaluation are fine-needle aspiration biopsy, immunohistochemistry, and ploidy and oncogene analysis.

Speiser, P. W. 2001. "Congenital adrenal hyperplasia: transition from childhood to adulthood." *Journal of Endocrinological Investigation* 24(9): 681-91.

Congenital adrenal hyperplasia (CAH) is a group of disorders caused by inborn errors of steroid metabolism. The most common form owing to 21-hydroxylase deficiency (CAH-21OHD) is present in about 1:10,000- 1:15,000 live births worldwide. In its classic salt-wasting form (-66-75 percent of cases) patients may suffer potentially lethal adrenal insufficiency. Non-salt-wasting forms of CAH-21 OHD are recognized by genital ambiguity in affected females, and by signs of androgen excess in later childhood in males. Non-classic CAH-21 OHD may be detected in up to 1-3 percent of certain populations, and is often mistaken for idiopathic precocious pubarche in children or polycystic ovary syndrome in young women. This chapter will address issues relating to transition of CAH care from the pediatric to the adult endocrinologist.

Speiser, P. W. 2001. "Molecular diagnosis of CYP21 mutations in congenital adrenal hyperplasia: implications for genetic counseling." *American Journal of Pharmacogenomics* 1(2): 101-10.

Congenital adrenal hyperplasia (CAH) is an inherited disorder of steroid biosynthesis most often attributable to mutations in CYP21 (also termed CYP21A2) encoding the active steroid 21-hydroxylase enzyme. This review focuses on clinical and genetic aspects of CAH, and updates the reader on current methodology and applications for molecular genetic diagnosis. Genotyping patients with CAH has revealed >50 mutations within CYP21, yet only 10 mutations account for approximately 95 percent of affected alleles. Many CYP21 mutations are gene conversions arising via transfer of gene sequences between the non-functional CYP21 pseudogene and CYP21. Phenotype is generally well-correlated with genotype. Historically, CAH has been divided into 3 types of disease: classic salt-wasting, classic simple-virilizing (non-salt-wasting), and non-classic. Recent findings support the notion that rather than discrete phenotypic categories, CAH is better represented as a continuum of phenotypes, from severe to mild. Molecular genetic diagnosis is most effectively employed now in prenatal diagnosis of classic CAH. As newborn screening for CAH becomes more widespread, genotyping may be implemented to resolve diagnostic difficulties encountered with hormonal testing. As automated methods of DNA diagnosis such as microarrays or gene chips are refined, it is likely that genetic screening will become less expensive and more readily available. The clinician should be aware of the potential for both false negatives and false positives with PCR-based gene screening. In short, whereas molecular genetic diagnosis is a valuable tool, it cannot replace clinical acumen and hormonal assays.

Speiser, P. W., E. S. Knochenhauer, et al. 2000. "A multicenter study of women with non-classical congenital adrenal hyperplasia: relationship between genotype and phenotype." *Molecular Genetics and Metabolism* 71(3): 527-34.

Characteristic presentation of non-classical adrenal hyperplasia (NCAH) due to 21-hydroxylase deficiency was compared between women carrying a severe and a mild CYP21 mutation (Group 1, N = 26) versus homozygotes for mild mutations (Group 2, N = 8). The diagnosis was based on elevated ACTH-stimulated 17OH-progesterone (17-OHP). Genotyping for 10 mutations was performed by PCR-based techniques. Jewish patients predominated among

Group 2 (25% vs 11.5% in Group 1); however, 85% of all patients were non-Jewish Caucasians. Average age of presentation was 23-25 years, and did not differ between groups. Hirsutism, and to a lesser extent oligomenorrhea and acne, were more prevalent among Group 1 women. There was a trend to higher basal 17-OHP among Group 1 patients (mean +/- SEM; 1354+/-323 vs 714+/-129 ng/dl, P< or =0.25). The lack of significant difference was perhaps due to the relatively few homozygotes for 2 mild mutations (24%). V281L was carried on approximately 48% of all alleles, and about 16% carried either P30L or P453S. Approximately 38% of alleles and 77% of patients carried a classic mutation. These data have important implications for genetic counseling. In summary, we describe differences in clinical, hormonal, and genetic characteristics among a multiethnic group of females with NCAH.

Speiser, P. W., and P. C. White. 2003. "Congenital adrenal hyperplasia." *New England Journal of Medicine* 349(8): 776-88.

Stikkelbroeck, N. M., B. A. Van't Hof-Grootenboer, et al. (2003). "Growth inhibition by glucocorticoid treatment in salt wasting 21-hydroxylase deficiency: in early infancy and (pre)puberty." *Journal of Clinical Endocrinology and Metabolism* 88(8): 3525-30.

In patients with congenital adrenal hyperplasia (CAH) due to 21-hydroxylase deficiency, adult height is below target height. This may result from growth inhibition by glucocorticoid treatment. Previous studies suggest that glucocorticoids have a dose-dependent negative effect on growth in CAH patients and that this effect is age dependent. This study analyzed the correlation between glucocorticoid dose and growth in these patients. A retrospective study was carried out on growth data from 48 patients with classic salt-wasting 21-hydroxylase deficiency who all had been diagnosed in the first year of life and treated from the moment of diagnosis with glucocorticoids and mineralocorticoids. Analysis of the effect of prescribed glucocorticoid dose on growth was performed in age intervals, by analysis of covariance (ANCOVA). The dependent variables height for age z-score (HAZ), weight for age z-score (WAZ) (both corrected for secular trend), and weight for height z-score (WHZ), at 10 selected ages (1, 2, 4, 6, 8, 10, 12, 14, 16, and 18 yr) were explained by 1) mean daily glucocorticoid dose per body surface in the preceding age interval; 2) HAZ, WAZ, or WHZ value at the beginning of the age interval; 3) HAZ, WAZ, or WHZ value 1 yr before the beginning of the considered age interval; and 4) midparental height (only for HAZ). ANCOVA showed that the daily glucocorticoid dose had significant negative effects on HAZ between the ages of 6 and 12 months and between the age of 8-10 and 12-14 yr (and a trend toward significance between 10-12 yr). The negative glucocorticoid effect on HAZ in the age interval of 12-14 yr was as large as in the interval between 6 and 12 months of age. Weight and weight for height were not significantly influenced by glucocorticoid dose in any of the age intervals. We conclude that in CAH patients in the first year of life and between the ages of 8 and 14 yr, there is a dose-dependent negative effect of glucocorticoids on linear growth. Therefore, the daily glucocorticoid dose in these periods should be sufficient to avoid androgen excess, but as low as possible to allow optimal linear growth and adult height.

Talbot, N. B., A. B. Butler, et al. 1942. "Adrenal cortical hyperplasia with virilization: diagnosis, course and treatment." *Journal of Clinical Investestigation* 21: 559-71.

Tanner, J. M., and P. S. Davies. 1985. "Clinical longitudinal standards for height and height velocity for North American children [see comments]." *Journal of Pediatrics* 107(3): 317-29.

Longitudinally-based height and height velocity charts for North American children are presented. Centiles are given for early, middle, and late maturers. The shape of the curves is taken from a review of longitudinal studies, and the prepubertal and adult centiles for height attained are taken from National Center for Health Statistics data. The charts are suitable for following an individual child's progress during observation or treatment throughout the growth period, including puberty.

Van Wyk, J. J., and E. M. Ritzen. 2003. "The role of bilateral adrenalectomy in the treatment of congenital adrenal hyperplasia." *Journal of Clinical Endocrinology and Metabolism* 88(7): 2993-98.

This report summarizes follow-up studies in 18 patients who underwent bilateral adrenalectomy for congenital adrenal hyperplasia. Three of these patients were young children with null/null mutations of CYP21, and the other 15 were adrenalectomized because of difficulties in their management on conventional therapy. The average duration of follow-up was 59 months and represents an aggregate of 90 postoperative years. The adrenals were removed laparoscopically in 13 patients and by open flank incisions in five. Adrenal crises associated with severe illnesses occurred in five patients at times when their glucocorticoid substitution was suboptimal. All were responsive to appropriate therapy. Two of these patients were young children who had hypoglycemia during gastroenteritis or febrile illness associated with poor food intake or vomiting. Significant elevations of adrenal steroid precursors, presumably from ectopic adrenal rests, were observed postoperatively in eight of the patients. Patients and parents were nearly unanimous in their enthusiasm for adrenalectomy. In most, signs of androgen excess have decreased, and obesity has become less of a problem with lowering the dose of glucocorticoid. We conclude that adrenalectomy is a safe and efficacious method of managing congenital adrenal hyperplasia in selected patients. Prophylactic adrenalectomy in young children with double null mutations remains experimental.

Weise, M., B. Drinkard, et al. (2004). "Stress dose of hydrocortisone is not beneficial in patients with classic congenital adrenal hyperplasia undergoing short-term, high-intensity exercise." *Journal of Clinical Endocrinology and Metabolism* 89(8): 3679-84.

Classic congenital adrenal hyperplasia (CAH) is associated with impaired function of the adrenal cortex and medulla leading to decreased production of cortisol and epinephrine. As a result, the normal exercise-induced rise in blood glucose is markedly blunted in such individuals. We examined whether an extra dose of hydrocortisone, similar to that given during other forms of physical stress such as intercurrent illness, would normalize blood glucose levels during exercise in patients with CAH. We studied hormonal, metabolic, and cardiorespiratory parameters in response to a standardized high-intensity exercise protocol in nine adolescent patients with classic CAH. Patients were assigned to receive either an additional morning dose of hydrocortisone or placebo, in addition to their usual glucocorticoid and mineralocorticoid replacement in a randomized, double-blind, crossover design 1 h before exercising. Although plasma cortisol levels approximately doubled after administration of the additional hydrocortisone dose compared with the usual single dose, fasting and exercise-induced blood glucose levels did not differ. In addition, no differences were observed in the serum concentrations of the glucose-modulating hormones epinephrine, insulin, glucagon, and GH and of the metabolic parameters lactate and free fatty acids. Although maximal heart rate was slightly higher after stress dosing (193 +/- 3 vs. 191 +/- 3 beats/min, mean +/- sem, $P < 0.05$), this did not affect exercise performance or perceived exertion. We conclude that patients with classic CAH do not benefit from additional hydrocortisone during short-term, high-intensity exercise. Although this has not been tested with long-term exercise, a high degree of caution should be used when considering the frequent use of additional hydrocortisone administration with exercise, given the adverse side effects of glucocorticoid excess.

Weise, M., S. L. Mehlinger, et al. (2004). "Patients with classic congenital adrenal hyperplasia have decreased epinephrine reserve and defective glucose elevation in response to high-intensity exercise." *Journal of Clinical Endocrinology and Metababolism* 89(2): 591-7.

Classic congenital hyperplasia (CAH) is characterized by impaired adrenocortical function with a decrease in cortisol and aldosterone secretion and an increase in androgen secretion. Adrenomedullary function is also compromised due to developmental defects in the formation of the adrenal medulla, leading to decreased production of epinephrine. To examine the response to a natural stressful stimulus in patients with classic CAH, we studied hormonal, metabolic, and cardiorespiratory parameters in response to a standardized high-intensity exercise protocol in nine adolescent patients with CAH and nine healthy controls matched for gender, age, and percent body fat. The same relative workload was applied, based on individual maximal aerobic capacity, and all patients received their usual glucocorticoid and mineralocorticoid replacement. When compared with their normal counterparts, patients with CAH had significantly lower epinephrine levels both at baseline and at peak exercise ($P < 0.01$), whereas norepinephrine levels did not differ. Blood glucose concentrations were similar at baseline, but the normal exercise-induced rise observed in the healthy controls was significantly blunted in the CAH patients ($P < 0.01$). Peak heart rate was also lower in CAH patients than healthy controls ($P < 0.05$). As expected, the normal exercise-induced increase in cortisol was not observed in patients with CAH. No significant differences were found in serum levels of insulin, glucagon, GH, lactate and free fatty acids, blood pressure, or ability to sustain exercise between the two groups. Patients with CAH replaced with glucocorticoids have decreased adrenomedullary reserve and impaired exercise-induced changes in glucose but normal short-term high-intensity exercise performance. Whether the combination of epinephrine and cortisol deficiency poses a risk for hypoglycemia and/or decreased endurance during long-term physical stress has to be determined.

White, P. C. 2001. "Congenital adrenal hyperplasias." *Best Practice and Research Clinical Endocrinology and Metabolism* 15(1): 17-41.

Congenital adrenal hyperplasia syndromes result from deficiencies of enzymes involved in corticosteroid biosynthesis. Most commonly, they are due to mutations in 21-hydroxylase. This chapter describes the clinical diagnosis and management of congenital adrenal hyperplasias throughout life, including in the fetus, child and adult. These clinical recommendations are explained in the context of the molecular and biochemical characteristics of the diseases.

White, P. C., and P. W. Speiser. 2002. "Long-term consequences of childhood-onset congenital adrenal hyperplasia." *Best Practice and Research Clinical Endocrinology and Metabolism* 16(2): 273-88.

Congenital adrenal hyperplasia (CAH) is a general term applied to several diseases caused by inherited defects of cortisol synthesis. The most common of these is steroid 21-mono-oxygenase (also termed 21-hydroxylase) deficiency (CAH-21OHD), found in approximately 1:10 000-1:15 000 live births. Potentially lethal adrenal insufficiency is characteristic of about two-thirds to three-quarters of patients with the classic salt-wasting form of CAH-21OHD. Non-salt-wasting forms of CAH-21OHD may be diagnosed based in part on genital ambiguity in affected newborn females, and/or by later evidence of androgen excess in members of either sex. Non-classical CAH-21OHD may be detected in up to 1-3 percent of certain populations, and is often mistaken for idiopathic precocious pubarche in children or polycystic ovary syndrome in young women. This chapter addresses issues relating to long-term consequences in adult life of CAH-21OHD diagnosed in early childhood or adolescence.

Wilkins, L., R. A. Lewis, et al. 1950. "Suppression of androgen secretion by cortisone in a case of congenital adrenal hyperplasia." *Bulletin of Johns Hopkins Hospital* 86: 249-255.

Winterer, J., G. P. Chrousos, et al. 1985. "Effect of hydrocortisone dose schedule on adrenal steroid secretion in congenital adrenal hyperplasia." *Annals of the New York Academy of Sciences* 458: 182-92.

Young, M. C., J. A. Robinson, et al. 1988. "17OH-progesterone rhythms in congenital adrenal hyperplasia." *Archives of Disease in Childhood* 63(6): 617-23.

Serial blood spot and saliva samples were collected at home by 18 patients being treated for congenital adrenal hyperplasia to determine the circadian rhythm of 17OH-progesterone as an index of therapeutic control. There was a strong correlation between the magnitude of the circadian fall and a single morning measurement of the plasma testosterone concentration taken near the time of the 17OH-progesterone rhythm samples. Poor control in pubertal girls produced an exaggerated circadian fall in 17OH-progesterone concentrations that were raised at all sampling times. Optimal control (plasma testosterone 1.5-2.5 nmol/l) was associated with blood spot and salivary 170H-progesterone concentrations at 0800 hours of between 30-70 nmol/l and 260-1000 pmol/l, respectively, falling thereafter to less than 10 nmol/l and less than 150 pmol/l, respectively. Similar results were obtained in prepubertal patients. Nomograms have been constructed to interpret the daily profiles of blood spot or salivary measurements of 17OH- progesterone, or both. The analysis of 17OH-progesterone circadian rhythms is useful in monitoring treatment in patients with congenital adrenal hyperplasia, particularly those who may be over-treated.

Young, M. C., N. Cook, et al. 1989. "The pharmacokinetics of low-dose dexamethasone in congenital adrenal hyperplasia." *European Journal of Clinical Pharmacology* 37(1): 75-7.

The pharmacokinetics of dexamethasone, given at low dose, were studied in 13 patients with congenital adrenal hyperplasia (CAH) to ascertain whether kinetics differed in this inherited disorder of cortisol metabolism from those seen in healthy individuals. Changes in plasma dexamethasone concentration after intravenous bolus, measured using a simple novel radioimmunoassay, were well described by a two-compartment open model with first-order kinetics. Values for lambda 2: 0.206 h-1, t1/2: 3.53 h, Vc: 24.41 and f: 0.64 were similar to those previously reported for normal subjects. There were considerable interindividual differences in parameter values and Cmaxp.o. (range 22-67 nmol/l). As suppression of the hypothalamo-pituitary-adrenal axis correlates with plasma dexamethasone levels, this variability may partly explain the differing dose and dose schedule requirements necessary to achieve adequate therapeutic control in the clinical management of CAH.

Young, M. C., J. Ribeiro, et al. 1989. "Growth and body proportions in congenital adrenal hyperplasia." *Archives of Disease in Childhood* 64(11): 1554-8.

Total height, sitting height, and subischial leg length were measured in 27 patients (19 girls and eight boys aged 4.3-21.1 years) with congenital adrenal hyperplasia to determine the influence of chronic hyperandrogenaemia on body proportions. Proportions were normal in 24 patients with classical congenital adrenal hyperplasia who had received steroid treatment since birth, but one of three patients with non-classical (late-onset) congenital adrenal hyperplasia had a disproportionately large trunk. Eleven patients with classical congenital adrenal hyperplasia had completed growth, of whom seven had height standard deviation (SD) scores for chronological age less than zero, and one had extremely short stature (SD score -3.25). In 13 patients who were still growing, nine had height SD scores for chronological age of less than zero despite having mean (SD) advances in bone age over chronological age of 1.64 (1.68) years. Height SD scores for bone age were less than 0 in all 13 patients, indicating a loss of height despite advanced skeletal maturation. Doses of glucocorticoid that permit mild chronic or intermittent hyperandrogenaemia also seem to be associated with mild growth retardation. An adult height below average may be an inevitable consequence for many patients with congenital adrenal hyperplasia receiving conventional glucocorticoid treatment.

Young, M. C. and I. A. Hughes. 1990. "Dexamethasone treatment for congenital adrenal hyperplasia." *Archives of Disease in Childhood* 65(3): 312-14.

Ten patients with congenital adrenal hyperplasia (three males, seven females; aged 12-29 years) had their usual glucocorticoid treatment changed to dexamethasone in three crossover dosage regimens. A starting dose of 5 micrograms/kg/day is suggested but as no one dose regimen resulted in adequate control the timing of the dose must be decided for each patient.

Zachmann, M., B. Sobradillo, et al. 1978. "Bayley-Pinneau, Roche-Wainer-Thissen, and Tanner height predictions in normal children and in patients with various pathologic conditions." *Journal of Pediatrics* 93(5): 749-55.

Bayley-Pinneau, Roche-Wainer-Thissen, and Tanner height predictions at various chronologic ages were compared with final adult height in

56 normal subjects and in 34 patients with abnormal growth pattern (11 with familial tall stature, 7 with idiopathic precicious puberty, 6 with Turner syndrome, and 10 with primordial small stature or Silver-Russell syndrome). The two recent methods (Roche-Wainer-Thissen and Tanner) gave very accurate results and were superior to the Bayley- Pinneau method in normal subjects and in patients with familial tall stature. However, they overestimated adult height grossly in precocious puberty and moderately in Turner syndrome and in primordial small stature. It is concluded that calculations based on coefficients and regression equations obtained from normal children (as in the Roche-Wainer-Thissen and Tanner methods) can only be used in normal children or in patients with normal growth potential under adequate treatment. Calculations based on percentages of adult height (as in the Bayley-Pinneau method) are preferable in conditions in which the growth potential in relation to bone maturation is inherently reduced and cannot be corrected by treatment.

# Index

## B



## C

**D**



**E**

**F**



**G**



**H**

## I



## K



## L



## M



## N

O



P



R



S

## T



## U



## V



## W

**Y**



**Z**

# About The Authors

**C. Y. Hsu** is the mother of a child with Congenital Adrenal Hyperplasia. She holds a Bachelor of Science degree from the Massachusetts Institute of Technology in Cambridge, Massachusetts, and a Master of Architecture degree from Harvard University. Ms. Hsu is a licensed Architect who has practiced in Boston, New York, and Williamsburg, Virginia. Currently, she has her own small architecture firm in Connecticut.

**Scott A. Rivkees**, MD, is Professor of Pediatrics at the Yale University School of Medicine in New Haven, Connecticut, and Director of the Yale Child Health Research Center, a think tank devoted to finding treatments and cures for childhood diseases and illnesses. He is also Associate Chair of Pediatrics for Research, and Chief of the Section of Developmental Endocrinology and Biology at the Yale School of Medicine.

Dr. Rivkees has published more than 100 original research papers in the fields of pediatric endocrinology and neuroscience. His work in CAH includes "Dexamethasone Treatment of Virilizing Congenital Adrenal Hyperplasia: The Ability to Achieve Normal Growth" (*Pediatrics*, October 2000) and "Home Monitoring of 17- Hydroxyprogesterone Levels in Congenital Adrenal Hyperplasia with Filter Paper Blood Samples" (*Journal of Pediatrics*, February 1999).

Dr. Rivkees is a fellow of the American Academy of Pediatrics; a member of the American Society of Clinical Investigators; a member of the Connecticut Genetics Advisory Committee; and past Drug Committee Chair of the Lawson Wilkins Pediatric Endocrine Society. He sits on the scientific review boards at the National Institutes of Health and the *Journal of Clinical Endocrinology and Metabolism* and in 2002, testified in front of the U.S. Senate as an expert witness on newborn screening. Dr. Rivkees is a member of the scientific advisory board for CARES (Congenital Adrenal hyperplasia Research, Education and Support) Foundation, Inc.

Made in the USA